DESIGNER CROCHET

32 PATTERNS TO ELEVATE YOUR STYLE

SIZES SMALL TO 5X

SHANNON MULLETT-BOWLSBY

LARK
New York

LARK

New York

An Imprint of Sterling Publishing
1166 Avenue of the Americas
New York, NY 10036

ISBN 978-1-4547-0872-8

Distributed in Canada by Sterling Publishing
c/o Canadian Manda Group, 664 Annette Street
Toronto, Ontario, Canada M6S 2C8
Distributed in the United Kingdom by GMC Distribution Services
Castle Place, 166 High Street, Lewes, East Sussex, England BN7 1XU
Distributed in Australia by Capricorn Link (Australia) Pty. Ltd.
P.O. Box 704, Windsor, NSW 2756, Australia

For information about custom editions, special sales, and premium and corporate purchases,
please contact Sterling Special Sales at 800-805-5489 or specialsales@sterlingpublishing.com.

Manufactured in China

2 4 6 8 10 9 7 5 3 1

larkcrafts.com

CONTENTS

INTRODUCTION

If you are reading this, you are holding a copy of my book in your hands. This means the passion and hard work our team has poured into creating this book for the past year was successful insomuch as you are holding an actual published copy. WOOHOO!!

Now what? Now you will probably read through this introduction, then flip through the pages looking at the photos of the finished projects, making that most difficult of decisions: Which one do I make first?

While the photography is beautiful (if we do say so ourselves!), the true beauty of this book is more than skin deep. So, before you start page turning, let me tell you what you can expect to find on the pages that follow.

DESIGNS MADE IN LIGHTWEIGHT YARNS.

One of the aspects of being a crochet and hand knitwear designer that excites me the most is the unique ability I have to create custom fabrics for each of my designs. From fiber to finished garment, I love the total control I have over every aspect of making the fabrics that are incorporated into the finished designs you see in this book.

I love exploring this manipulation and control of fibers to create different fabrics and, for this book, I wanted to concentrate on using lightweight yarns to create my fabrics. Why use lightweight yarns? I'm glad you asked!

I decided to use lightweight yarns for the designs in this book because lightweight yarns allow me more flexibility with the weight of the fabrics I create.

If I start out with heavyweight yarns to make my fabrics, I am limited to making thicker and more substantial fabrics unless I want to incorporate a lot of lace stitch patterns. There's nothing wrong with that . . . everything has its time

and place . . . but that's not the direction I wanted to take this book.

On the other hand, if I start with lightweight yarns, I can always "bulk up" the stitches to create more substantial fabrics when I want. I can also make those stunning solid textured fabrics that I like using in my designs and still have fabrics that drape and move beautifully.

Lightweight yarns can always be made heavier, but it just isn't always practical to try to make heavyweight yarns into lightweight fabrics.

PATTERNS THAT FIT THE SIZES THEY ARE WRITTEN FOR.

We have carefully designed each of the pieces in this book to ensure that your finished projects will look good whether you are making the size medium or the size 5X.

Everyone deserves to have well-thought-out, properly proportioned patterns that make him or her look and feel FAB regardless of body shape or size. While it is true that

we can't anticipate every curve and every line of ALL your bodies, we have made every effort to write the patterns for our designs so they fit a wide range of sizes to begin with. Then, we have provided extensive sizing information within each pattern through the use of schematics and notes so you have the opportunity, either on your own or with a little help, to customize a length here or an armhole or waistline there to give yourself an even more custom fit.

Our number one design and patterning priority is proper proportional fit—no matter the size of the finished garment or the body type of the wearer. To demonstrate this, we have made the garment samples in *Designer Crochet* in sizes ranging from small to 2X and have photographed them on women with a variety of body types and shapes. To take it one step further, you can head over to ShibaguyzDesignz.com where we will have a gallery of images showing the sample garments from Designer Crochet styled in various ways to show how they fit a variety of body types and lifestyles.

STITCH CHARTS

Those things that look like a cross between your crochet stitches and alien hieroglyphics? Those are stitch charts! If this is your first time encountering these wonderful little tools, stitch charts are visual representations of the stitches you are making with your yarn and hooks.

We have provided these stitch charts for stitches we feel would benefit from a little visual cue or two. Even if you've never read a stitch chart before, take a look at the key and think of them as the print representation for the stitch you are making right there with your two hands. Often, stitchers find this visual cue, in combination with the project photos and the written pattern, just what they need to help them out with a stitch they aren't familiar with or a stitch that might be giving them a little bit of a challenge.

SCHEMATICS

Schematics are those line drawings included with most of the patterns in this book that provide you with a visual representation of the pieces of the projects you are making. Schematics kind of resemble a sewing pattern and are given as a reference for blocked dimensions and as a guide if you wish to alter one of the measurements in the garment you are making.

You can think of schematics the same way you would think of the blueprints for a house. Each of the shapes in these line drawings represents one of the pieces you are making in the pattern you are working on. Along the sides of each shape, there are lines drawn that represent a distance between two points on the shape. The numbers next to these lines show the distance between those two points in inches. You will use these schematic measurements to block your finished pieces into shape once you are finished making them.

Schematics are just another FAB reference tool to help make our patterns more accessible and to assist you in finishing your project successfully!

TUTORIALS

We have included some of the same tutorials in the Special Techniques section that are featured in our most popular classes we teach.

First, you will find photo tutorials and graphics that give you an actual visual reference for how to make foundation stitches, how to set in a sleeve, and how to sew clean and professional-looking seams. We have even included a graphic for how to cut a zipper to the perfect size for your finished project.

Next, we have included extensive notes within each pattern that will coach you through the points you should be mindful of while you are making your project. These are notes that we often make to ourselves in the margins of our patterning notes, and we have included them here for you, in each pattern, to help you along the way.

Finally, there is an entire section with tips and pointers from our classes on increasing and decreasing. This section will help you through the shaping in your projects even when you are increasing and decreasing while stitching some of the more intricate pattern stitches in this book.

Use these tutorials as a reference tool often while you work through your projects. It is our hope that these teaching tools we have included will give you the boost you need to try more advanced techniques than you have ever tried before and maybe even take your crochet skills to the next level!

There you have it! From the very first sketch to the last numbers in the written patterns, we have created this book of designs and patterns with YOU in mind.

We have created designs we know you will be proud to wear, and we have provided tools, coaching, and tutorials to supplement our written patterns to help you start smart and finish FAB!

We hope you enjoy making these projects as much as we enjoyed designing them for you.

Stitch On!

GETTING STARTED

Before you dive in to the patterns in this book, here are a few guides to help you pick the right project, stash up the right yarn, and brush up some techniques to finish FAB and have a project you are proud to show off.

WHICH PROJECT IS RIGHT FOR YOU?

We have worked diligently to ensure this book has a little something for crocheters of every experience level. Whether you have worked on potholders and scarves or if you are an experienced garment maker, you will find projects here that challenge and excite you.

Each project is labeled with a skill level, so use this guide to understand the experience and knowledge involved in each pattern.

BEGINNER

You know your basic skills like making chains, single crochet, half double crochet, and double crochet stitches. You've probably made basic projects like potholders, scarves, and afghans, but this is your first garment.

Patterns written for the Beginner level have either little or very easy shaping. There might be a couple of new stitches for the less experienced crocheter, but the Beginner patterns use stitch patterns with easy repeats. Finishing will involve sewing easy, straight seams, or sewing on a button, but there are no shaped sleeve caps or zippers to deal with.

This is a great gateway pattern for your first garment. Work on these to upgrade your garment-making skills; then you can go on to projects that require more experience.

More experienced crocheters will find these patterns easy to finish and will have a garment in a relatively short period of time to show off.

INTERMEDIATE

Your crochet skills include more complicated stitches like lace patterns and colorwork. You have probably made a garment or two before.

Patterns written for the Intermediate level have shaping in the body panels, armhole, and neckline. There might be a few new techniques, and there are set-in sleeves and maybe even a zipper to sew in.

Crocheters who have made their first garment will find these patterns a welcome challenge. More experienced crocheters who have made garments before will have no trouble completing these patterns.

ADVANCED

Your crochet skills include complex stitch patterns with longer repeats and color changes. This is not your first garment, and you are ready to show off your skills.

Patterns written for the Advanced level have more complex shaping instructions, and finishing includes buttons, zippers, and set-in sleeves.

Crocheters who have made a few garments will find these patterns a welcome challenge and will feel that rush of accomplishment when they weave in that last end.

Crocheters with minimal garment-making experience will still find they can complete these patterns with great results with a little patience and attention to the detailed pattern instructions and tutorials.

CHOOSING YARNS

How to pick the right yarn to create the right fabric

One of the most important parts of our design process is choosing the fabrics our designs are made from. As crochet and knitwear designers, we have the unique ability to work with an endless combination of stitches and yarns with different fiber contents to always create custom fabrics for our designs.

For many different valid reasons, you might not want to use the exact yarn we used to create the original samples

CYCA Standard Yarn Weight System chart

	LACE **0**	SUPER FINE **1**	FINE **2**	LIGHT **3**	MEDIUM **4**
	Fingering 10-count crochet thread	Sock, Fingering, Baby	Sport, Baby	DK, Light Worsted	Worsted, Afghan Aran
Crochet Gauge* Ranges in Single Crochet to 4 inch	32–42 double crochets	21–32 sts	16–20 sts	12–17 sts	11–14 sts
Recommended Hook in Metric Size Range	Steel 1.6–1.4 mm	2.25—3.5 mm	3.5—4.5 mm	4.5—5.5 mm	5.5—6.5 mm
Recommended Hook US Size Range	Steel 6, 7, 8 Regular hook B–1	B–1 to E–4	E–4 to 7	7 to I–9	I–9 to K–10½

for the patterns in this book . . . and that's okay! Sometimes, however, the task of substituting yarns can be daunting and too often it is difficult to know the right yarn to choose for your project.

Luckily, we have tools for creating a common language for communicating with crocheters and knitters when discussing yarn that will make your choices much easier. For *Designer Crochet*, we have used the Craft Yarn Council of America's (CYCA) Standard Yarn Weight System chart as our Rosetta stone. We will use this chart to let you know what yarn we are using and how to make a good decision about what yarn to use when making your own versions of our designs.

To that end, there are three factors you should consider in order to choose an appropriate yarn substitute for your project: yarn weight, yarn content, and the finished fabric.

YARN WEIGHT

To check the weight of the yarn we used for a specific pattern, look under the Materials section in the pattern and you will see, under Yarn, one of the yarn symbols from the chart. Each weight of yarn has its own designation, and you will use these designations as your guide when substituting yarn for your project.

If, for example, you look at the pattern for the Cables and Lace Tunic and see the pattern indicates the yarn used for this pattern has the symbol for a CYCA 1, you can go online or head to the store where you buy yarn and look for the CYCA 1 symbol on the ball band of the yarn. Or, if you just fall in love with a particular yarn that you THINK might be the right weight but doesn't have the CYCA number designation on it, you can check your handy dandy chart and see if the stitches per inch gauge or the recommended hook or needle size matches up.

Still not sure if that luscious ball of yarny goodness will work for your project? Take a look at the CYCA Standard Yarn Weight System chart again. You will see that a CYCA 1 yarn also says it is called sock or fingering weight yarn. Words like sport, sock, fingering, and DK are all just another way to communicate in a common language.

Whether you use the CYCA number, or the common name like fingering or DK, most everyone communicates using one of these methods of identifying yarn weight. All it takes is a little bit of investigating on your part to see how the yarn seller communicates their yarn weight to you, then use that language to make your choice.

YARN CONTENT

The content of the yarn is just as important as choosing the correct weight. While it might seem obvious that a bulky weight yarn will not create the same fabric as a fingering or DK weight yarn, it might not occur to folks that a 100% cotton yarn will not create the same fabric as an alpaca/wool/nylon blend.

If the yarn you are substituting doesn't have the same fiber content as the yarn we used to create the design, make sure you are choosing a close approximation and not a yarn that is going to make a completely different fabric.

For example, for our Duster we knew we would need a yarn that would be lightweight enough to not become hard, heavy, and stiff on the solid stitch panels but that would hold its shape in the lace sections. The yarn we chose had the perfect balance of weight and fiber content to give us the final fabric we wanted. If you were substituting yarns, you might want to choose a wool/nylon blend or a superwash wool, or an acrylic or acrylic blend that would give you the same type of lightweight strength but still have drape and movement. Choosing a yarn that is too soft or stretchy would cause your finished garment to stretch out of proportion and sag rather than drape.

Since you are investing time and love into stitching this project, you might as well put just as much time and love into picking a yarn that will give you a finished garment you'll never want to take off. In the end it doesn't matter how much you dream about that yarn you found at the store that was just calling your name. If it isn't the right weight or has the wrong fiber content for your project, it just isn't going to create the right fabric in the end.

GAUGE

Obtaining the correct stitch gauge (or tension, depending on what part of the world you are in) is essential to making sure your finished garment fits properly. You will notice we list the "Blocked Gauge" for each project in this book. This means you will make your swatch then block that swatch to obtain your stitch and row gauge. In most cases, this means you will stitch slightly tighter than your blocked gauge requires.

Making sure you can meet this gauge will ensure your finished project comes out with the same fabric as our original design. Before you dive in to your project, make the sample swatch(es) as written in the pattern, then wet or steam block your swatch to the measurements given in the pattern. After you count your stitches and rows, check out your handiwork and see if the finished fabric is too stretched or too loose. If you aren't happy with the fabric, make another swatch and change your tension or hook size accordingly. Remember: It takes a relatively short amount of time to check your gauge and get your project right the first time!

BLOCKING

Once you have blocked your swatch, checked your gauge, and made the individual pieces for your garment, you will notice each of the patterns include a Finishing section where you will be instructed to "Block all pieces to finished measurements." As with your swatch, use either a wet or steam method to block your components into their final shapes.

This makes sewing the pieces together much easier and will ensure your finished garment fits properly.

In addition to ensuring a proper fit, blocking also adds clarity and definition to your stitches by opening up lacework and by setting close stitches into place allowing your stitching prowess to really show.

You will notice that your fibers become more pliable and sumptuous after blocking. Wools will open up and "bloom" with steam or wet blocking, and acrylic blends will soften and drape beautifully with a little steam.

FINISHING

The Finishing section will also tell you to sew buttons or zippers, sew sleeves, and set in sleeves and collars. The Special Techniques section on page 197 provides step-by-step photo tutorials to show you how to set in a sleeve, how to sew your best seams with a locking mattress stitch technique, and more. Do yourself a favor and invest in a set of locking stitch markers or pins, a yarn needle, and follow the photo tutorials. You will be finishing like a pro in no time and will carry this knowledge over into your other projects.

ABBREVIATION CHART

Most of these abbreviations should already be familiar to you, but just in case, we're providing you with an easy-to-use chart of all the basic abbreviations used in this book.

Have fun and happy stitching!

ABBREVIATIONS

2 dc-cluster	2 double crochet cluster	**FPqtr**	Front Post quadruple treble crochet	**sc2tog**	single crochet 2 together
3-dc Cl	3 double crochet Cluster	**FPtr**	Front Post treble crochet	**sc tbl**	single crochet through back loop only
BPdc	Back Post double crochet	**Fsc**	Foundation single crochet	**Sc V-St**	Single crochet V-Stitch
BPhdc	Back Post half double crochet	**Hdc**	Half double crochet	**sk**	skip
ch	chain	**hdc tbl**	half double crochet through back loop only	**sl**	slip
dc	double crochet	**Hdc-v**	Half double crochet v stitch	**sl st**	slip stitch
dc2tog	double crochet 2 together	**hdc2tog**	half double crochet 2 together	**sp**	space
dc3tog	double crochet 3 together	**Hhdc**	Herringbone half double crochet	**sps**	spaces
dec	decrease	**lp**	loop	**st**	stitch
dtr	double treble crochet	**lps**	loops	**sts**	stitches
Fhdc	Foundation half double crochet	**pm**	place marker	**tbl**	through back loop
First-tr	First treble crochet	**rem**	remaining	**tr**	treble crochet
First-dc	First double crochet	**rep**	repeat	**tr2tog**	treble crochet 2 together
First-dtr	First double treble crochet	**rnd**	round	**V-St**	V-Stitch
FPdc	Front Post double crochet	**rnds**	rounds	**var**	variation
FPdtr	Front Post double treble crochet	**RS**	Right Side	**WS**	Wrong Side
FPhdc	Front Post half double crochet	**sc**	single crochet	**yo**	yarn over

US TO UK CROCHET CONVERSION CHART

US Terminology	UK Terminology	US Terminology	UK Terminology
single crochet (sc)	Double crochet (Dc)	Double treble (Dtr)	Triple treble (Trtr)
Half double crochet (Hdc)	Half treble (Htr)	skip	miss
Double crochet (Dc)	Treble (Tr)	gauge	tension
Treble (Tr)	Double treble (Dtr)	yarn over (yo)	yarn over hook (yoh)

OUTERWEAR

DUSTER

The long, graceful line of the classic duster silhouette is a look that compliments bodies of all different shapes and sizes. In this version, we used a graphic mix of lace and solid stitch pattern combined with a lightweight yarn and two stylish back pleats to create a garment with a lot of dramatic style.

Each section is made separately so you can customize this jacket to fit your personal style. Work fewer rows in the first three lower sections of the coat to make a shorter jacket, or really go all out and work more repeats for the look of a formal cover up.

SKILL LEVEL: Intermediate
SIZES: S (M, L, XL, 2X, 3X, 4X, 5X)
Sample shown in size small

FINISHED MEASUREMENTS

To Fit Bust: 32 (36, 40, 44, 48, 52, 56, 60) inches/81.5 (91.5, 101.5, 112, 122, 132, 142, 152.5) cm.
Finished Bust: 36 (41, 45, 48¼, 52, 56, 60, 64¾) inches/91.5 (104, 114.5, 122.5, 132, 142, 152.5, 164.5) cm.
Finished Length: 43 (43¾, 43¾, 43¾, 44, 44, 44½, 44½) inches/109 (111, 111, 111, 112, 112, 113, 113) cm.

MATERIALS AND TOOLS

■ Sample uses Berroco, Ultra Alpaca Fine (50% Wool/20% Alpaca/30% Nylon; 3.5 ounces/100 g = 433 yards/400 m); 7 (8, 8, 9, 10, 11, 11, 12) skeins in color Pea Soup Mix #1275 or 3031 (3464, 3464, 3897, 4330, 4763, 4763, 5196) yards/2772 (3167, 3167, 3563, 3959, 4355, 4355, 4751) m of superfine weight yarn

■ Crochet hook: 3.25mm (size D-3) or size to obtain gauge
■ Yarn needle
■ Stitch markers

BLOCKED GAUGES

Cables and lace: 54 sts = 10 inches/25.5 cm; 13 rows = 5 inches/12.5 cm

Woven hdc: 30 sts = 6 inches/15 cm; 24 rows = 5¼ inches/13.5 cm

Cross and cluster lace: 41 sts = 5¾ inches/14.5 cm; 13 rows = 5¾ inches/14.5 cm

Always take time to check your gauge.

GAUGE SWATCHES

Cables and lace stitch swatch

Foundation Row: Work 54 Fsc, turn.

Row 1 (RS): First hdc, hdc in each st across, turn.

Rows 2–13: Work even in cables and lace pattern st.

Cross and cluster lace stitch swatch

Foundation Row (WS): Work 41 Fsc, turn.

Rows 1–13: Work even in cross and cluster lace pattern st.

Woven hdc stitch swatch

Row 1: Work 30 Fsc, turn.

Rows 2–24: Work even in woven hdc pattern st.

STITCH GUIDE

Foundation single crochet (Fsc): Ch 2, insert hook in 2nd ch from hook, yo and draw up a loop, yo and draw through 1 loop (first "chain" made), yo and draw through 2 loops on hook (first sc made), *insert hook under 2 loops of the "chain" just made, yo and draw up a loop, yo and draw through 1 loop ("chain" made), yo and draw through 2 loops on hook (sc made); rep from * for indicated number of foundation sts.

Foundation half double crochet (Fhdc): Ch 3, yo, insert hook in 3rd ch from hook, yo and draw up a loop, yo and draw through 1 loop (first "chain" made), yo and draw through all 3 loops on hook (first hdc made), *yo, insert hook under 2 loops of the "chain" just made, yo and draw up a loop, yo and draw through 1 loop ("chain" made), yo and draw through all 3 loops on hook (hdc made); rep from * for indicated number of foundation sts.

First double crochet (First-dc): Sc in first st, ch 2. Note: Use this st whenever the first st of a row is a dc. When working back in the First-dc at the end of the following row, insert hook into the second ch of the ch-2.

Reverse single crochet (rev sc): Working from left to right, sc in opposite direction by inserting hook in next st to the right, yo and draw up a loop, yo and draw through both loops on hook.

Left dc-cross (worked over 3 sts): Sk next 2 sts, dc in ch-1 sp, ch 1, working in front of dc just made, dc in first skipped ch-1 sp.

3-double crochet cluster (3-dc Cl): Yo, insert hook in indicated st or sp and draw up a loop, yo and draw through 2 loops on hook (2 loops remain on hook), [yo, insert hook in same st or sp and draw up a loop, yo and draw through 2 loops on hook] 2 times, yo and draw through all 4 loops on hook.

Back Post double crochet (BPdc): Yo, insert hook from back to front then to back again around post of indicated st, yo and draw up a loop, [yo and draw through 2 loops on hook] twice.

Front Post treble crochet (FPtr): Yo (twice), insert hook from front to back and then to front again around post of designated st, yo and draw up a loop, [yo and draw through 2 loops on hook] 3 times.

2-over-2 FPtr left cross cable (worked over 4 sts): Sk next 2 sts, FPtr around each of next 2 sts; working in front of FPtr just made, FPtr around each of 2 skipped sts.

PATTERN STITCHES

For Master Chart Key, see page 206.

Cables and lace (worked on a multiple of 16 + 6 sts) Ⓐ

Row 1 (WS): Ch 1, First-dc in first st, *dc in each of next 5 sts, ch 3, sk next 2 sts, sc in next st, ch 3, sk next 2 sts, 3 dc in next st, sk next 4 sts, 3 dc in next st; rep from * across to last 5 sts, dc in each of last 5 sts, turn.

Row 2 (RS): Ch 1, First-dc in first st, *work 2-over-2 FPtr left cross cable, dc in next st, ch 3, sk next 2 dc, sc in sp before next dc, ch 3, sk next 2 dc, 3 dc in next dc, sk next ch-3 space, 3 dc in next dc; rep from * across to last 5 sts, work 2-over-2 FPtr left cross cable, dc in last st, turn.

Row 3: Ch 1, First-dc in first st, *BPdc around the post of each of next 4 sts, dc in next st, ch 3, sk next 2 dc, sc in space before next dc, ch 3, sk next 2 dc, 3 dc in next st, sk next ch-3 space, 3 dc in next st; rep from * across to last 5 sts, BPdc around the post of each of next 4 sts, dc in last st, turn.

Rep last 2 rows for pattern st.

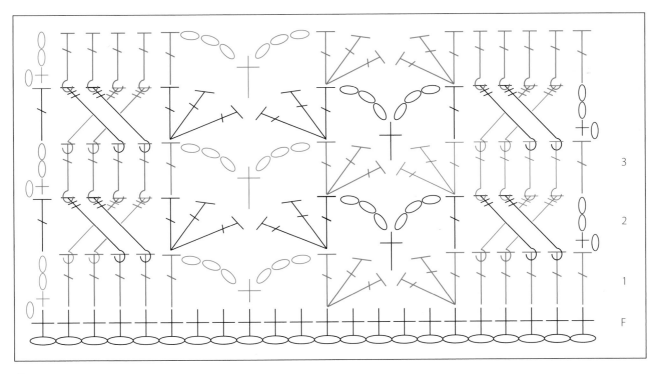

A Cables and lace stitch chart

Cross and cluster lace (worked on a multiple of 3 + 2 sts) **B**

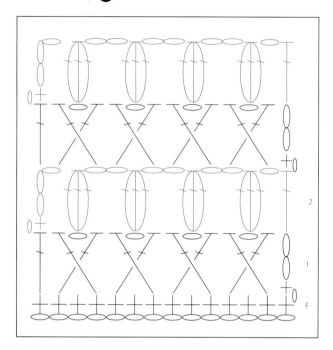

B Cross and cluster lace stitch chart

Row 1 (WS): First-dc in first st, work left dc-cross to last st, dc in last st, turn.
Row 2: First-dc, ch 1, sk next st, 3-dc Cl in next ch-1 sp, *ch 2, sk next 2 sts, 3-dc Cl in next ch-1 sp; rep from * to last 2 sts, ch 1, sk next st, dc in last st, turn.
Rep rows 1 and 2 for pattern st.

Woven hdc (worked on any number of sts)
Row 1: Ch 1, hdc in each st across, turn.
Row 2: Ch 1, hdc in first st, sk next st, hdc in space bet skipped st and next st, hdc in each space bet sts to last st, hdc in last st, turn.
Rep row 2 for pattern st.

SPECIAL TECHNIQUE
Locking mattress stitch (see Special Techniques, page 200)
Setting in a sleeve (See Special Techniques, page 201)

NOTES
1. When instructed to work in st 2 rows below, insert hook in indicated stitch in the row numbered 2 less than the row you are working. For example, if you are working row 5, a stitch "2 rows" below is in row 5–2 = row 3.
2. Left Side and Right Side refer to left and right side as worn.
3. Garment is made from the bottom up starting with two wide panels, then main body is worked in three separate panels of right and left front and back panels.
4. When instructed to work in a pattern stitch "as established," work the next row of pattern stitch and ensure that the stitches line up as in previous rows.
5. For the purpose of this pattern, all chain spaces count as 1 stitch.
6. When instructed to "decrease X number of sts," use dc2tog, hdc2tog, or sc2tog (see Stitch Guide) according to the pattern row you are working on. For example: if you are about to work a row of Dc-V stitches, you would dc2tog where the pattern reads "decrease 1 st."
7. When instructed to "increase X number of sts," work 2 dc, 2 hdc or 2 sc in first st according to the pattern row you are working on. For example: if you are about to work a row of Dc-V stitches, you would work 2 dc in first st where the pattern reads "inc 1 st."
8. If after a decrease the next stitch is a chain space, work 1 stitch in pattern stitch in the place of that chain space, then continue as instructed.

A Note on Increasing
1. The cross and cluster lace pattern stitch has a 2-row repeat. Ensure that this 2-row rep continues.

2. The cross and cluster lace pattern stitch has a pattern rep in multiples of 3 + 2 stitches. Once you have increased a total of 3 stitches on each side of your established pattern, you will have enough increase stitches to begin working additional 3-stitch pattern repeats of the cross and cluster lace pattern stitch on the next row.

INSTRUCTIONS

LOWER BODY

PANEL #1

Foundation Row: Work 242 (272, 287, 316, 331, 346, 375, 390) Fhdc, turn.

Rows 1–30: Work row 2 of woven hdc pattern st.

PANEL #2

Foundation Row: Work 262 (294, 310, 342, 358, 374, 406, 422) Fsc, turn.

Row 1 (RS): First-dc in first st, dc in each st to end of row, turn.

Rows 2–34: Work even in cables and lace pattern st.

Fasten off.

PANEL #3

Foundation Row: Work 242 (272, 287, 316, 331, 346, 375, 390) Fhdc, turn.

Rows 1–30: Work row 2 of woven hdc pattern st.

UPPER BODY

LEFT FRONT

Foundation Row (RS): Work 65 (74, 80, 86, 95, 101, 107, 116) Fsc, turn.

Rows 1–22 (22, 22, 22, 22, 20, 18, 18): Work even in cross and cluster lace pattern st.

BEGIN LEFT FRONT NECKLINE SHAPING

Row 1 (WS): First dc in first st, [dc2tog over next 2 sts] twice, dc in next st, work in pattern st as established across, turn—63 (72, 78, 84, 93, 99, 105, 114) sts.

Row 2 (RS): Work in pattern st as established to last 6 sts, dc in next st, dc2tog twice, dc in last st, turn—61 (70, 76, 82, 91, 97, 103, 112) sts.

SIZES S (M, L, 2X) ONLY

Row 3: Rep row 1—59 (68, 74, 89) sts.

SIZES XL (3X, 4X, 5X) ONLY

Rows 3–6 (6, 8, 8): Rep last 2 rows (2 [2, 3, 3] times)—74 (89, 91, 100) sts at end of last row.

SIZES 4X (5X) ONLY

Row 9: Rep row 1—89 (98) sts.

SECOND DECREASE SECTION

SIZES S (M, L, 2X, 4X, 5X) ONLY

Row 4 (4, 4, 4, 10, 10) (RS): Work in pattern st as established to last 6 sts, sk next st, dc2tog twice, dc in last st, turn—56 (65, 71, 86, 86, 95) sts.

Row 5 (5, 5, 5, 11, 11) (WS): First dc, [dc2tog over next 2 sts] twice, sk next st, work in pattern st as established across, turn—53 (62, 68, 83, 83, 92) sts.

SIZES XL (3X) ONLY

Row 7 (WS): First dc, [dc2tog over next 2 sts] twice, sk next st, work in pattern st as established across, turn—71 (86) sts.

Row 8 (RS): Work in pattern st as established to last 6 sts, sk next st, [dc2tog over next 2 sts] twice, dc in last st, turn—68 (83) sts.

ALL SIZES

Rows 6 (6, 6, 9, 6, 9, 12, 12)–7 (9, 9, 10, 11, 12, 13, 15): Rep last 2 rows 1 (2, 2, 1, 3, 2, 1, 2) times—47 (50, 56, 62, 65, 71, 77, 80) sts at end of last row.

SIZES S (4X) ONLY

Row 8 (14): Rep row 4 (10)—44 (74) sts.

Fasten off.

ALL SIZES

Fasten off.

SHOULDER SECTION

Foundation Row: Work 29 (34, 39, 43, 45, 48, 51, 56) Fhdc, turn.

Rows 1–19: Work row 2 of woven hdc pattern st. Fasten off.

RIGHT FRONT

Foundation Row (RS): Work 65 (74, 80, 86, 95, 101, 107, 116) Fsc, turn.

Rows 1–22 (22, 22, 22, 22, 20, 18, 18): Work even in cross and cluster lace pattern st.

BEGIN RIGHT FRONT NECKLINE SHAPING

Row 1 (WS): Work in pattern st as established to last 6 sts, dc in next st, [dc2tog over next 2 sts] twice, dc in last st, turn—63 (72, 78, 84, 93, 99, 105, 114) sts.

Row 2 (RS): First-dc in first st, [dc2tog over next 2 sts] twice, dc in next st, work in pattern st as established across, turn—61 (70, 76, 82, 91, 97, 103, 112) sts.

SIZES S (M, L, 2X) ONLY

Row 3: Rep row 1—59 (68, 74, 89) sts.

SIZES XL (3X, 4X, 5X) ONLY

Rows 3–6 (6, 8, 8): Rep last 2 rows 2 (2, 3, 3) times—74 (89, 91, 100) sts at end of last row.

SIZES 4X (5X) ONLY

Row 9: Rep row 1—89 (98) sts.

SECOND DECREASE SECTION

SIZES S (M, L, 2X, 4X, 5X) ONLY

Row 4 (4, 4, 4, 10, 10) (RS): First-dc in first st, [dc2tog over next 2 sts] twice, sk next st, work in pattern st as established across, turn—56 (65, 71, 86, 86, 95) sts.

Row 5 (5, 5, 5, 11, 11) (WS): Work in pattern st as established across to last 6 sts, sk next st, [dc2tog over next 2 sts] twice, dc in last st, turn—53 (62, 68, 83, 83, 92) sts.

SIZES XL (3X) ONLY

Row 7 (WS): Work in pattern st as established to last 6 sts, sk next st, [dc2tog over next 2 sts] twice, dc in last st, turn—71 (86) sts.

Row 8 (RS): First-dc, [dc2tog over next 2 sts] twice, sk next st, work in pattern st as established across, turn—68 (83) sts.

ALL SIZES

Rows 6 (6, 6, 9, 6, 9, 12, 12)–7 (9, 9, 10, 11, 12, 13, 15): Rep last 2 rows 1 (2, 2, 1, 3, 2, 1, 2) times—47 (50, 56, 62, 65, 71, 77, 80) sts at end of last row.

SIZES S (4X) ONLY

Row 8 (14): Rep row 4 (10)—44 (74) sts.

ALL SIZES

Fasten off.

SHOULDER SECTION

Foundation Row: Work 29 (34, 39, 43, 45, 48, 51, 56) Fhdc, turn.

Rows 1–19: Work row 2 of woven hdc pattern st. Fasten off.

BACK

Foundation Row (RS): Work 128 (143, 158, 173, 185, 200, 215, 230) Fsc, turn.

Rows 1–29 (31, 31, 31, 32, 32, 33, 33): Work even in cross and cluster lace pattern st. Fasten off.

SHOULDER SECTION

Foundation Row: Work 90 (100, 113, 121, 130, 140, 151, 161) Fhdc, turn.

Rows 1–19: Work row 2 of woven hdc pattern st. Fasten off.

SLEEVE (MAKE 2)

CUFF

Row 1: Work 48 (52, 52, 56, 65, 69, 69, 69) Fhdc turn.

Rows 2–9: Work row 2 of woven hdc pattern st. Fasten off.

MAIN SLEEVE

Foundation Row: Work 68 (68, 74, 80, 92, 98, 98, 98) Fsc, turn.

Rows 1–7 (5, 2, 2, 3, 3, 2, 2): Work even in cross and cluster lace pattern st.

BEGIN SLEEVE SHAPING

Row 1: (First dc, dc) in first st, work in pattern st as established across to last st, 2 dc in last st, turn—70 (70, 76, 82, 94, 100, 100, 100) sts.

Row 2: (First-dc, dc) in first st, 2 dc in next st, work in pattern st as established across to last 2 sts, 2 dc in each of last 2 sts, turn—74 (74, 80, 86, 98, 104, 104, 104) sts.

Row 3: Work even in pattern st as established.

Rows 4–18 (21, 24, 24, 24, 24, 27, 27): Rep last 3 rows 5 (6, 7, 7, 7, 7, 8, 8) times—104 (110, 122, 128, 140, 146, 152, 152) sts at end of last row.

TOP OF SLEEVE

Row 1: Work 73 (78, 85, 90, 98, 102, 107, 113) Fhdc, turn.

Rows 2–28: Work row 2 of woven hdc pattern st.

Fasten off.

FINISHING

Block all pieces to schematic measurements.

Sew Panels 1, 2, and 3 together according to schematic.

FIRST PLEAT

With RS facing find center of Panel 3 and place Marker #1. Measure 3¾ (4, 4¼, 4½, 4½, 4½, 4½, 4½)"/9.5 (10.25, 10.75, 11.5, 11.5, 11.5, 11.5, 11.5) cm to the right of Marker #1, place Marker #2. Measure 6¼ (6¾, 6¼, 7½, 7¼, 6½, 7½, 6½)"/ 16 (17, 16, 19, 18.5, 16.5, 19, 16.5) cm to the right of Marker #2, place Marker #3. Fold Marker #3 to Marker #2 holding excess fabric to back of work. Flatten excess fabric so that half of the stitches are on either side of point where Markers #3 and #2 meet. Ensure the stitches of both layers of fabric match.

Working from RS, use Locking Mattress Stitch to sew the sts of the top edge of the folded section to corresponding sts of excess fabric. Note: you will be sewing through 3 layers of stitches.

SECOND PLEAT

With RS facing, measure 3¾ (4, 4¼, 4½, 4½, 4½, 4½, 4½)"/9.5 (10.25, 10.75, 11.5, 11.5, 11.5, 11.5, 11.5) cm to the left of Marker #1, place Marker #2. Measure 6¼ (6¾, 6¼, 7½, 7¼, 6½, 7½, 6½)"/ 16 (17, 16, 19, 18.5, 16.5, 19, 16.5) cm to the left of Marker #2, place Marker #3. Folder Marker #3 to Marker #2 holding excess fabric to back of work.

Sew all remaining Duster panels together according to schematic as follows:

Sew Front Solid Panels to Front Lace Panels.

Sew Back Solid Panel to Back Lace Panel.

Sew completed Front Panels to Completed Back Panel leaving 7 (7.5, 8, 8.5, 9, 9.5, 10, 10.5)" for armhole openings.

Sew completed upper body to completed lower body.

With WS facing, fold Front Panels to Back Panels and sew shoulder seam of 6 (7, 8, 8.5, 9, 9.5, 10, 11)"

Place sleeves in armholes and sew in place.

Sew Sleeve seams.

Weave in ends.

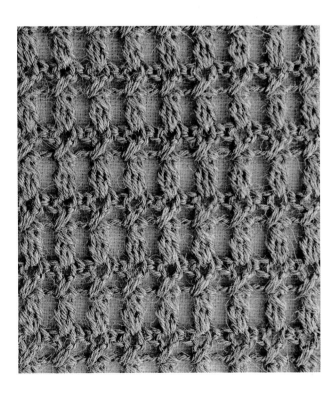

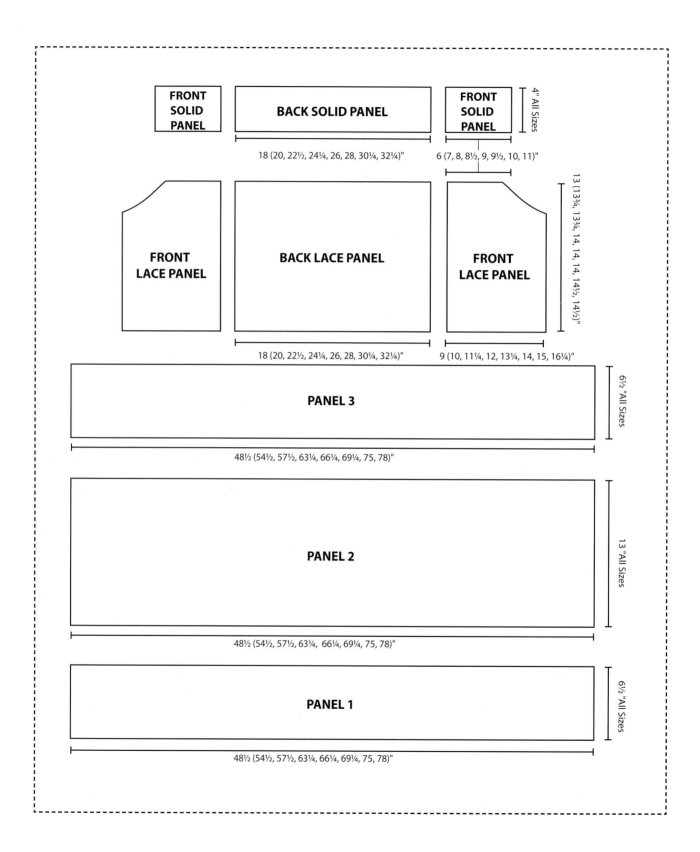

FRONT SOLID PANEL

BACK SOLID PANEL

FRONT SOLID PANEL

4" All Sizes

18 (20, 22½, 24¼, 26, 28, 30¼, 32¼)"

6 (7, 8, 8½, 9, 9½, 10, 11)"

13 (13¾, 13¾, 14, 14, 14, 14½, 14½)"

FRONT LACE PANEL

BACK LACE PANEL

FRONT LACE PANEL

18 (20, 22½, 24¼, 26, 28, 30¼, 32¼)"

9 (10, 11¼, 12, 13¼, 14, 15, 16¼)"

PANEL 3

6½" All Sizes

48½ (54½, 57½, 63¼, 66¼, 69¼, 75, 78)"

PANEL 2

13" All Sizes

48½ (54½, 57½, 63¼, 66¼, 69¼, 75, 78)"

PANEL 1

6½" All Sizes

48½ (54½, 57½, 63¼, 66¼, 69¼, 75, 78)"

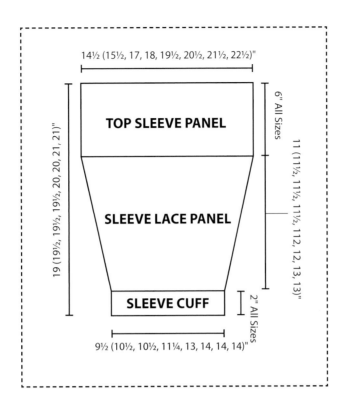

14½ (15½, 17, 18, 19½, 20½, 21½, 22½)"

TOP SLEEVE PANEL

6" All Sizes

11 (11½, 11½, 11½, 112, 12, 13, 13)"

SLEEVE LACE PANEL

19 (19½, 19½, 20, 20, 21, 21)"

SLEEVE CUFF

2" All Sizes

9½ (10½, 10½, 11¼, 13, 14, 14, 14)"

CLOAKED HOOD HOODIE

We have given the beloved classic hoodie a boost with design elements like asymmetrical overlapping front panels, a generous hood, an exposed zipper, longer body styling, and ribbed forearms. Make this piece and show people you have a flash of edge to your style, but you like to keep it comfy too.

SKILL LEVEL: Intermediate
SIZES: S (M, L, XL, 2X, 3X, 4X, 5X)
Sample shown in size small

FINISHED MEASUREMENTS

To Fit Bust: 32 (36, 40, 44, 48, 52, 56, 60) inches/81.5 (91.5, 101.5, 112, 122, 132, 142, 152.5) cm
Finished Bust: 36 (40, 44, 48, 52½, 56, 60, 64½) inches/91.5 (101.5, 112, 122, 133.5, 142, 152.5, 164) cm
Finished Length: 32 (32, 32½, 33, 33, 33, 33½, 33½) inches/81.5 (81.5, 82.5, 84, 84, 84, 85, 85) cm

MATERIALS AND TOOLS

- Sample uses Knit Picks, Capretta (80% Fine Merino Wool, 10% Cashmere, 10% Nylon; 1.8 ounces/50 g = 230 yards/210 m; 11 (12, 13, 14, 16, 17, 18, 19) skeins in color #25946 Wine—2530 (2760, 2990, 3220, 3680, 3910, 4140, 4370) yards/2310 (2520, 2730, 2940, 3360, 3570, 3780, 3990) m of lightweight yarn

- Crochet hook: 3.5 mm (size E-4) or size to obtain gauge
- Yarn needle
- Sewing needle
- Thread in matching color for sewing in zipper
- Separating zipper: 32 (32, 32½, 33, 33, 33, 33½, 33½) inches/81.5 (81.5, 82.5, 84, 84, 84, 85, 85) cm long

BLOCKED GAUGES

Sc linen stitch var 1 pattern: 33 sts = 5¼ inches/13.5 cm; 21 rows = 3¾ inches/9.5 cm

Sc ribbing pattern: 20 sts = 3½ inches/9 cm; 19 rows = 3¼ inches/8.5 cm

Always take time to check your gauge.

STITCH GUIDE

Foundation single crochet (Fsc): Ch 2, insert hook in 2nd ch from hook, yo and draw up a loop, yo and draw through 1 loop (first "chain" made), yo and draw through 2 loops on hook (first sc made), *insert hook under 2 loops of the "chain" just made, yo and draw up a loop, yo and draw through 1 loop ("chain" made), yo and draw through 2 loops on hook (sc made); rep from * for indicated number of foundation sts.

Single crochet through back loop only (sc-tbl): Insert hook in back loop of indicated st, yo and draw up a loop, yo and draw through 2 loops on hook.

PATTERN STITCHES

For Master Chart Key, see page 206.

Single crochet linen stitch variation 1 (sc linen st var 1) (worked on a multiple of 2 + 1 sts) Ⓐ

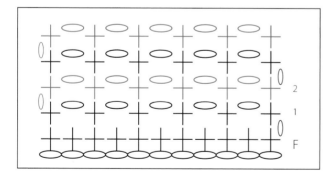

Ⓐ Single crochet linen stitch variation 1 stitch chart

Row 1 (RS): Ch 1, sc in first st, *ch 1, sk next st, sc in next st; rep from * across, turn.

Row 2: Ch 1, sc in first st, *ch 1, sk next ch-1 sp, sc in next st; rep from * across, turn.

Rep row 2 for pattern st.

Single crochet ribbing (sc ribbing) (worked on any number of sts) Ⓑ

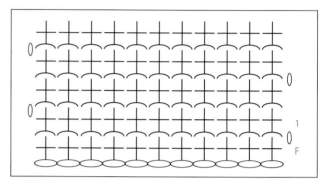

Ⓑ Single crochet ribbing stitch chart

Row 1: Ch 1, sc in both loops of first st, sc-tbl in each st across to last st, sc in both loops of last st, turn.

Rep row 1 for pattern st.

SPECIAL TECHNIQUE

Locking mattress stitch (see Special Techniques, page 200)

Setting in a sleeve (see Special Techniques, page 201)

Sewing in a zipper (see Special Techniques, page 202)

NOTES

1. Left Side and Right Side refer to left and right side as worn.
2. When instructed to work in a pattern stitch "as established," work the next row of pattern stitch and ensure that the stitches line up as in previous rows.
3. For the purpose of this pattern, all chain spaces count as 1 stitch.
4. Ribbing section is worked first from side to side, then stitches for main body are worked in side of ribbing rows.

INSTRUCTIONS

BACK PANEL

BOTTOM HEM RIBBING

Row 1: Work 34 Fsc, turn.

Rows 2–105 (118, 129, 140, 153, 165, 176, 189): Work in sc ribbing pattern st.

Do not fasten off. At end of last row, rotate work ¼ turn to the right for working in row-end sts of ribbing.

MAIN BODY

Row 1 (RS): Ch 1, working in row-end sts of ribbing, sc in each of first 11 (11, 11, 10, 11, 11, 10, 10) sts, [2 sc in next st, sc in each of next 11 (11, 11, 11, 11, 12, 12, 12) sts] 7 (8, 9, 10, 11, 11, 12, 13) times, 2 sc in next st, sc in each of next 9 (10, 9, 9, 9, 10, 9, 9) sts, turn—113 (127, 139, 151, 165, 177, 189, 203) sts.

Rows 2–106 (104, 104, 102, 100, 98, 98, 94): Work even in sc linen st var 1 pattern st.

BEGIN ARMHOLE SHAPING

Row 1: Ch 1, sl st in first 8 (7, 6, 8, 8, 8, 9, 10) sts, ch 1, sc in next st, work in pattern st as established across to last 9 (8, 7, 9, 9, 9, 10, 11) sts, sc in next st, turn, leaving last 8 (7, 6, 8, 8, 8, 9, 10) sts unworked—97 (113, 127, 135, 149, 161, 171, 183) sts.

Row 2: Ch 1, sc2tog, sc in next st, work in pattern st as established across to last 3 sts, sc in next st, sc2tog, turn—95 (111, 125, 133, 147, 159, 169, 181) sts.

Row 3: Ch 1, [sc2tog in next 2 sts] twice, sc in next st, work in pattern st as established across to last 5 sts, sc in next st, [sc2tog in next 2 sts] twice, turn—91 (107, 121, 129, 143, 155, 165, 177) sts.

SIZES M (L, XL, 2X, 3X, 4X, 5X) ONLY

Rows 4 and 5: Rep last 2 rows—101 (115, 123, 137, 149, 159, 171) sts at end of last row.

SIZES L (XL, 2X, 3X, 4X, 5X) ONLY

Rows 6–9 (9, 13, 17, 19, 23): Rep last 2 rows 2 (2, 4, 6, 7, 9) times—103 (111, 113, 113, 117, 117) sts at end of last row.

ALL SIZES

Rows 4 (6, 10, 10, 14, 18, 20, 24)–34 (36, 38, 42, 44, 46, 48, 52): Work even in pattern st as established.

BEGIN BACK NECKLINE SHAPING

FIRST SIDE

Row 1 (RS): Ch 1, work in pattern st as established across first 31 (36, 37, 41, 39, 37, 38, 38) sts, sc in next st, turn, leaving last 59 (64, 65, 69, 73, 75, 78, 78) sts unworked, turn—32 (37, 38, 42, 40, 38, 39, 39) sts.

Row 2: Ch 1, sc in first st, sk next st, [sc2tog in next 2 sts] twice, work in pattern st as established across to end of row, turn—29 (34, 35, 39, 37, 35, 36, 36) sts.

Row 3: Ch 1, work in pattern st as established to last 6 sts, [sc2tog in next 2 sts] twice, sk next st, sc in last st, turn—26 (31, 32, 36, 34, 32, 33, 33) sts.

Rows 4 and 5: Rep last 2 rows—20 (25, 26, 30, 28, 26, 27, 27) sts.

SIZES L (XL, 2X, 3X, 4X, 5X) ONLY

Row 6: Rep row 2—23 (27, 25, 23, 24, 24) sts.

ALL SIZES

Row 6 (6, 7, 7, 7, 7, 7, 7): Work even in pattern st as established.

SIZES 4X (5X) ONLY

Row 8: Work even in pattern st as established.

ALL SIZES

Fasten off.

SECOND SIDE

With RS facing, skip first 27 (27, 27, 27, 33, 37, 39, 39) unworked sts at center of neckline, join yarn in next stitch; first st of row 1 is worked in same st as joining.

Row 1 (RS): Ch 1, work in pattern st as established to end of row, turn—32 (37, 38, 42, 40, 38, 39, 39) sts.

Row 2: Ch 1, work in pattern st as established to last 6 sts, sc2tog twice, sk next st, sc in last st, turn—29 (34, 35, 39, 37, 35, 36, 36) sts.

Row 3: Ch 1, sc in first st, sk next st, sc2tog twice, work in pattern st as established to end of row, turn—26 (31, 32, 36, 34, 32, 33, 33) sts.

Rows 4 and 5: Rep last 2 rows—20 (25, 26, 30, 28, 26, 27, 27) sts at end of last row.

SIZES L (XL, 2X, 3X, 4X, 5X) ONLY

Row 6: Rep row 2—23 (27, 25, 23, 24, 24) sts.

ALL SIZES

Row 6 (6, 7, 7, 7, 7, 7, 7): Work even in pattern st as established.

SIZES 4X (5X) ONLY

Row 8: Work even in pattern st as established.

ALL SIZES

Fasten off.

LEFT FRONT PANEL

BOTTOM HEM RIBBING

Row 1: Work 34 Fsc, turn.

Rows 2–53 (59, 64, 70, 77, 83, 88, 94): Work in sc ribbing pattern st.

Do not fasten off. At end of last row, rotate work ¼ turn to the right for working in row-end sts of ribbing.

MAIN BODY

Row 1 (RS): Ch 1, working in row-end sts of ribbing, sc in each of first 10 (12, 10, 11, 11, 11, 11, 11) sts, [(2 sc in next st, sc in each of next 10 (11, 10, 11, 10, 11, 10, 11) sts] 3 (3, 4, 4, 5, 5, 6, 6) times, 2 sc in next st, sc in each of next 9 (10, 9, 10, 10, 11, 10, 10) sts, turn—57 (63, 69, 75, 83, 89, 95, 101) sts.

Rows 2–106 (104, 104, 102, 100, 98, 98, 94): Work even in sc linen st var 1 pattern st.

BEGIN ARMHOLE SHAPING

Row 1 (RS): Ch 1, sl st in first 8 (7, 6, 8, 8, 8, 9, 10) sts, ch 1, sc in next st, work in pattern st as established across, turn—49 (56, 63, 67, 75, 81, 86, 91) sts.

Row 2 (WS): Ch 1, work in pattern st as established to last 2 sts, sc2tog, turn—48 (55, 62, 66, 74, 80, 85, 90) sts.

Row 3: Ch 1, [sc2tog in next 2 sts] twice, work in pattern st as established to end of row, turn—46 (53, 60, 64, 72, 78, 83, 88) sts.

SIZES M (L, XL, 2X, 3X, 4X, 5X) ONLY

Rows 4 and 5: Rep last 2 rows—50 (57, 61, 69, 75, 80, 85) sts.

SIZES L (XL, 2X, 3X, 4X, 5X) ONLY

Rows 6–9 (9, 13, 17, 19, 23): Rep last 2 rows 2 (2, 4, 6, 7, 9) times—51 (55, 57, 57, 59, 58) sts.

ALL SIZES

Rows 4 (6, 10, 10, 14, 18, 20, 24)–32 (34, 36, 40, 42, 44, 46, 50): Work even in pattern st as established.

BEGIN LEFT FRONT NECKLINE SHAPING

Row 1 (RS): Ch 1, work in pattern st as established to last 9 (8, 11, 11, 12, 11, 12, 11) sts, sc in next st, turn, leaving last 8 (7, 10, 10, 11, 10, 11, 10) sts unworked—38 (43, 41, 45, 46, 47, 48, 48) sts.

Row 2 (WS): Ch 1, sc2tog, sk next st, sc2tog, work in pattern st as established across, turn—35 (40, 38, 42, 43, 44, 45, 45) sts.

Row 3: Ch 1, work in pattern st as established to last 5 sts, sc2tog, sk next st, sc2tog, turn—32 (37, 35, 39, 40, 41, 42, 42) sts.

Rows 4–7 (7, 7, 7, 8, 8, 8): Rep last 2 rows 2 (2, 2, 2, 3, 3, 3) times, turn—20 (25, 23, 27, 28, 23, 24, 24) sts at end of last row.

SIZE 2X ONLY

Row 8: Rep row 2—25 sts.

ALL SIZES

Row 8 (8, 8, 8, 9, 9, 9, 9): Work even in pattern st as established.

SIZES L (XL, 4X, 5X) ONLY

Row 9 (9, 10, 10): Work even in pattern st as established.

ALL SIZES

Fasten off.

RIGHT FRONT PANEL

BOTTOM HEM RIBBING

Row 1: Work 34 Fsc, turn.

Rows 2–77 (83, 88, 94, 100, 105, 111, 118): Work even in sc ribbing pattern st.

Do not fasten off. At end of last row, rotate work ¼ turn to the right for working in row-end sts of ribbing.

MAIN BODY

Row 1 (RS): Ch 1, working in row-end sts of ribbing, sc in each of first 11 (12, 11, 11, 11, 11, 14, 11) sts, [2 sc in next st, sc in each of next 10 (11, 10, 11, 12, 11, 11, 11)] 5 (5, 6, 6, 6, 7, 7, 8) times, 2 sc in next st, sc in each of next 10 (10, 10, 10, 10, 9, 12, 10) sts, turn—83 (89, 95, 101, 107, 113, 119, 127) sts.

Rows 2–106 (104, 104, 102, 100, 98, 98, 94): Work even in sc linen st var 1 pattern st.

BEGIN ARMHOLE SHAPING

Row 1 (RS): Ch 1, work in pattern st across to last 9 (8, 7, 9, 9, 9, 10, 11) sts, sc in next st, turn, leaving last 8 (7, 6, 8, 8, 8, 9, 10) sts unworked—75 (82, 89, 93, 99, 105, 110, 117) sts.

Row 2 (WS): Ch 1, sc2tog, work in pattern st as established across, turn—74 (81, 88, 92, 98, 104, 109, 116) sts.

Row 3: Ch 1, work in pattern st as established to last 4 sts, [sc2tog in next 2 sts] twice, turn—72 (79, 86, 90, 96, 102, 107, 114) sts.

SIZES M (L, XL, 2X, 3X, 4X, 5X) ONLY

Rows 4 and 5: Rep last 2 rows—76 (83, 87, 93, 99, 104, 111) sts at end of last row.

SIZES L (XL, 2X, 3X, 4X, 5X) ONLY

Rows 6–9 (9, 13, 17, 19, 23): Rep last 2 rows 2 (2, 4, 6, 7, 9) times—77 (81, 81, 81, 83, 84) sts.

ALL SIZES

Rows 4 (6, 10, 10, 14, 18, 20, 24)–32 (34, 36, 40, 42, 44, 46, 50): Work even in pattern st as established.
Fasten off.

BEGIN RIGHT FRONT NECKLINE SHAPING

With RS facing, sk first 34 (33, 36, 36, 35, 34, 35, 36) unworked stitches at center of neckline, join yarn with sl st in next st; first st of row 1 is worked in same st as joining.

Row 1 (RS): Ch 1, work even in pattern stitch as established to end of row, turn—38 (43, 41, 45, 46, 47, 48, 48) sts.

Row 2 (WS): Ch 1, work in pattern st as established to last 5 sts, sc2tog, sk next st, sc2tog, turn—35 (40, 38, 42, 43, 44, 45, 45) sts.

Row 3: Ch 1, sc2tog, sk next st, sc2tog, work in pattern st as established across, turn—32 (37, 35, 39, 40, 41, 42, 42) sts.

Rows 4–7 (7, 7, 7, 7, 8, 8, 8): Rep last 2 rows 2 (2, 2, 2, 2, 3, 3, 3) times, turn—20 (25, 23, 27, 28, 23, 24, 24) sts.

SIZE 2X ONLY

Row 8: Rep row 2 one more time—25 sts.

ALL SIZES

Row 8 (8, 8, 8, 9, 9, 9, 9): Work even in pattern st as established.

SIZES L (XL, 4X, 5X) ONLY

Row 9 (9, 10, 10): Work in pattern st as established.

ALL SIZES

Fasten off.

SLEEVE (MAKE 2)

FOREARM RIBBING

Row 1: Work 51 Fsc, turn.

Rows 2–8 (10, 8, 6, 8, 6, 8, 8): Work even in sc ribbing pattern stitch.

Row 9 (11, 9, 7, 9, 7, 9, 9) (first row of short-row shaping): Ch 1, sc in first st, sc-tbl in each of next 16 sts, sl st tbl of next st, turn wrapping yarn to back of work—17 sc, 1 sl st.

Row 10 (12, 10, 8, 10, 8, 10, 10) (second row of short-row shaping): Do not ch 1, skip sl st, sc-tbl of first st and each st across to last st, sc in last st, turn—17 sc.

Row 11 (13, 11, 9, 11, 9, 11, 11): Ch 1, sc in first st, sc-tbl in each of next 16 sts, sc in side of wrap and sl st, sc-tbl of next st and each st across to last st, sc in last st, turn—51 sc.

Rows 12 (14, 12, 10, 12, 10, 12, 12)–14 (16, 14, 12, 14, 12, 14, 14): Work in sc ribbing pattern st.

Row 15 (17, 15, 13, 15, 13, 15, 15): Rep row 9.

Row 16 (18, 16, 14, 16, 14, 16, 16): Rep row 10.

Row 17 (19, 17, 15, 17, 15, 17, 17)–40 (42, 52, 62, 64, 68, 70, 76): Rep last 6 rows 4 (4, 6, 8, 8, 9, 9, 10) times.

Row 41 (43, 53, 63, 65, 69, 71, 77): Rep row 11.

Rows 42 (44, 54, 64, 66, 70, 72, 78)–48 (52, 60, 68, 70, 76, 78, 84): Work even in sc ribbing pattern st.

Do not fasten off. At end of last row, rotate work ¼ turn to the right for working in row-end sts of ribbing.

UPPER ARMS

Set-up row (RS): Ch 1, working in row-end sts of ribbing, sc in each of first 6 (6, 8, 8, 7, 10, 7, 10) sts, (2 sc in next st, sc in next st) 18 (20, 22, 26, 28, 28, 32, 32) times, 2 sc in next st, sc in each of first 5 (5, 7, 7, 6, 9, 6, 9) sts, turn—67 (73, 83, 95, 99, 105, 111, 117) sts.

BEGIN UPPER ARM SHAPING

Rows 1–4 (4, 4, 5, 5, 5, 5, 5): Work even in pattern st.

Row 5 (5, 5, 6, 6, 6, 6, 6): Ch 1, 2 sc in first st, work in pattern st as established to last st, 2 sc in last st, turn—69 (75, 85, 97, 101, 107, 113, 119) sts.

Rows 6 (6, 6, 7, 7, 7, 7, 7)–50 (35, 25, 18, 66, 48, 54, 54): Working in pattern st as established, rep last 5 (5, 5, 6, 6, 6, 6, 6) rows 9 (6, 4, 2, 10, 7, 8, 8) times—87 (87, 93, 101, 121, 121, 129, 135) sts.

Rows 51 (36, 26, 19, 67, 49, 55, 55)–55 (40, 30, 24, 72, 54, 60, 60): Work in pattern st as established.

Row 56 (41, 31, 25, 73, 55, 61, 61): Ch 1, 2 sc in first st, work in pattern st as established to last st, 2 sc in last st, turn—89 (89, 95, 103, 123, 123, 131, 137) sts.

SIZES S (M, L, XL, 3X, 4X, 5X) ONLY

Rows 57 (42, 32, 26, 56, 62, 62)–62 (65, 67, 67, 76, 82, 82): Working in pattern st as established, rep last 6 (6, 6, 7, 7, 7, 7) rows 1 (4, 6, 6, 3, 3, 3) times—91 (97, 107, 115, 123, 129, 137, 143) sts at end of last row.

ALL SIZES

Rows 63 (66, 68, 68, 74, 77, 83, 83)–73 (76, 78, 78, 84, 87, 93, 93): Work even in pattern st as established.

BEGIN SLEEVE CAP SHAPING

Row 1: Ch 1, sl st in each of first 7 (7, 8, 8, 8, 10, 10, 10) sts, ch 1, sc in next st, work in pattern st as established across to last 8 (8, 9, 9, 9, 11, 11, 11) sts, sc in next st, turn, leaving last 7 (7, 8, 8, 8, 10, 10, 10) sts unworked—77 (83, 91, 99, 107, 109, 117, 123) sts.

Row 2: Ch 1, sc2tog, work in pattern st as established to last 2 sts, sc2tog, turn—75 (81, 89, 97, 105, 107, 115, 121) sts.

Row 3: Ch 1, [sc2tog in next 2 sts] twice, work in pattern st as established to last 4 sts, [sc2tog in next 2 sts] twice, turn—71 (77, 85, 93, 101, 103, 111, 117) sts.

Row 4: Work even in pattern st as established.

Rows 5–19 (19, 22, 25, 28, 28, 22, 16): Rep last 3 rows 5 (5, 6, 7, 8, 8, 6, 4) times—41 (47, 49, 51, 53, 55, 75, 93) sts at end of last row.

Rows 20 (20, 23, 26, 29, 29, 23, 17)–23 (23, 26, 29, 32, 32, 32, 32): Rep row 2 and 3 (2 [2, 2, 2, 2, 2, 5, 8] times)—29 (35, 37, 39, 41, 43, 45, 45) sts at end of last row.

Rows 24 (24, 27, 30, 33, 33, 33, 33)–25 (25, 28, 31, 34, 34, 34, 34): Ch 1, sc2tog, sk next st, sc2tog, work in pattern st as established across to last 5 sts, sc2tog, sk next st, sc2tog, turn—17 (23, 25, 27, 29, 31, 33, 33) sts at end of last row. Fasten off.

FINISHING

Block all pieces to finished measurements.

Sew shoulder seams using locking mattress stitch in preparation for working Hood.

HOOD

With RS facing, join yarn with sl st in right front corner st; first st of row 1 is worked in same st as joining.

Row 1 (RS): Ch 1, work 52 (51, 54, 54, 56, 58, 59, 60) sc evenly spaced across Right Front neck edge, work 51 (51, 57, 57, 63, 67, 69, 69) sc evenly spaced across Back neck edge, work 26 (25, 28, 28, 32, 34, 35, 34) sc evenly spaced across Left Front neck edge, turn—129 (127, 139, 139, 151, 159, 163, 163) sts.

Row 2: Ch 1, sc in each of first 8 (7, 3, 3, 2, 6, 8, 8) sts, [2 sc in next st, sc in each of next 5 (5, 6, 6, 6, 6, 6, 6) sts] 19 (19, 19, 19, 21, 21, 21, 21) times, 2 sc in next st, sc in each of last 6 (5, 2, 2, 1, 5, 7, 7) sts, turn—149 (147, 159, 159, 173, 181, 185, 185) sts.

Rows 3–78: Work even in sc linen st var 1 pattern st. Fasten off.

FINISHING

Block hood to finished measurements.

Fold hood in half and sew top seam.

Sew zipper into front of garment 3 inches/7.5 cm from front edge of Left Front Panel. Weave in ends.

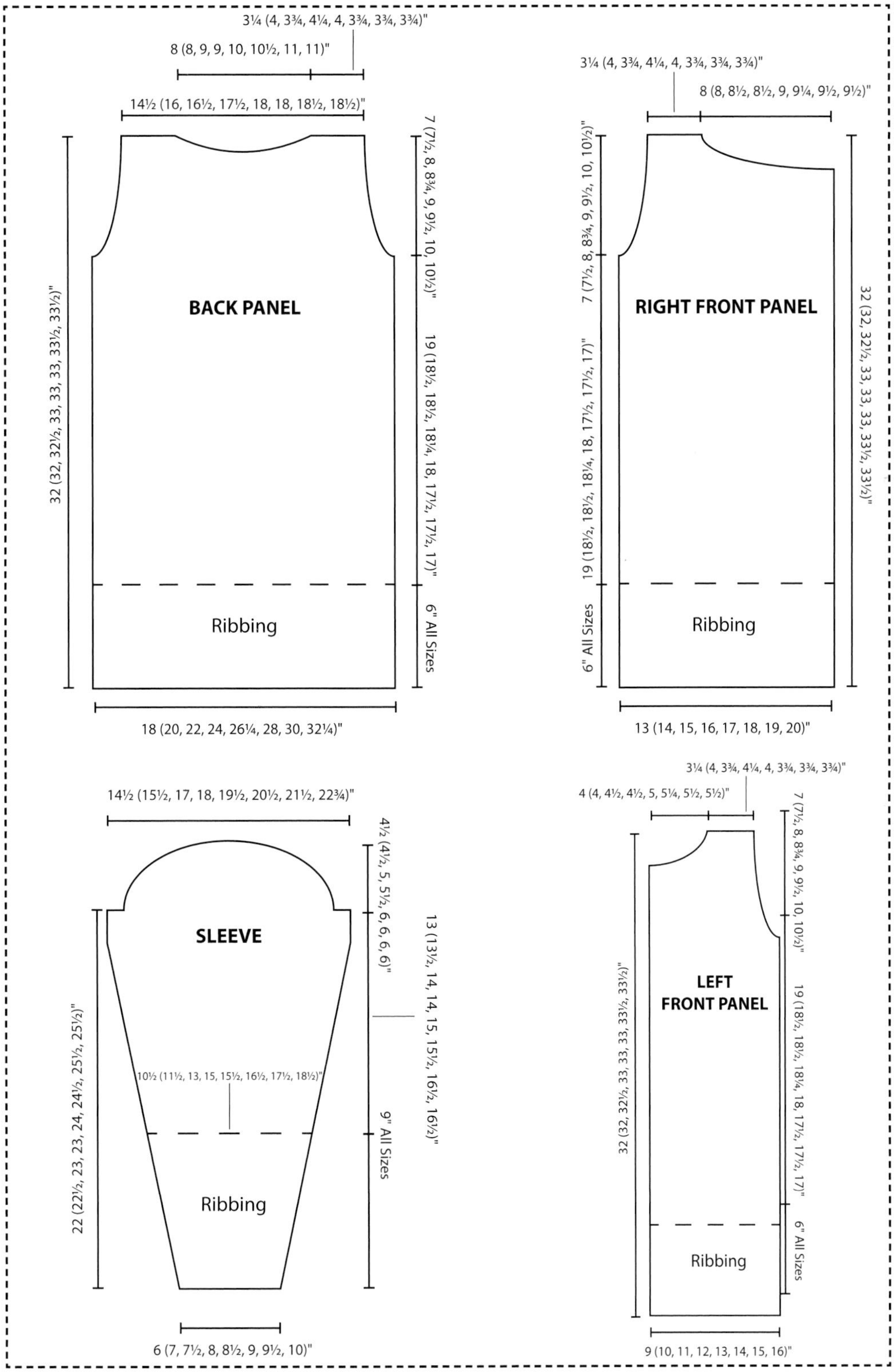
3¼ (4, 3¾, 4¼, 4, 3¾, 3¾, 3¾)"
8 (8, 9, 9, 10, 10½, 11, 11)"
14½ (16, 16½, 17½, 18, 18, 18½, 18½)"
7 (7½, 8, 8¾, 9, 9½, 10, 10½)"
32 (32, 32½, 33, 33, 33, 33½, 33½)"
BACK PANEL
19 (18½, 18½, 18¼, 18, 17½, 17½, 17)"
Ribbing
6" All Sizes
18 (20, 22, 24, 26¼, 28, 30, 32¼)"
3¼ (4, 3¾, 4¼, 4, 3¾, 3¾, 3¾)"
8 (8, 8½, 8½, 9, 9¼, 9½, 9½)"
7 (7½, 8, 8¾, 9, 9½, 10, 10½)"
RIGHT FRONT PANEL
32 (32, 32½, 33, 33, 33, 33½, 33½)"
19 (18½, 18½, 18¼, 18, 17½, 17½, 17)"
Ribbing
6" All Sizes
13 (14, 15, 16, 17, 18, 19, 20)"
14½ (15½, 17, 18, 19½, 20½, 21½, 22¾)"
4½ (4½, 5, 5½, 6, 6, 6, 6)"
SLEEVE
13 (13½, 14, 14, 15, 15½, 16½, 16½)"
22 (22½, 23, 23, 24, 24½, 25½, 25½)"
10½ (11½, 13, 15, 15½, 16½, 17½, 18½)"
9" All Sizes
Ribbing
6 (7, 7½, 8, 8½, 9, 9½, 10)"
3¼ (4, 3¾, 4¼, 4, 3¾, 3¾, 3¾)"
4 (4, 4½, 4½, 5, 5¼, 5½, 5½)"
7 (7½, 8, 8¾, 9, 9½, 10, 10½)"
LEFT FRONT PANEL
32 (32, 32½, 33, 33, 33, 33½, 33½)"
19 (18½, 18½, 18¼, 18, 17½, 17½, 17)"
6" All Sizes
Ribbing
9 (10, 11, 12, 13, 14, 15, 16)"

SLEEVELESS HOODIE

Who doesn't love a good hoodie? Here we have created a sleeveless version of the classic hoodie to make this the perfect layering piece. A zip-front closure and internal pockets make this fashion favorite even more functional and stylish, ensuring this will be your grab-and-go wardrobe favorite.

SKILL LEVEL: Intermediate

SIZES: S (M, L, XL, 2X, 3X, 4X, 5X)
Sample shown in size small

FINISHED MEASUREMENTS

To Fit Bust: 32 (36, 40, 44, 48, 52, 56, 60) inches/81.5 (91.5, 101.5, 112, 122, 132, 142, 152.5) cm

Finished Bust: 36 (40½, 44½, 48, 52, 56, 60½, 64½) inches/91.5 (103, 113, 122, 132, 142, 153.5, 164) cm

Finished Length from Shoulder: 26 (26, 26½, 27, 27, 27, 27½, 27½) inches/66 (66, 67.5, 68.5, 68.5, 68.5, 70, 70) cm

MATERIALS AND TOOLS

- Sample uses Cascade, Heritage Silk (85% Superwash Merino Wool, 15% Mulberry Silk; 3.5 ounces/100 g = 437 yards/400 m): 5 (5, 6, 6, 7, 7, 8, 8) skeins in color Cerulean #5637—2185 (2185, 2622, 2622, 3059, 3059, 3496, 3496) yards/2000 (2000, 2400, 2400, 2800, 2800, 3200, 3200) m of superfine weight yarn

- Crochet hooks: 3.25mm (size D-3) and 3.5mm (size E-4) or sizes to obtain gauge
- Yarn needle
- Sewing needle
- Thread in matching color for sewing in zipper
- Separating zipper: 26 (26, 26½, 27, 27, 27, 27½, 27½) inches/66 (66, 67.5, 68.5, 68.5, 68.5, 70, 70) cm long
- Pins

BLOCKED GAUGE

Sc linen stitch var 1 pattern: With larger hook, 53 sts = 7 inches/18 cm; 32 rows = 5 inches/12.5 cm

Always take time to check your gauge.

GAUGE SWATCH

Sc linen stitch variation 1 stitch swatch

Row 1: Work 53 Fsc, turn.

Rows 2–32: Work even in sc linen st var 1 pattern st.

STITCH GUIDE

Foundation single crochet (Fsc): Ch 2, insert hook in 2nd ch from hook, yo and draw up a loop, yo and draw through 1 loop (first "chain" made), yo and draw through 2 loops on hook (first sc made), *insert hook under 2 loops of the "chain" just made, yo and draw up a loop, yo and draw through 1 loop ("chain" made), yo and draw through 2 loops on hook (sc made); rep from * for indicated number of foundation sts.

PATTERN STITCH

For Master Chart Key, see page 206.

Single crochet linen stitch variation 1 (sc linen st var 1) (worked on multiple of 2 + 1 sts) Ⓐ

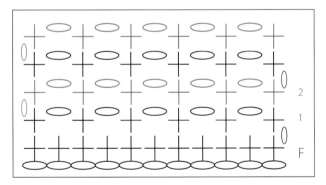

Ⓐ Single crochet linen stitch variation 1 stitch chart

Row 1: Ch 1, sc in first st, *ch 1, sk next st, sc in next st; rep from * across, turn.

Row 2: Ch 1, sc in first st, *ch 1, sk next ch-1 sp, sc in next st; rep from * across, turn.

Rep row 2 for pattern.

SPECIAL TECHNIQUES

Locking mattress stitch (see Special Techniques, page 200)

Custom zipper creation (see Special Techniques, pages 198–199)

NOTES

1. When instructed to work in pattern stitch "as established," work the next row of pattern stitch and ensure that the stitches line up as in previous rows.

2. Left Side and Right Side refer to left and right side as worn.

INSTRUCTIONS

BACK

Row 1 (WS): With larger hook, work 137 (153, 167, 183, 197, 213, 229, 243) Fsc, turn.

Rows 2–121 (119, 119, 119, 115, 111, 113, 109): Work in sc linen st var 1 pattern st.

BEGIN BACK ARMHOLE SHAPING

Row 1 (RS): Ch 1, sl st in each of first 8 (10, 9, 10, 9, 8, 8, 9) sts, ch 1, sc in next st, work in pattern st as established to last 9 (11, 10, 11, 10, 9, 9, 10) sts, sc in next st, turn, leaving last 8 (10, 9, 10, 9, 8, 8, 9) sts unworked—121 (133, 149, 163, 179, 197, 213, 225) sts.

Row 2 (WS): Ch 1, sc2tog, sc in next st, work in pattern st as established across to last 3 sts, sc in next st, sc2tog, turn—119 (131, 147, 161, 177, 195, 211, 223) sts.

Row 3: Ch 1, [sc2tog over next 2 sts] twice, sc in next st, work in pattern st as established to last 5 sts, sc in next st, [sc2tog over next 2 sts] twice, turn—115 (127, 143, 157, 173, 191, 207, 219) sts.

Rows 4–5 (5, 9, 11, 15, 21, 25, 29): Rep last 2 rows 1 (1, 3, 4, 6, 9, 11, 13) times—109 (121, 125, 133, 137, 137, 141, 141) sts at end of last row.

Rows 6 (6, 10, 12, 16, 22, 26, 30)–40 (42, 45, 48, 52, 56, 58, 62): Work even in pattern st as established.

BEGIN BACK NECKLINE SHAPING

FIRST SIDE

Row 1 (RS): Ch 1, work even in pattern st as established across 36 (42, 41, 45, 43, 41, 41, 41) sts, turn, leaving last 73 (79, 84, 88, 94, 96, 100, 100) sts unworked—36 (42, 41, 45, 43, 41, 41, 41) sts.

Row 2: Ch 1, sc2tog, sk next st, sc2tog, sc in next st, work in pattern st as established across to end of row, turn—33 (39, 38, 42, 40, 38, 38, 38) sts.

Row 3: Ch 1, work in pattern st as established to last 6 sts, sc in next st, sc2tog, sk next st, sc2tog, turn—30 (36, 35, 39, 37, 35, 35, 35) sts.

Rows 4 and 5: Rep last 2 rows—24 (30, 29, 33, 31, 29, 29, 29) sts at end of last row.

Row 6: Work even in pattern st as established.

Fasten off.

SECOND SIDE

With larger hook and RS facing, sk next 37 (37, 43, 43, 51, 55, 59, 59) unworked sts, join yarn with sl st in next unworked st. First st of row 1 is worked in same st as joining.

Row 1 (RS): Ch 1, sc in first st, work in pattern st as established across, turn—36 (42, 41, 45, 43, 41, 41, 41) sts.

Row 2 (WS): Ch 1, work in pattern st as established across to last 6 sts, sc in next st, sc2tog, sk next st, sc2tog, turn—33 (39, 38, 42, 40, 38, 38, 38) sts.

Row 3: Ch 1, sc2tog, sk next st, sc2tog, sc in next st, work in pattern st as established across, turn—30 (36, 35, 39, 37, 35, 35, 35) sts.

Rows 4 and 5: Rep last 2 rows—24 (30, 29, 33, 31, 29, 29, 29) sts at end of last row.

Row 6: Work even in pattern st as established.

Fasten off.

LEFT FRONT PANEL

Row 1 (WS): With larger hook, work 69 (77, 85, 91, 99, 107, 115, 123) Fsc, turn.

Rows 2–38: Work even in sc linen st var 1 pattern st.

BEGIN POCKET OPENING SHAPING

FIRST SIDE

Row 1 (WS): Ch 1, work in pattern st across first 48 sts, sc in next st, turn—49 sts.

Rows 2 and 3: Work even in pattern st as established.

Row 4 (RS): Ch 1, sc2tog, work in pattern st as established across, turn—48 sts.

Rows 5 and 6: Work even in pattern st as established.

Row 7 (WS): Ch 1, work in pattern st as established across to last 4 sts, [sc2tog in next 2 sts] twice, turn—46 sts.

Rows 8 and 9: Work even in pattern st as established.

Rows 10–33: Rep last 6 rows (4 times)—34 sts at end of last row.

Rows 34 and 35: Work even in pattern st as established.

SECOND SIDE

With WS facing, join yarn with sl st in next unworked st after last st of First Side row 1; First st of Second Side row 1 worked in same st as joining.

Row 1 (WS): Ch 1, sc in first st, work even in pattern st as established across, turn—20 (28, 36, 42, 50, 58, 66, 74) sts.

Rows 2 and 3: Work even in pattern st as established.

Row 4 (RS): Ch 1, work in pattern st as established to last st, 2 sc in last st, turn—21 (29, 37, 43, 51, 59, 67, 75) sts.

Rows 5 and 6: Work even in pattern st as established.

Row 7 (WS): Ch 1, 2 sc in first st, 2 sc in next st, work in pattern st as established across, turn—23 (31, 39, 45, 53, 61, 69, 77) sts.

Rows 8 and 9: Work even in pattern st as established.

Rows 10–33: Rep last 6 rows (4 times)—35 (43, 51, 57, 65, 73, 81, 89) sts at end of last row.

Rows 34 and 35: Work even in pattern st as established.

JOINING ROW

Row 36 (RS): Ch 1, work in pattern st as established across first 34 sts, sc in next st, working in st just worked and first st on First Side of Front, sc2tog to join top of pocket, sc in next st, continue to work in pattern st as established across, turn—69 (77, 85, 91, 99, 107, 115, 123) sts.

Row 37: Ch 1, work pattern st (reestablished) across row.

Rows 38–83 (81, 81, 81, 77, 73, 75, 71): Work even in pattern st as established.

BEGIN ARMHOLE SHAPING

Row 1 (RS): Ch 1, sl st in each of first 8 (10, 9, 10, 9, 8, 8, 9) sts, ch 1, sc in next st, work in pattern st as established across, turn—61 (67, 76, 81, 90, 99, 107, 114) sts.

Row 2 (WS): Ch 1, work in pattern st as established across to last 3 sts, sc in next st, sc2tog, turn—60 (66, 75, 80, 89, 98, 106, 113) sts.

Row 3: Ch 1, [sc2tog in next 2 sts] twice, sc in next st, work in pattern st as established across, turn—58 (64, 73, 78, 87, 96, 104, 111) sts.

Rows 4–5 (5, 9, 11, 15, 21, 25, 29): Rep last 2 rows 1 (1, 3, 4, 6, 9, 11, 13) more times—55 (61, 64, 66, 69, 69, 71, 72) sts.

Rows 6 (6, 10, 12, 16, 22, 26, 30)–46 (48, 51, 54, 58, 62, 64, 68): Work even in pattern st as established.
Fasten off.

RIGHT FRONT PANEL

Row 1 (WS): With larger hook, work 69 (77, 85, 91, 99, 107, 115, 123) Fsc, turn.

Rows 2–38: Work even in sc linen st var 1 pattern st.

BEGIN POCKET OPENING SHAPING

FIRST SIDE

Row 1 (WS): Ch 1, work in pattern st across first 19 (27, 35, 41, 49, 57, 65, 73) sts, sc in next st, turn—20 (28, 36, 42, 50, 58, 66, 74) sts.

Rows 2 and 3: Work even in pattern st as established.

Row 4 (RS): Ch 1, sc in first st, 2 sc in next st, work in pattern st as established across, turn—21 (29, 37, 43, 51, 59, 67, 75) sts.

Rows 5 and 6: Work even in pattern st as established.

Row 7 (WS): Ch 1, work in pattern st as established across to last 2 sts, 2 sc in each of next 2 sts—23 (31, 39, 45, 53, 61, 69, 77) sts.

Rows 8 and 9: Work even in pattern st as established.

Rows 10–33: Rep last 6 rows (4 times)—35 (43, 51, 57, 65, 73, 81, 89) sts at end of last row.

Rows 34 and 35: Work even in pattern st as established.

SECOND SIDE

With WS facing, join yarn in next unworked st after last st of First Side row 1; first st of Second Side row 1 worked in same st as joining.

Row 1 (WS): Ch 1, sc in first st, work in pattern st as established across, turn—49 sts.

Rows 2 and 3: Work even in pattern st as established.

Row 4 (RS): Ch 1, work in pattern st as established to last 2 sts, sc2tog, turn—48 sts.

Rows 5 and 6: Work even in pattern st as established.

Row 7 (WS): Ch 1, [sc2tog in next 2 sts] twice, work in pattern st as established across, turn—46 sts.

Rows 8 and 9: Work even in pattern st as established.

Rows 10–33: Rep last 6 rows (4 times)—34 sts at end of last row.

Rows 34 and 35: Work even in pattern st as established.

JOINING ROW

Row 36 (RS): Ch 1, work in pattern st as established across first 33 sts, sc in next st, working in st just worked and first st of First Side of Front, sc2tog to join top of pocket, sc in next st, continue to work in pattern st as established across, turn—69 (77, 85, 91, 99, 107, 115, 123) sts.

Row 37: Ch 1, work in reestablished pattern st across row.

Rows 38–83 (81, 81, 81, 77, 73, 75, 71): Work even in pattern st as established.

BEGIN ARMHOLE SHAPING

Row 1 (RS): Ch 1, work in pattern st across first 60 (66, 75, 80, 89, 98, 106, 113) sts, sc in next st, turn, leaving 8 (10, 9, 10, 9, 8, 8, 9) sts unworked—61 (67, 76, 81, 90, 99, 107, 114) sts.

Row 2 (WS): Ch 1, sc in first st, sc2tog, sc in next st, work in pattern st as established across, turn—60 (66, 75, 80, 89, 98, 106, 113) sts.

Row 3: Ch 1, work in pattern st as established to last 6 sts, sc in next st, [sc2tog in next 2 sts] twice, sc in last st, turn—58 (64, 73, 78, 87, 96, 104, 111) sts.

Rows 4–5 (5, 9, 11, 15, 21, 25, 29): Rep last 2 rows 1 (1, 3, 4, 6, 9, 11, 13) times—55 (61, 64, 66, 69, 69, 71, 72) sts at end of last row.

Rows 6 (6, 10, 12, 16, 22, 26, 30)–46 (48, 51, 54, 58, 62, 64, 68): Work even in pattern st as established.

Fasten off.

FINISHING

Block all pieces to schematic measurements.

Sew shoulder seams using locking mattress stitch in preparation for working Hood.

Sew side seams.

HOOD

With RS facing and larger hook, join yarn with sl st in right front corner st; first st of row 1 is worked in same st as joining.

Row 1 (RS): Ch 1, work 31 (31, 35, 33, 38, 40, 42, 34) sc evenly spaced across Right Front neck edge, work 61 (61, 67, 67, 75, 79, 83, 83) sc evenly spaced across Back neck edge, work 31 (31, 35, 33, 38, 40, 42, 34) sc evenly spaced across Left Front neck edge, turn—123 (123, 137, 133, 151, 159, 167, 151) sts.

Row 2: Ch 1, sc in each of first 4 (4, 11, 17, 14, 2, 11, 8) sts, [2 sc in next st, sc in each of next 3 (3, 3, 2, 3, 4, 4, 2) sts] 29 (29, 29, 33, 31, 31, 29, 45) times, 2 sc in next st, sc in each of next 2 (2, 9, 16, 12, 1, 10, 7) sts, turn—153 (153, 167, 167, 183, 191, 197, 197) sts.

Rows 3–84: Work even in sc linen st var 1 pattern st.

Fasten off.

Block Hood to schematic measurements.

Fold Hood in half widthwise and sew top seam.

POCKET INTERIOR (MAKE 2)

Row 1: With larger hook, work 53 Fsc, turn.

Rows 2–25: Work even in sc linen st var 1 pattern st.

Row 26: Ch 1, sc2tog, sc in next st, work in pattern st as established across, turn—52 sts.

Row 27: Work even in pattern st as established.

Rows 28–53: Rep last 2 rows (13 times)—39 sts at end of last row.

Rows 54–58: Work even in pattern st as established.

Fasten off.

With WS of Front Panel facing, lay Pocket Interior so it overlaps diagonal Pocket Opening by 1 inch/2.5 cm, and pin in place. Sew Pocket in place working through sts of Pocket Interior and the corresponding front loops (as it faces you) of Front Panel.

Rep for other Pocket.

FRONT BORDER

With RS facing and smaller hook, join yarn with sl st in bottom Right Front corner; first st is made in same st as joining.

Row 1: Ch 1, working in row-end sts, sc in each st up Right Front, sc in each st around hood, sc in each st down Left Front. Fasten off.

ARMHOLE BORDER

With RS facing and smaller hook, join yarn with sl st in bottom seam of armhole; first st is made in same st as joining.

Rnd 1: Ch 1, working in sts of underarm and in row-end sts, sc evenly around armhole, join with duplicate stitch.

Rep for Armhole Border around other armhole.

FINISHING

Weave in ends. Sew zipper into front of garment.

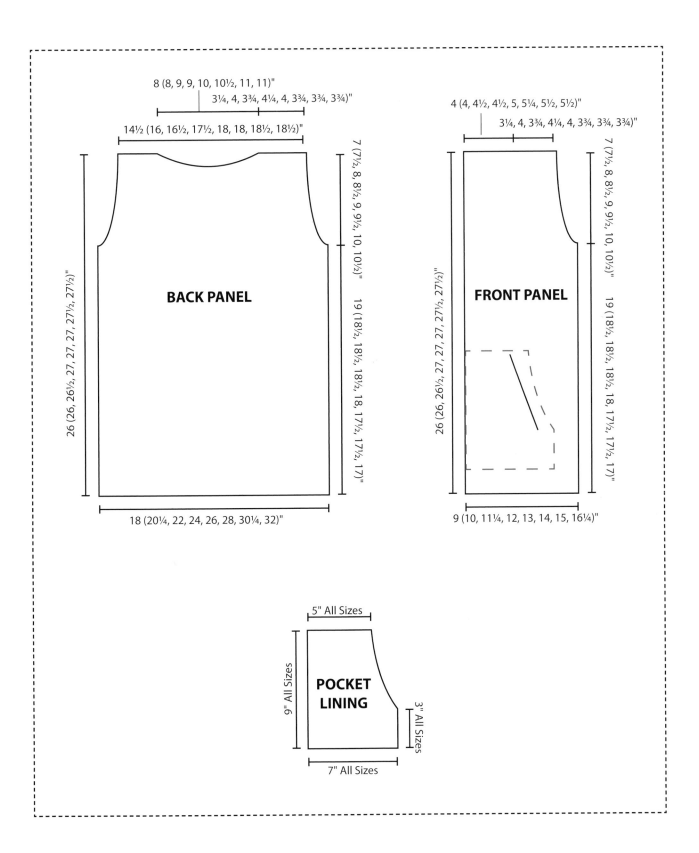

8 (8, 9, 9, 10, 10½, 11, 11)"

3¼, 4, 3¾, 4¼, 4, 3¾, 3¾, 3¾)"

14½ (16, 16½, 17½, 18, 18, 18½, 18½)"

7 (7½, 8, 8½, 9, 9½, 10, 10½)"

BACK PANEL

26 (26, 26½, 27, 27, 27, 27½, 27½)"

19 (18½, 18½, 18, 17½, 17½, 17)"

18 (20¼, 22, 24, 26, 28, 30¼, 32)"

4 (4, 4½, 4½, 5, 5¼, 5½, 5½)"

3¼, 4, 3¾, 4¼, 4, 3¾, 3¾, 3¾)"

7 (7½, 8, 8½, 9, 9½, 10, 10½)"

FRONT PANEL

26 (26, 26½, 27, 27, 27, 27½, 27½)"

19 (18½, 18½, 18, 17½, 17½, 17)"

9 (10, 11¼, 12, 13, 14, 15, 16¼)"

5" All Sizes

9" All Sizes

POCKET LINING

3" All Sizes

7" All Sizes

TURTLENECK PONCHO

Start by making two rectangles in a graphic stitch pattern and color combination that you will enjoy watching unfold as you stitch along with your yarn and hook. Next, follow the schematic for easy assembly. Finally, finish up by stitching your turtleneck collar onto the assembled body. TAADAA!! Customize your piece with color combinations or monotone hues that suit your personal taste and individual style.

SKILL LEVEL: Intermediate
SIZES: One Size

FINISHED MEASUREMENTS

Each Panel: 31 inches/79 cm x 20 inches/51 cm
Turtleneck: 21 inches/53.5 cm in circumference x 8 inches/20.5 cm deep

MATERIALS AND TOOLS

- Sample uses Cascade 220 Superwash Sport (100% Superwash Merino Wool; 1.75 ounces/50 g = 136.5 yards/125 m): 8 skeins each of (A) Burnt Orange #823 and (B) Ginger #858—1092 yards/1000 m of fine weight yarn in each color

- Crochet hook: 3.75mm (size F-5) or size to obtain gauge
- Yarn needle

BLOCKED GAUGE

37 sts = 8½ inches/21.5 cm; 30 rows = 5¼ inches/13.5 cm in pattern

Always take time to check your gauge.

STITCH GUIDE

Foundation single crochet (Fsc): Ch 2, insert hook in 2nd ch from hook, yo and draw up a loop, yo and draw through 1 loop (first "chain" made), yo and draw through 2 loops on hook (first sc made), * insert hook under 2 loops of the "chain" just made, yo and draw up a loop, yo and draw through 1 loop ("chain" made), yo and draw through 2 loops on hook (sc made); rep from * for indicated number of foundation sts.

Spike: Insert hook in next st in indicated number of rows below, draw up a loop, yo and draw through 2 loops on hook. Do not work into the corresponding st of the current row (it should be covered by the spike stitch).

Spike-Wedge (worked over 5 sts): Spike in next st 6 rows below, Spike in next st 5 rows below, Spike in next st 4 rows below, Spike in next st 3 rows below, Spike in next st 2 rows below.

PATTERN STITCHES

For Master Chart Key, see page 206.

Spike-Wedge stitch pattern in rows (worked on a multiple of 10 + 5 sts) Ⓐ

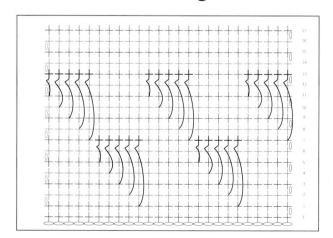

Ⓐ Spike-Wedge stitch pattern in rows stitch chart

WITH COLOR A

Rows 1–6: Ch 1, sc in each st across, turn. Fasten off A, join B.

WITH COLOR B

Row 7: Ch 1, sc in first 5 sts, *Spike-Wedge over next 5 sts, sc in next 5 sts; rep from * across, turn.

Rows 8–12: Ch 1, sc in each st to end of row, turn. Fasten off B, join A.

WITH COLOR A

Row 13: Ch 1, Spike-Wedge over first 5 sts, *sc in next 5 sts, Spike-Wedge over next 5 sts; rep from * across, turn.

Rows 14–18: Ch 1, sc in each st to end of row, turn.

Repeat rows 7–18 for Spike-Wedge pattern in rows. Fasten off A, join B.

Spike-Wedge stitch pattern in rnds (worked on a multiple of 10 sts)

WITH COLOR A

Rnd 1: Ch 1, starting in first st, *sc in next 5 sts, Spike-Wedge over next 5 sts; rep from * around, join with sl st in first sc, turn.

Rnds 2–6: Ch 1, sc in each st around, join with sl st in first sc, turn. Fasten off A, join B.

WITH COLOR B

Rnd 7: Ch 1, starting in first st, *Spike-Wedge over first 5 sts, sc in next 5 sts; rep from * around, join with sl st in first sc, turn.

Rnds 8–12: Ch 1, sc in each st around, join with sl st in first sc, turn.

Repeat rnds 1–12 for Spike-Wedge pattern in rnds. Fasten off B, join A.

SPECIAL TECHNIQUE

Locking mattress stitch (see Special Techniques, page 200)

NOTES

1. Main panels are worked in rows then sewn together to make main body of poncho.
2. Turtleneck is worked in turned rnds. Turned rnds are worked back and forth like rows but joined with a sl st like rnds before turning.

3. When instructed to work in st X rows below, insert hook in indicated stitch in the row numbered X less than the row you are working. For example, if you are working row 5, a stitch "3 rows" below is in row 5 − 3 = row 2.

INSTRUCTIONS

MAIN PANEL (MAKE 2)

WITH COLOR A

Foundation Row: Work 87 Fsc, turn.

Rows 1–6: Ch 1, sc in each st across, turn.

WITH COLOR B

Row 7: Ch 1, sc in first 5 sts, *Spike-Wedge over next 5 sts, sc in next 5 sts; rep from * across, turn.

Rows 8–12: Ch 1, sc in each st across, turn.

WITH COLOR A

Row 13: Ch 1, Spike-Wedge over first 5 sts, *sc in next 5 sts, Spike-Wedge over next 5 sts; rep from * across, turn.

Rows 14–18: Ch 1, sc in each st to end of row, turn.

Rows 19–180: Rep rows 7–18 (13 times); then rep rows 7–12 (once).

Fasten off.

FINISHING

Block all pieces to schematic measurements.

Using locking mattress stitch, sew panels together following assembly diagram.

TURTLENECK

Turtleneck is worked in turned rnds.

With RS facing, join yarn in any sc on top edge of poncho; first st of rnd 1 is worked in same st as joining.

Rnd 1: Work 130 sc evenly spaced around neckline, join with sl st in first sc, turn.

Rnd 2: Ch 1, sc in each st around, join with sl st in first sc, turn.

Rnd 3: Ch 1, starting in same st, *sc in each of next 11 sts, sc2tog; rep from * around, join with sl st to first sc, turn—120 sts.

Rnd 4: Ch 1, starting in same st, *sc in each of next 10 sts, sc2tog; rep from * around, join rnd with sl st to first sc made, turn—110 sts.

Rnd 5: Ch 1, starting in same st, *sc in each of next 9 sts, sc2tog; rep from * around, join rnd with sl st to first sc made, turn—100 sts.

Rnd 6: Ch 1, starting in same st, *sc in each of next 8 sts, sc2tog; rep from * around, join rnd with sl st to first sc made, turn—90 sts.

Rnd 7: Ch 1, sc in each st around, join with sl st to first sc, turn. Fasten off A, join B.

Rnds 8–49: Working in Spike-Wedge pattern st, work rnds 1–12 (3 times); then rep rnds 1–6 (once).

Fasten off.

Block Turtleneck to 10½ inches/26.5 cm wide x 8 inches/20.5 cm deep.

Weave in ends.

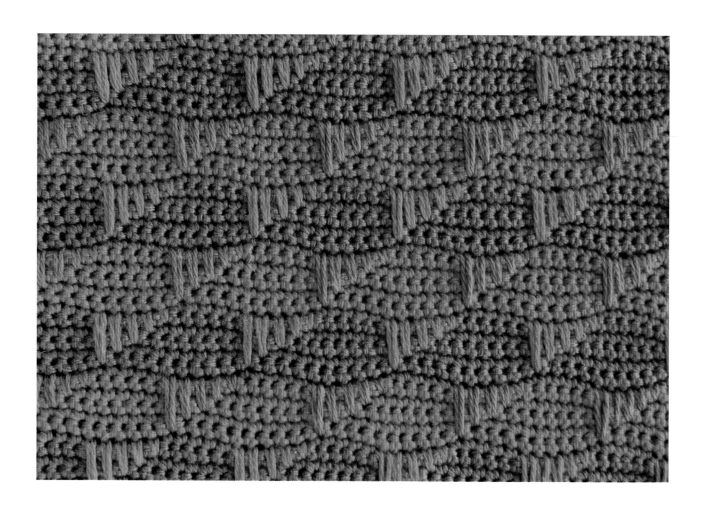

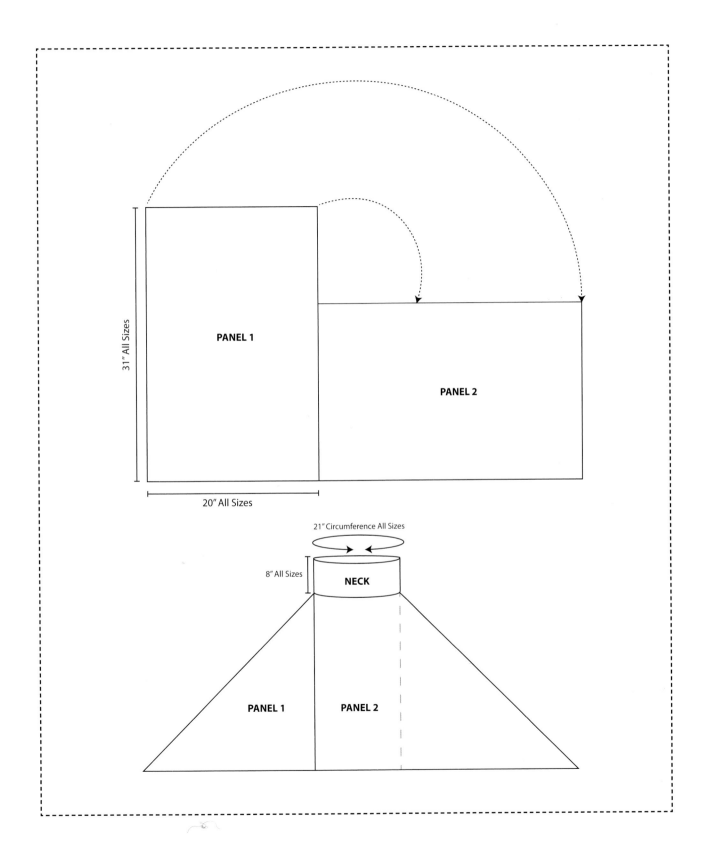

31" All Sizes

PANEL 1

PANEL 2

20" All Sizes

21" Circumference All Sizes

8" All Sizes

NECK

PANEL 1

PANEL 2

BELTED RUANA

Our ruana is a timeless classic that will add a flash of sweeping drama to your wardrobe. We have combined the perfect mix of graphic lace and textured solid stitches to make this a definite statement piece, while maximizing the functionality of a grand dame-style layering piece.

SKILL LEVEL: Intermediate

SIZES: S/M (L/XL, 2X/3X, 4X/5X)

Sample shown in size L/XL

FINISHED MEASUREMENTS

To Fit Bust: 32-36 (40-44, 48-52, 56-60) inches/81.5-91.5 (101.5-112, 122-132, 142-152.5) cm

Finished Width: 47½ (51½, 53½, 57½) inches/120.5 (131, 136, 146) cm

Finished Length: 41 inches/104 cm

Belt Length: 72 (80, 88, 96) inches/183 (203, 223.5, 244) cm

MATERIALS AND TOOLS

▨ Sample uses Cascade 220 Superwash Sport (100% Superwash Merino Wool; 1.75 ounces/50 g = 136.5 yards/125 m): 33 (36, 37, 40) skeins in color Plum Crazy #882 or approximately 4504.5 (4914, 5050.5, 5460) yards/4125 (4500, 4625, 5000) m of fine weight yarn

▨ Crochet hook: 4.0mm (size G-6) or size to obtain gauge

▨ Yarn needle

BLOCKED GAUGES

Hdc/sl st Crunch stitch: 30 sts = 7 inches/18 cm; 25 rows = 5 inches/12.5 cm

Lace pattern: 33 sts = 7¾ inches/19.5 cm; 23 rows = 6 inches/15 cm

Always take time to check your gauge.

GAUGE SWATCHES

Lace stitch swatch

Row 1: Work 33 Fsc, turn.

Rows 2–11: Work rows 2–11 of Lace pattern stitch.

Rows 12 and 13: Rep rows 2 and 3 of Lace pattern stitch.

Hdc/sl st Crunch stitch swatch

Row 1: Work 30 Fsc, turn.

Rows 2–25: Work in Hdc/sl st Crunch pattern stitch.

STITCH GUIDE

Foundation single crochet (Fsc): Ch 2, insert hook in 2nd ch from hook, yo and draw up a loop, yo and draw through 1 loop (first "chain" made), yo and draw through 2 loops on hook (first sc made), *insert hook under 2 loops of the "chain" just made, yo and draw up a loop, yo and draw through 1 loop ("chain" made), yo and draw through 2 loops on hook (sc made); rep from * for indicated number of foundation sts.

First double crochet (First-dc): Sc in first st, ch 2. Note: Use this stitch whenever the first stitch of a row is a dc.

5-double crochet cluster (5-dc Cl): Yo, insert hook in indicated st or sp and draw up a loop, yo and draw through 2 loops on hook (2 loops remain on hook), [yo, insert hook in same st or sp and draw up a loop, yo and draw through 2 loops on hook] 4 times, yo and draw through all 6 loops on hook.

PATTERN STITCHES

For Master Chart Key, see page 206.

Hdc/sl st Crunch (worked on any even number of stitches) A

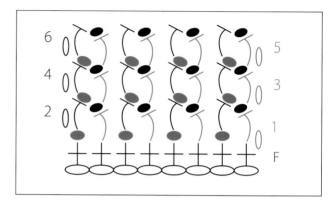

A Hdc/sl st Crunch stitch chart

Row 1: Ch 1, hdc in first st, sl st in next st, *hdc in next st, sl st in next st; rep from * across, turn.

Rep row 1 for pattern.

Lace (worked on a multiple of 8 + 1 sts) B

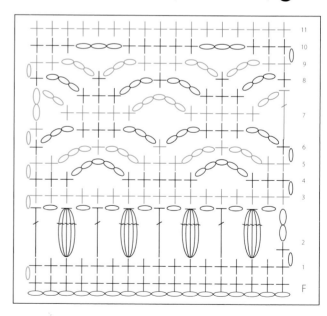

B Lace stitch chart

Row 1: Fsc.

Row 2 (RS): First-dc in first st, *ch 1, sk next st, 5-dc Cl in next st, ch 1, sk next st, dc in next st; rep from * across, turn.

Row 3: Ch 1, sc in each st and each ch-1 sp across, turn.

Row 4: Ch 1, sc in first st, *sc in each of next 2 sts, ch 5, sk next 3 sts, sc in each of next 3 sts; rep from * across, turn.

Row 5: Ch 1, sc in first st, *sc in next st, ch 3, sc in next ch-5 sp, ch 3, sk next sc, sc in each of next 2 sc; rep from * across, turn.

Row 6: Ch 1, sc in first st, *ch 3, sc in next ch-3 sp, sc in next st, sc in next ch-3 sp, ch 3, sk next sc, sc in next st; rep from * across, turn.

Row 7: First-dc in first st, ch 2, sc in next ch-3 sp, sc in each of next 3 sts, sc in next ch-3 sp, *ch 5, sc in next ch-3 sp, sc in each of next 3 sts, sc in next ch-3 sp; rep from * across to last st, ch 2, dc in last st, turn.

Row 8: Ch 1, sc in first st, ch 3, sk next ch-2 sp, sc in each of next 3 sts, ch 3, *sc in next ch-5 sp, ch 3, sk next st, sc in each of next 3 sts, ch 3; rep from * across to last st, sc in last st, turn.

Row 9: Ch 1, sc in first st, *sc in next ch-3 sp, ch 3, sk next sc, sc in next st, ch 3, sc in next ch-3 sp, sc in next sc; rep from * across, turn.

Row 10: Ch 1, sc in first st, *sc in next st, sc in next ch-3 sp, ch 3, sc in next ch-3 sp, sc in each of next 2 sts; rep from * across, turn.

Row 11: Ch 1, sc in first st, *sc in each of next 2 sts, 3 sc in next ch-3 sp, sc in each of next 3 sts; rep from * across, turn.

SPECIAL TECHNIQUE

Locking mattress stitch (see Special Techniques, page 200)

NOTES

1. Garment is made from side to side in three panels: Right Front, Left Front, and Back.

2. Left Side and Right Side refer to left and right side as worn.

INSTRUCTIONS

FRONT (MAKE 2)

SECTION 1 (LACE)

Row 1 (WS): Work 177 Fsc, turn.

Rows 2–21: Work rows 2–11 of Lace pattern stitch (twice).

Rows 22 and 23: Rep rows 2 and 3 of Lace pattern stitch (once).

SECTION 2 (CRUNCH)

Row 1 (RS): Ch 1, sc in first st, 2 sc in next st, sc in each st across, turn—178 sts.

Rows 2–13 (17, 21, 25): Work in Hdc/sl st Crunch pattern stitch.

SECTION 3 (LACE)

Row 1 (WS): Ch 1, sc in first st, sc2tog, sc in each st across, turn—177 sts.

Rows 2–31: Work rows 2–11 of Lace pattern stitch (3 times).

Rows 32 and 33: Rep row 2 and 3 of Lace pattern stitch (once).

SECTION 4 (CRUNCH)

Row 1 (RS): Ch 1, sc in first st, 2 sc in next st, sc in each st across, turn—178 sts.

Rows 2–13 (17, 21, 25): Work in Hdc/sl st Crunch pattern stitch.

SECTION 5 (LACE)

Row 1 (WS): Ch 1, sc in first st, sc2tog, sc in each st across, turn—177 sts.

Rows 2–21: Work rows 2–11 of Lace pattern stitch (twice).

Rows 22 and 23: Rep rows 2 and 3 of Lace pattern stitch (once). Fasten off.

BACK

SECTION 1 (LACE)

Row 1 (WS): 177 Fsc, turn.

Rows 2–21: Work rows 2–11 of Lace pattern stitch (twice).

Rows 22 and 23: Rep rows 2 and 3 or Lace pattern stitch (once).

SECTION 2 (CRUNCH)

Row 1 (RS): Ch 1, sc in first st, 2 sc in next st, sc in each st across, turn—178 sts.

Rows 2–13 (17, 21, 25): Work in Hdc/sl st Crunch pattern stitch.

SECTION 3 (LACE)

Row 1 (WS): Ch 1, sc in first st, sc2tog, sc in each st across, turn—177 sts.

Rows 2–31: Work rows 2–11 of Lace pattern stitch (3 times).

Rows 32 and 33: Rep rows 2 and 3 of Lace pattern stitch (once).

SECTION 4 (CRUNCH)

Row 1 (RS): Ch 1, sc in first st, 2 sc in next st, sc in each st across, turn—178 sts.

Rows 2–13 (17, 21, 25): Work in Hdc/sl st Crunch pattern stitch.

SECTION 5 (LACE)

Row 1 (WS): Ch 1, sc in first st, sc2tog, sc in each st across, turn—177 sts.

Rows 2–31: Work rows 2–11 of Lace pattern stitch (3 times).

Rows 32 and 33: Rep rows 2 and 3 of Lace pattern stitch (once).

SECTION 6 (CRUNCH)

Row 1 (RS): Ch 1, sc in first st, 2 sc in next st, sc in each st across, turn—178 sts.

Rows 2–13 (17, 21, 25): Work in Hdc/sl st Crunch pattern stitch.

SECTION 7 (LACE)

Row 1 (WS): Ch 1, sc in first st, sc2tog, sc in each st across, turn—177 sts.

Rows 2–31: Work rows 2–11 of Lace pattern stitch (3 times).

Rows 32 and 33: Rep rows 2 and 3 of Lace pattern stitch (once).

SECTION 8 (CRUNCH)

Row 1 (RS): Ch 1, sc in first st, 2 sc in next st, sc in each st across, turn—178 sts.

Rows 2–13 (17, 21, 25): Work in Hdc/sl st Crunch pattern stitch.

SECTION 9 (LACE)

Row 1 (WS): Work 177 Fsc, turn.

Rows 2–21: Work rows 2–11 of Lace pattern stitch (twice).

Rows 22 and 23: Rep rows 2 and 3 of Lace pattern stitch (once). Fasten off.

BELT

Row 1: Work 308 (344, 378, 412) Fsc, turn.

Rows 2–6: Work Hdc/sl st Crunch pattern stitch.

Row 7: Ch 1, sc in each st across. Fasten off.

FINISHING

Block all pieces to finished measurements.

Sew shoulder seams, leaving center 7½ (8, 9½, 10) inches/19 (20.5, 24, 25.5) cm open for neckline.

Weave in ends.

Pull Belt through holes in lace panels, and snug around waistline.

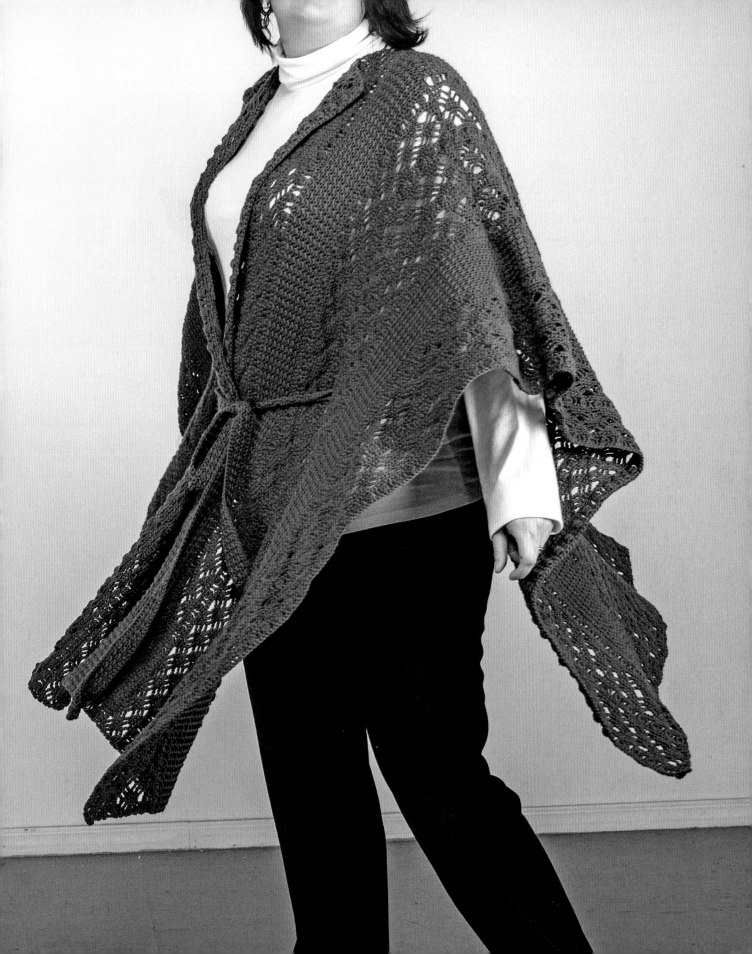

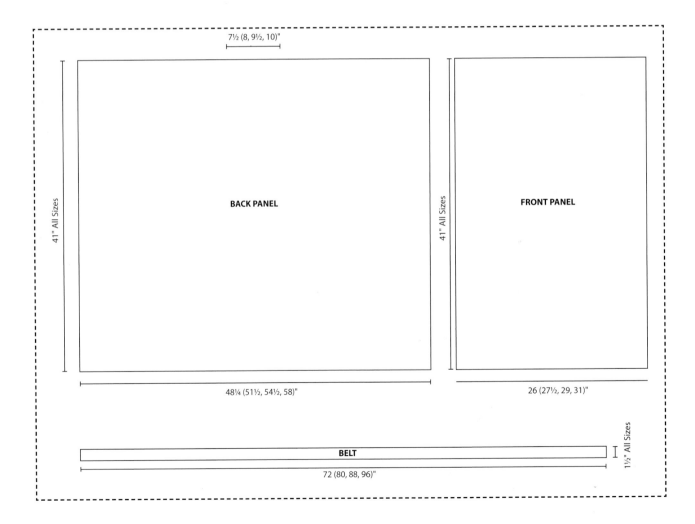

7½ (8, 9½, 10)"

41" All Sizes

BACK PANEL

41" All Sizes

FRONT PANEL

48¼ (51½, 54½, 58)"

26 (27½, 29, 31)"

1½" All Sizes

BELT

72 (80, 88, 96)"

CARDIGANS
& PULLOVERS

CARDI WITH ATTACHED SCARF

Above all else, I love to create beautiful clothes that make the wearer feel special and even more beautiful than they already are. Here I use simple, elegant lines combined with a variation of our unique Non-Stick Lace pattern stitch to create a garment that is truly exquisite. Wear the attached scarf pinned in front or tied for a great work look or dress it up for a special occasion.

SKILL LEVEL: Intermediate

SIZES: S (M, L, XL, 2X, 3X, 4X, 5X)

Sample shown in size small

FINISHED MEASUREMENTS

To Fit Bust: 32 (36, 40, 44, 48, 52, 56, 60) inches/81.5 (91.5, 101.5, 112, 122, 132, 142, 152.5) cm

Finished Bust: 36 (40¼, 45, 48¾, 52½, 57¼, 61½, 64¾) inches/91.5 (102, 114.5, 124, 133.5, 145.5, 156, 164.5) cm

Length From Shoulder: 29 (29, 29, 29, 29, 31, 31, 31) inches/73.5 (73.5, 73.5, 73.5, 73.5, 79, 79, 79) cm

MATERIALS AND TOOLS

■ Sample uses Mirasol Yarn, Nuna (40% Merino Wool/40% Silk/20% Bamboo; 3.5 ounces/100 g = 191 yards/175 m): 12 (13, 14, 16, 17, 18, 20, 21) skeins in color Sangria #42 or 2292 (2483, 2674, 3056, 3247, 3438, 3820, 4011) yards/2100 (2275, 2450, 2800, 2975, 3150, 3500, 3675) m of superfine weight yarn

■ Crochet hook: 3.5mm (size E-4) or size to obtain gauge

■ Yarn needle

■ Four ⅞ inch/2.2 cm decorative buttons

■ Four ⅝ inch/1.6 cm shirt buttons for backing

BLOCKED GAUGE

Non-stick lace variation 1 pattern: 47 sts = 7½ inches/19 cm; 18 rows = 7¼ inches/18.5 cm

Always take time to check your gauge.

GAUGE SWATCH

Non-stick lace variation 1 stitch swatch (worked on a multiple of 5 + 2 sts and a multiple of 4 rows)

Row 1: Work 47 Fsc, turn.

Row 2 (RS): Ch 1, First-tr, *yo, [insert hook into next st, yo and pull up a loop to height of first tr] 5 times (7 loops on hook), yo and draw through 6 loops on hook, yo and draw through remaining 2 loops on hook, sc 4 under last 6 loops ("eye" of loops), rep from * across to last st, tr in last st, turn.

Row 3: Ch 1, sc in first st, ch 1, sk next st, *sc in each of next 3 sts, ch 2, sk next 2 sts; rep from * across to last 5 sts, sc in each of next 3 sts, ch 1, sc in last st, turn.

Row 4: Ch 1, First-dc, sk next 2 sts, 5 dc in next st, *sk next 4 sts, 5 dc in next st; rep from * across to last 3 sts, sk next 2 sts, dc in last st, turn.

Row 5: Ch 1, sc in each st across, turn.

Rows 6–17: Rep rows 2–5.

Row 18: Rep row 2.

STITCH GUIDE

Foundation single crochet (Fsc): Ch 2, insert hook in 2nd ch from hook, yo and draw up a loop, yo and draw through 1 loop (first "chain" made), yo and draw through 2 loops on hook (first sc made), *insert hook under 2 loops of the "chain" just made, yo and draw up a loop, yo and draw through 1 loop ("chain" made), yo and draw through 2 loops on hook (sc made); rep from * for indicated number of foundation sts.

First double crochet (First-dc): Sc in first st, ch 2. Note: Use this stitch whenever the first stitch of a row is a dc.

First treble crochet (First-tr): Sc in first st, ch 3. Note: Use this stitch whenever the first stitch of a row is a tr.

PATTERN STITCH

For Master Chart Key, see page 206.

Non-stick lace variation 1 (work on a multiple of 5 + 2 sts and a multiple of 4 rows) Ⓐ

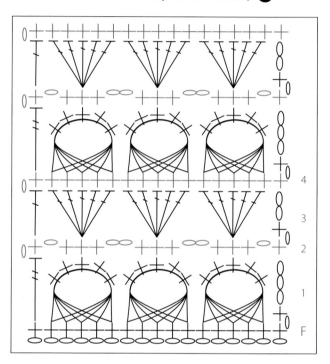

Ⓐ Non-stick lace variation 1 stitch chart

Row 1 (RS): Ch 1, First-tr, *yo, [insert hook into next st, yo and pull up a loop to height of first tr] 5 times (7 loops on hook), yo and draw through 6 loops on hook, yo and draw through remaining 2 loops on hook, sc 4 under last 6 loops ("eye" of loops), rep from * across to last st, tr in last st, turn.

Row 2: Ch 1, sc in first st, ch 1, sk next st, *sc in each of next 3 sts, ch 2, sk next 2 sts; rep from * across to last 5 sts, sc in each of next 3 sts, ch 1, sc in last st, turn.

Row 3: Ch 1, First-dc, sk next 2 sts, 5 dc in next st, *sk next 4 sts, 5 dc in next st; rep from * across to last 3 sts, sk next 2 sts, dc in last st, turn.

Row 4: Ch 1, sc in each st across, turn.

Rep rows 1–4 for pattern st.

SPECIAL TECHNIQUE

Locking mattress stitch (see Special Techniques, page 200)

Setting in a sleeve (see Special Techniques, page 201)

NOTES

1. For the purpose of this pattern, all chain spaces count as 1 stitch.

2. When instructed to work in side of stitch, insert hook from front to back into the indicated stitch between the 2 vertical strands of yarn directly below the first wrap, catching 2 side strands of yarn.

3. When instructed to work in a pattern stitch "as established," work the next row of pattern stitch and ensure that the stitches line up as in previous rows.

4. Scarf is made from the center out.

5. When working back into First-tr or First-dc sts, insert hook into top chain stitch of First-tr or First-dc.

6. When instructed to "decrease X number of sts," use tr2tog, dc2tog, or sc2tog (see Stitch Guide) according to the pattern row you are working on. For example: If you are about to work a row that begins with a dc, where the pattern reads "decrease 1 st," you would work dc2tog.

7. When instructed to "increase X number of sts", work 2 tr, 2 dc, or 2 sc in first st according to the pattern row you are working on. For example: If you are about to work a row of dc-v stitches, where the pattern reads "increase 1 st," you would work 2 dc in first st.

8. If, after a decrease, the next stitch is a chain space, work 1 st in pattern stitch in the place of that chain space; then continue as instructed.

9. Left Side and Right Side refer to left and right side as worn.

10. Generally, when instructed to decrease "in pattern st as established," you will work the first stitch of the row as in pattern stitch, then work two stitches together, then work the same type of stitch until another repeat of the pattern stitch can be established. For example: if you are working on a row that begins with a dc, you would dc in the first st, dc2tog, then dc until you can start another repeat of the 5-stitch pattern repeat of the Non-stick lace variation 1 pattern stitch. Likewise at the end of a row, you would work in pattern stitch as established, then work dc over any partial sections of the 5-stitch pattern repeat of the Non-stick lace variation 1 pattern stitch, dc2tog, then dc in the last stitch.

A Note On Increasing

1. The Non-stick lace variation 1 pattern stitch has a 4-row repeat. Ensure that this 4-row repeat continues.

2. The Non-stick lace variation 1 pattern stitch has a pattern rep in multiples of 5+2 stitches. Once you have increased a total of 5 stitches on each side of your established pattern, you will have enough increase stitches to begin working pattern repeats of the Gradient V-Stitch pattern stitch on the next row.

INSTRUCTIONS

BACK PANEL

Foundation Row (WS): Work 112 (127, 137, 152, 167, 177, 192, 202) Fsc, turn.

Rows 1–72 (72, 72, 72, 72, 76, 76, 76): Work even in Non-stick lace var 1 pattern st.

Fasten off.

FRONT PANEL (MAKE 2)

Foundation Row (WS): Work 57 (62, 72, 77, 82, 92, 97, 102) Fsc, turn.

Rows 1–72 (72, 72, 72, 72, 76, 76, 76): Work even in Non-stick lace var 1 pattern st.

SLEEVE (MAKE 2)

Foundation Row (WS): Work 77 (77, 82, 82, 87, 92, 92, 97) Fsc, turn.

Rows 1–15: Work even in Non-stick lace var 1 pattern st.

BEGIN SLEEVE SHAPING

Row 16 (inc row): Inc 1 in first st, work in pattern st as established to last st, inc 1 in last st, turn—79 (79, 84, 84, 89, 94, 94, 99) sts.

Row 17: Work even in pattern st as established.

Rows 18–19 (31, 35, 29, 33, 23, 23, 23): Rep last 2 rows 1 (7, 9, 6, 8, 3, 3, 3) times—81 (93, 102, 96, 105, 100, 100, 105) sts at end of last row.

Row 20 (32, 36, 30, 34, 24, 24, 24) (inc row): Inc 1 in first st, work in pattern st as established to last st, inc 1 in last st—83 (95, 104, 98, 107, 102, 102, 107) sts.

SIZES S (M) ONLY

Row 21 (33)–22 (34): Work even in pattern st as established.

Rows 23 (35)–34 (37): Rep last 3 rows 4 (1) times—91 (97) sts at end of last row.

SIZE L

Row 37: Rep last row—106 sts.

SIZES XL (2X, 3X, 4X, 5X) ONLY

Rows 31 (35, 25, 25, 25)–37 (37, 38, 41, 41): Rep last row 7 (3, 14, 17, 17) times—112 (113, 130, 136, 141) sts at end of last row.

ALL SIZES

Rows 35 (38, 38, 38, 38, 39, 42, 42)–41 (42, 42, 42, 42, 43, 46, 46): Work even in pattern st as established.

Fasten off.

SCARF

FIRST HALF

Foundation Row (WS): Work 27 Fsc, turn.

Rows 1–65: Work even in Non-stick lace var 1 pattern st.

Fasten off.

SECOND HALF

With RS facing, working across opposite side of Foundation Row, join yarn in bottom of first st of Foundation Row.

Rows 1–65: Work even in Non-stick lace var 1 pattern st.

Fasten off.

FINISHING

Block all pieces to schematic measurements.

Using locking mattress stitch technique, leaving center 6 (7, 7, 7½, 8½, 10, 11, 11) inches/15 (18, 18, 19, 21.5, 25.5, 28, 28) cm on Back unjoined for neck, sew shoulder seams. Fold Sleeves in half lengthwise. Matching fold to shoulder seam, sew top of Sleeves to Front and Back. Sew side and underarm seams. Center one long edge of Scarf across Back neck edge, and sew in place.

Weave in ends.

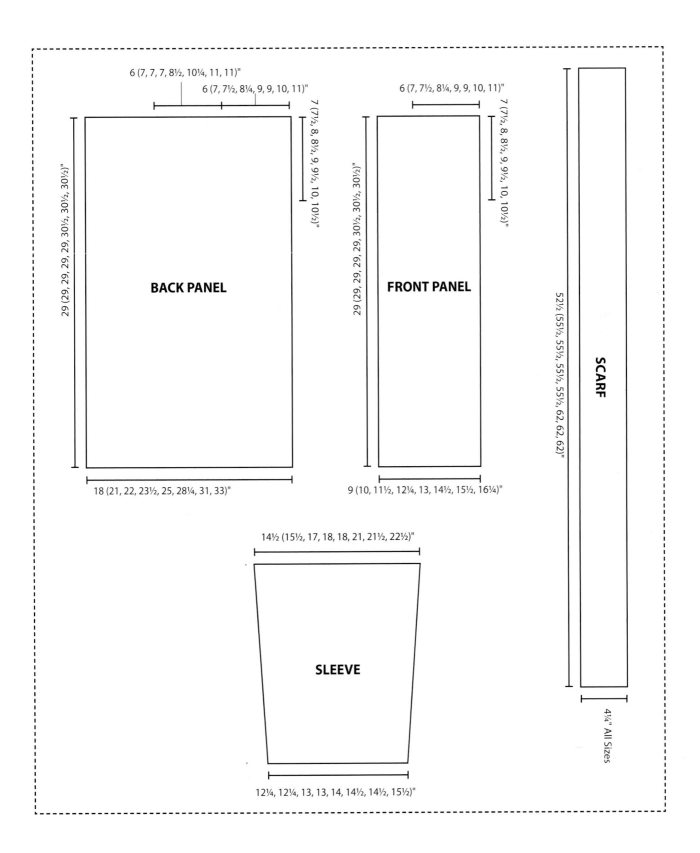

6 (7, 7, 7, 8½, 10¼, 11, 11)"

6 (7, 7½, 8¼, 9, 9, 10, 11)"

7 (7½, 8, 8½, 9, 9½, 10, 10½)"

BACK PANEL

29 (29, 29, 29, 30½, 30½, 30½)"

18 (21, 22, 23½, 25, 28¼, 31, 33)"

6 (7, 7½, 8¼, 9, 9, 10, 11)"

7 (7½, 8, 8½, 9, 9½, 10, 10½)"

FRONT PANEL

29 (29, 29, 29, 30½, 30½, 30½)"

9 (10, 11½, 12¼, 13, 14½, 15½, 16¼)"

SCARF

52½ (55½, 55½, 55½, 55½, 62, 62, 62)"

4¼" All Sizes

14½ (15½, 17, 18, 18, 21, 21½, 22½)"

SLEEVE

12¼, 12¼, 13, 13, 14, 14½, 14½, 15½)"

THREE-QUARTER SLEEVE PULLOVER

Everyone has that one wardrobe staple they reach for time after time. We designed this pullover to be the first thing you think of when you want something cozy and comfy enveloping you as you make your way through your day. This will become your grab-and-go pullover, so you'd better make two . . . or three . . . for every occasion!

SKILL LEVEL: Beginner

SIZES: S (M, L, XL, 2X, 3X, 4X, 5X)

Sample shown in size large

FINISHED MEASUREMENTS

To Fit Bust: 32 (36, 40, 44, 48, 52, 56, 60) inches/81.5 (91.5, 101.5, 112, 122, 132, 142, 152.5) cm

Finished Bust: 36 (40, 44, 48½, 53, 56, 60, 64½) inches/ 91.5, (101.5, 112, 123, 134.5, 142, 152.5, 164) cm

Finished Length: 25 (25¼, 25½, 25½, 26, 26, 26½, 26¾) inches/63.5 (64, 65, 65, 66, 66, 67.5, 68) cm

MATERIALS AND TOOLS

▪ Sample uses Crystal Palace, Mini Mochi Solid (80% Merino Wool, 20% Nylon; 1.75 ounces/50 g = 195 yards/180 m): 12 (13, 14, 16, 17, 18, 19, 21) skeins in color Purple Rain #1103—2340 (2535, 2730, 3120, 3315, 3510, 3705, 4095) yards/2160 (2340, 2520, 2880, 3060, 3240, 3420, 3780) m superfine weight yarn

▪ Crochet hook: 3.25mm (size D-3) or size to obtain gauge

▪ Yarn needle

BLOCKED GAUGE

Single crochet V-Stitch pattern: 41 sts = 5¾ inches/14.5 cm; 22 rows = 4¼ inches/11 cm

Always take time to check your gauge.

GAUGE SWATCH

Single crochet V-Stitch stitch swatch

Row 1: Work 41 Fsc, turn.

Rows 2–22: Work in Sc V-St pattern st.

STITCH GUIDE

Foundation single crochet (Fsc): Ch 2, insert hook in 2nd ch from hook, yo and draw up a loop, yo and draw through 1 loop (first "chain" made), yo and draw through 2 loops on hook (first sc made), *insert hook under 2 loops of the "chain" just made, yo and draw up a loop, yo and draw through 1 loop ("chain" made), yo and draw through 2 loops on hook (sc made); rep from * for indicated number of foundation sts.

Single crochet V-Stitch (Sc V-St): (Sc, ch 1, sc) in next st or sp.

Beginning feather: Yo, insert hook in last ch-1 space of previous rnd, yo and draw up a loop even with loops on hook (3 loops on hook), yo, insert hook in st or ch-1 sp one row below same sp, yo and draw up a loop even with loops on hook (5 loops on hook), yo, insert hook in next ch-1 sp, yo and draw up a loop even with loops on hook, yo and draw through all 7 loops on hook.

Feather: Yo, insert hook in same ch-1 sp as last feather, yo and draw up a loop even with loops on hook (3 loops on hook), yo, insert hook in skipped st or ch-1 sp one row below same sp, yo and draw up a loop even with loops on hook (5 loops on hook), yo, insert hook in next ch-1 sp, yo and draw up a loop even with loops on hook, yo and draw through all 7 loops on hook.

Last feather: Yo, insert hook in same ch-1 sp as last feather, yo and draw up a loop even with loops on hook (3 loops on hook), yo, insert hook in skipped st or ch-1 sp one row below same sp, yo and draw up a loop even with loops on

hook (5 loops on hook), yo, insert hook in same ch-1 sp as first loop of Beginning feather, and draw up a loop even with loops on hook, yo and draw through all 7 loops on hook.

PATTERN STITCH

For Master Chart Key, see page 206.

Single crochet V-Stitch (Sc V-St) (worked on a multiple of 3 + 2 sts) Ⓐ

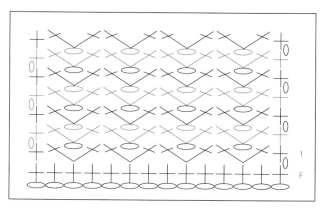

Ⓐ Single crochet V-Stitch stitch chart

Row 1: Ch 1, sc in first st, sk next st, *Sc V-St in next st, sk next 2 sts; rep from * across to last 3 sts, Sc V-St in next st, sk next st, sc in last st, turn.

Row 2: Ch 1, sc in first st, sk next st, *Sc V-St in next ch-1 sp, sk next 2 sts; rep from * across to last ch-1 sp, Sc V-St in last ch-1 sp, sk next st, sc in last st, turn.

Rep row 2 for pattern.

SPECIAL TECHNIQUES

Locking mattress stitch (see Special Techniques, page 200)
Duplicate stitch (see Special Techniques, page 199)
Setting in a sleeve (see Special Techniques, page 201)

INSTRUCTIONS

FRONT PANEL

Foundation Row: Work 128 (143, 158, 173, 188, 200, 215, 230) Fsc, turn.

Row 1 (RS): Ch 1, sc in first st, sk next st, *Sc V-St in next st, sk next 2 sts; rep from * across to last 3 sts, Sc V-St in next st, sk next st, sc in last st, turn.

Row 2 (WS): Ch 1, sc in first st, sk next st, *Sc V-St in next ch-1 sp, sk next 2 sts; rep from * across to last ch-1 sp, Sc V-St in last ch-1 sp, sk next st, sc in last st, turn.

Rows 3–94 (92, 90, 88, 88, 86, 86, 84): Rep row 2.

BEGIN ARMHOLE SHAPING

Row 1 (RS): Ch 1, sl st in first 5 (7, 7, 5, 5, 5, 5, 6) sts, ch 1, sc2tog, work in pattern st as established across to last 5 (7, 7, 5, 5, 5, 5, 6) sts, sc2tog, turn leaving last 5 (7, 7, 5, 5, 5, 5, 6) sts unworked—116 (127, 142, 161, 176, 188, 203, 216) sts.

Row 2: Ch 1, sc2tog, work in pattern st as established to last 2 sts, sc2tog, turn—114 (125, 140, 159, 174, 186, 201, 214) sts.

Row 3: Ch 1, sc2tog, sk next st, work in pattern st as established to last 3 sts, sk next st, sc2tog, turn—110 (121, 136, 155, 170, 182, 197, 210) sts.

Rows 4–5 (5, 9, 13, 17, 21, 25, 29): Rep last 2 rows 1 (1, 3, 5, 7, 9, 11, 13) times—104 (115, 118, 125, 128, 128, 131, 132) sts at end of last row.

Rows 6 (6, 10, 14, 18, 22, 26, 30)–28 (32, 34, 36, 38, 40, 42, 44): Work even in pattern st as established.

BEGIN FRONT NECKLINE SHAPING

FIRST SIDE

Row 1 (RS): Ch 1, work in pattern st as established across first 45 (49, 49, 52, 53, 51, 51, 54) sts, turn, leaving last 59 (66, 69, 73, 75, 77, 80, 78) sts unworked—45 (49, 49, 52, 53, 51, 51, 54) sts.

Row 2 (WS): Ch 1, sk first st, sc2tog, sk next st, work in pattern st as established across, turn—42 (46, 46, 49, 50, 48, 48, 51) sts.

Row 3 (RS): Ch 1, work in pattern st as established across to last 5 sts, sc2tog, sk next st, sc2tog, turn—39 (43, 43, 46, 47, 45, 45, 48) sts.

Rows 4–5 (5, 5, 7, 7, 7, 7, 9): Rep last 2 rows 1 (1, 1, 2, 2, 2, 2, 3) times—33 (37, 37, 34, 35, 33, 33, 30) sts at end of last row.

SIZES S (M, L, 2X, 3X, 4X) ONLY

Row 6 (6, 6, 8, 8, 8): Rep row 2—30 (34, 34, 32, 30, 30) sts.

ALL SIZES

Row 7 (7, 7, 8, 9, 9, 9, 10): Work even in pattern st as established.

SIZES M (XL, 2X, 3X, 5X) ONLY

Fasten off.

SIZES S (L, 4X) ONLY

Row 8 (8, 10): Work even in pattern st as established.

Fasten off.

SECOND SIDE

With RS facing, sk first 14 (17, 20, 21, 22, 26, 29, 24) unworked sts at center of neckline, join yarn with sl st in next st; first st of row 1 is worked in same st as joining.

Row 1 (RS): Ch 1, work in pattern st as established across next 45 (49, 49, 52, 53, 51, 51, 54) sts, turn.

Row 2 (WS): Ch 1, work in pattern st as established across to last 5 sts, sc2tog, sk next st, sc2tog, turn—42 (46, 46, 49, 50, 48, 48, 51) sts.

Row 3 (RS): Ch 1, sk first st, sc2tog, sk next st, work in pattern st as established across, turn—39 (43, 43, 46, 47, 45, 45, 48) sts.

Rows 4–5 (5, 5, 7, 7, 7, 7, 9): Rep last 2 rows 1 (1, 1, 2, 2, 2, 2, 3) times—33 (37, 37, 34, 35, 33, 33, 30) sts at end of last row.

SIZES S (M, L, 2X, 3X, 4X)

Row 6 (6, 6, 8, 8, 8): Rep row 2—30 (34, 34, 32, 30, 30) sts.

ALL SIZES

Row 7 (7, 7, 8, 9, 9, 9, 10): Work even in pattern st as established.

SIZES M (XL, 2X, 3X, 5X) ONLY

Fasten off.

SIZES S (L, 4X) ONLY

Row 8 (8, 10): Work even in pattern st as established.

Fasten off.

BACK PANEL

Work same as Front Panel through row 5 (5, 9, 13, 17, 21, 25, 29) of Armhole Shaping.

Row 6 (6, 10, 14, 18, 22, 26, 30)–30 (32, 36, 38, 40, 42, 46, 48): Work even in pattern st as established.

BEGIN BACK NECKLINE SHAPING

FIRST SIDE

Row 1 (RS): Ch 1, work in pattern st as established across first 42 (46, 46, 46, 44, 42, 42, 42) sts, turn, leaving 62 (69, 72, 79, 84, 86, 89, 90) sts unworked—42 (46, 46, 46, 44, 42, 42, 42) sts.

Row 2 (WS): Ch 1, sk first st, sc2tog, sk next st, work in pattern st as established across, turn—39 (43, 43, 43, 41, 39, 39, 39) sts.

Row 3 (RS): Ch 1, work in pattern st as established across to last 5 sts, sc2tog, sk next st, sc2tog, turn—36 (40, 40, 40, 38, 36, 36, 36) sts.

Rows 4 and 5: Rep last 2 rows—30 (34, 34, 34, 32, 30, 30, 30) sts at end of last row.

Row 6: Work even in pattern st as established

SIZES S (L, XL, 4X, 5X) ONLY

Fasten off.

SIZES M (2X, 3X) ONLY

Row 7: Work even in pattern st as established.

Fasten off.

SECOND SIDE

With RS facing, sk first 20 (23, 26, 33, 40, 44, 47, 48) unworked sts at center of neckline, join yarn with sl st in next st; first st of row 1 is worked in same stitch as joining.

Row 1 (RS): Ch 1, work even in pattern st as established across, turn.

Row 2: Ch 1, work in pattern st as established to last 5 sts, sc2tog, sk next st, sc2tog, turn—39 (43, 43, 43, 41, 39, 39, 39) sts.

Row 3: Ch 1, sk first st, sc2tog, sk next st, work in pattern st as established across, turn—36 (40, 40, 40, 38, 36, 36, 36) sts.

Rows 4 and 5: Rep last 2 rows—30 (34, 34, 34, 32, 30, 30, 30) sts at end of last row.

Row 6: Work even in pattern st as established.

SIZES S (L, XL, 4X, 5X) ONLY

Fasten off.

SIZES M (2X, 3X) ONLY

Row 7: Work even in pattern st as established.

Fasten off.

SLEEVE (MAKE 2)

Foundation Row: Work 113 (122, 131, 140, 152, 158, 164, 173) Fsc, turn.

Rows 1–37 (37, 41, 45, 40, 45, 44, 44): Work even in Sc V-St pattern st.

BEGIN SLEEVE SHAPING

Row 1: Ch 1, sc2tog, work in pattern st as established to last 2 sts, sc2tog, turn—111 (120, 129, 138, 150, 156, 162, 171) sts.

Rows 2–7 (9, 8, 7, 12, 9, 10, 10): Rep last row 6 (8, 7, 6, 11, 8, 9, 9) times—99 (104, 115, 126, 128, 140, 144, 153) sts at end of last row.

UPPER ARM

Rows 1–21: Work even in pattern st as established.

BEGIN SLEEVE CAP SHAPING

Row 1: Ch 1, sl st in first 7 sts, ch 1, work in pattern st as established across to last 7 sts, turn, leaving last 7 sts unworked—85 (90, 101, 112, 114, 126, 130, 139) sts.

Row 2: Ch 1, sc2tog, work in pattern st as established to last 2 sts, sc2tog, turn—83 (88, 99, 110, 112, 124, 128, 137) sts.

Row 3: Ch 1, sc2tog, sk next st, work in pattern st as established across to last 3 sts, sk next st, sc2tog, turn—79 (84, 95, 106, 108, 120, 124, 133) sts.

Rows 4–17 (17, 21, 19, 23, 23, 25, 25): Rep last 2 rows 7 (7, 9, 8, 10, 10, 11, 11) times—37 (42, 41, 58, 48, 60, 58, 67) sts at end of last row.

SIZE SMALL ONLY

Rows 18 and 19: Work even in pattern st as established.

SIZE M

Rows 18 and 19: Rep row 2 (twice)—38 sts.

SIZE 2X ONLY

Row 24: Rep row 2—44 sts.

SIZES XL (3X, 4X, 5X) ONLY

Row 20 (24, 26, 26): Ch 1, sk first st, sl st in next 2 (5, 1, 2) sts, ch 1, sc2tog, work in pattern st as established to last 4 (8, 3, 5) sts, sc2tog, turn, leaving last 2 (6, 1, 3) sts unworked—51 (46, 53, 59) sts.

SIZES XL (4X, 5X) ONLY

Row 21 (27, 27): Rep last row—44 (48, 51) sts.

ALL SIZES

Rows 20 (20, 22, 22, 25, 25, 28, 28)–21 (21, 23, 23, 26, 26, 29, 29): Ch 1, sk first st, sl st in next 2 sts, ch 1, sc2tog, work in pattern st as established across to last 4 sts, sc2tog, turn, leaving last 2 sts unworked—23 (24, 27, 30, 30, 32, 34, 37) sts. Fasten off.

FINISHING

Block all pieces to schematic measurements.

Using locking mattress stitch technique, sew shoulder and side seams.

Set sleeves into armholes and sew in place.

Sew sleeve seams.

NECKLINE BORDER

With RS facing, join yarn with sl st in any st at shoulder seam; first st of round 1 is worked in same st as joining.

Rnd 1: Ch 1, sc in first st, ch 1, sk next st, *sc in next st, ch 1, sk next st; rep from * working evenly around neckline, join with sl st in first sc.

Rnd 2: Ch 1, work Beg feather, ch 1, *feather, ch 1; rep from * around to last ch-1 sp, work Last feather, join with duplicate stitch.

SLEEVE BORDER

With RS facing, join yarn in any st at Sleeve seam; first st of rnd 1 is worked in same st as joining.

Rnd 1: Ch 1, sc in first st, ch 1, sk next st, *sc in next st, ch 1, sk next st; rep from * working evenly around Sleeve edge, join with sl st in first sc.

Rnd 2: Ch 1, work Beg feather, ch 1, *feather, ch 1; rep from * around to last ch-1 sp, work Last feather, join with duplicate stitch.

Rep Sleeve Border around other Sleeve edge.

FINISHING

Gently block Neckline and Sleeve Borders to even out stitches if needed.

Weave in ends.

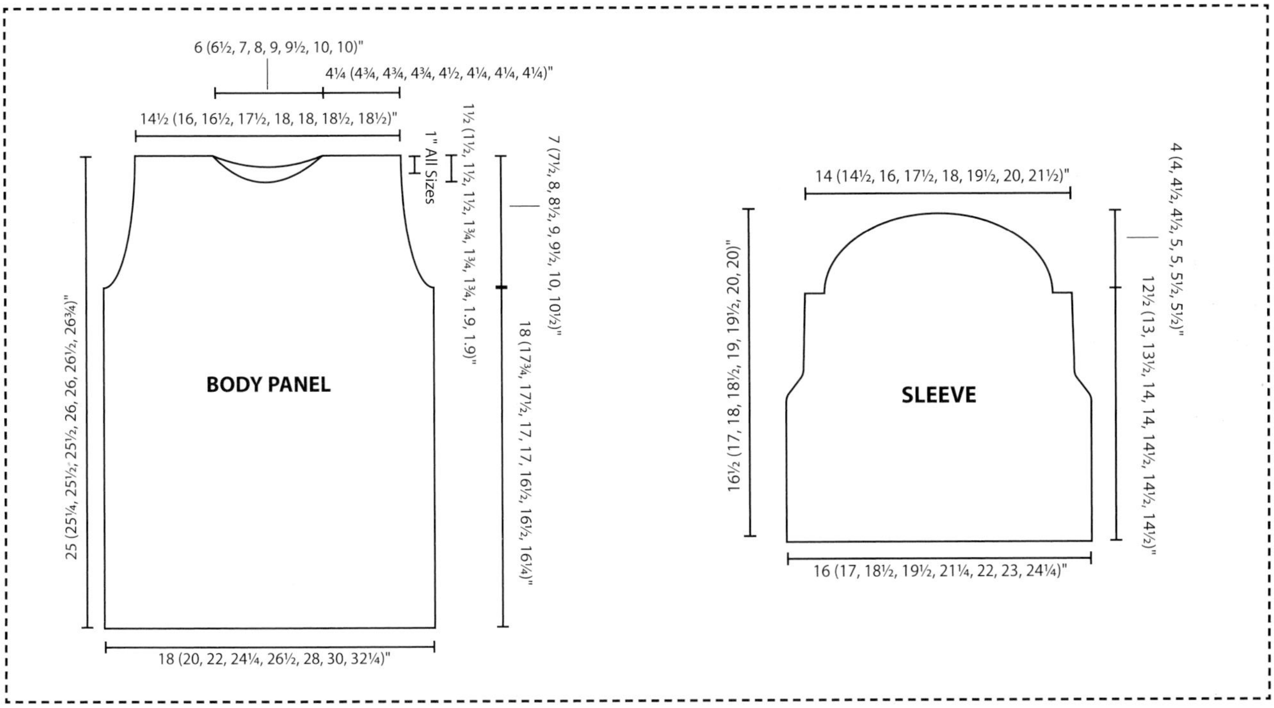

6 (6½, 7, 8, 9, 9½, 10, 10)"
4¼ (4¾, 4¾, 4¾, 4½, 4¼, 4¼, 4¼)"
14½ (16, 16½, 17½, 18, 18, 18½, 18½)"
1" All Sizes
1½ (1½, 1½, 1½, 1¾, 1¾, 1¾, 1.9, 1.9)"
7 (7½, 8, 8½, 9, 9½, 10, 10½)"
25 (25¼, 25½, 25½, 26, 26, 26½, 26¾)"
BODY PANEL
18 (17¾, 17½, 17, 17, 16½, 16½, 16¼)"
18 (20, 22, 24¼, 26½, 28, 30, 32¼)"
14 (14½, 16, 17½, 18, 19½, 20, 21½)"
4 (4, 4½, 4½, 5, 5, 5½, 5½)"
16½ (17, 18, 18½, 19, 19½, 20, 20)"
SLEEVE
12½ (13, 13½, 14, 14, 14½, 14½, 14½)"
16 (17, 18½, 19½, 21¼, 22, 23, 24¼)"

BEGINNER CARDI

If your crochet projects up to this point have all been scarves, afghans, and washcloths, this is the perfect project to introduce you to the world of garment making.

Made from six rectangles with easy shaping in the sleeves, this cardi is simple to make and construct but is big on visual impact, with a stunning ribbed shawl collar and luxuriously textured main body.

Both new and experienced stitchers will come back to this pattern over and over again for everything from special occasions to a grab-and-go wardrobe essential.

SKILL LEVEL: Beginner

SIZES: S (M, L, XL, 2X, 3X, 4X, 5X)

Sample shown in size small

FINISHED MEASUREMENTS

To Fit Bust: 32 (36, 40, 44, 48, 52, 56, 60) inches/81.5 (91.5, 101.5, 112, 122, 132, 142, 152.5) cm

Finished Bust: 35½ (40½, 44½, 48, 52, 57, 61, 64½) inches/90 (103, 113, 122, 132, 145, 155, 164) cm

Finished Length: 28 (28, 28, 29, 29, 29, 30, 30) inches/71 (71, 71, 73.5, 73.5, 73.5, 76, 76) cm

MATERIALS AND TOOLS

■ Sample uses Cascade 220 Superwash Sport (100% Superwash Merino Wool; 1.75 ounces/50g = 136.5 yards/125 m): 15 (17, 18, 20, 21, 23, 25, 26) skeins in color Really Red #809 or 2047.5 (2320.5, 2457, 2730, 2866.5, 3139.5, 3412.5, 3549) yards/1875 (2125, 2250, 2500, 2621, 2875, 3125, 3250) m of fine weight yarn

■ Crochet hook: 3.75mm (size F-5) or size to obtain gauge

■ Yarn needle

■ Pins or locking stitch markers

BLOCKED GAUGES

Sc/dc Crunch pattern stitch: 28 sts and 17 rows = 6¾ inches/17 cm x 5 inches/12.5 cm

Sc ribbing pattern: 24 sts and 22 rows = 4¾ inches/12 cm x 4¼ inches/11 cm

Always take time to check your gauge.

GAUGE SWATCHES

Sc/dc Crunch stitch swatch

Row 1: Work 28 Fsc, turn.

Row 2: Ch 1, sc in first st, dc in next st, *sc in next st, dc in next st; rep from * across, turn.

Rows 3–17: Work in Sc/dc Crunch pattern st.

Sc ribbing stitch swatch

Row 1: Work 24 Fsc, turn.

Rows 2–22: Work even in sc ribbing pattern st.

STITCH GUIDE

Foundation single crochet (Fsc): Ch 2, insert hook in 2nd ch from hook, yo and draw up a loop, yo and draw through 1 loop (first "chain" made), yo and draw through 2 loops on hook (first sc made), *insert hook under 2 loops of the "chain" just made, yo and draw up a loop, yo and draw through 1 loop ("chain" made), yo and draw through 2 loops on hook (sc made); rep from * for indicated number of foundation stitches.

PATTERN STITCHES

For Master Chart Key, see page 206.

Sc/dc Crunch (worked on any even number of sts) Ⓐ

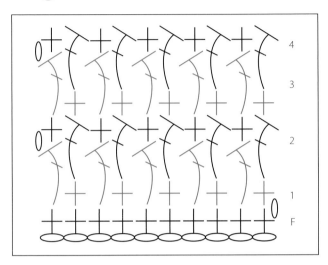

Ⓐ Sc/dc Crunch stitch chart

Row 1: Ch 1, sc in first st, dc in next st, *sc in next st, dc in next st; rep from * across.

Rep row 1 for pattern.

Single crochet ribbing (sc ribbing) (any number of sts)

Row 1: Ch 1, sc in both loops of first st, sc-tbl in each st across to last st, sc in both loops of last st, turn.

Rep row 1 for pattern.

SPECIAL TECHNIQUES

Locking mattress stitch (see Special Techniques, page 200)

Setting in sleeves (see Special Techniques, page 201)

INSTRUCTIONS

BACK PANEL

Foundation Row: Work 76 (84, 92, 100, 108, 118, 126, 134) Fsc.

Row 1: Ch 1, sc in first st, dc in next st, *sc in next st, dc in next st; rep from * across, turn.

Rows 2–95 (95, 95, 99, 99, 99, 102, 102): Work in Sc/dc Crunch pattern st.

Fasten off.

FRONT PANEL (MAKE 2)

Foundation Row: Work 24 (28, 30, 34, 36, 40, 42, 46) Fsc.

Row 1: Ch 1, sc in first st, dc in next st, *sc in next st, dc in next st; rep from * across, turn.

Rows 2–95 (95, 95, 99, 99, 99, 102, 102): Work in Sc/dc Crunch pattern st.

Fasten off.

SLEEVE (MAKE 2)

CUFF

Row 1: Work 40 (42, 46, 46, 48, 48, 50, 50) Fsc.

Rows 2–4 (5, 3, 5, 4, 4, 4, 4): Work in Sc/dc Crunch pattern st.

BEGIN SLEEVE INCREASES

Row 1: Ch 1, 2 sc in first st, dc in next st, *sc in next st, dc in next st; rep from * to last 2 sts, sc in next st, 2 dc in last st, turn—42 (44, 48, 48, 50, 50, 52, 52) sts.

Row 2: Ch 1, sc in first st, *sc in next st, dc in next st; rep from * to last st, dc in last st, turn.

Rows 3–6 (5, 5, 4, 4): Rep row 2.

SIZES 3X (4X, 5X) ONLY

Row 3: Rep row 2.

ALL SIZES

Row 7 (6, 6, 5, 5, 4, 4, 4): Ch 1, 2 sc in first st, *sc in next st, dc in next st; rep from * across to last st, 2 dc in last st, turn—44 (46, 50, 50, 52, 52, 54, 54) sts.

Rows 8 (7, 7, 6, 6, 5, 5, 5)–12 (10, 10, 8, 8, 6, 6, 6): Ch 1, sc in first st, dc in next st, *sc in next st, dc in next st; rep from * across, turn.

Rows 13 (11, 11, 9, 9, 7, 7, 7)–60 (60, 60, 56, 64, 60, 60, 66): Rep last 12 (10, 10, 8, 8, 6, 6, 6) rows 4 (5, 5, 6, 7, 9, 9, 10) times—60 (66, 70, 74, 80, 88, 90, 94) sts at end of last row.

SIZES S (L, XL, 2X, 3X, 4X, 5X) ONLY

Row 61 (61, 57, 65, 61, 61, 67)–66 (65, 60, 68, 63, 63, 69): Rep rows 1–6 (5, 5, 4, 4, 3, 3, 3) once—62 (72, 76, 82, 90, 92, 96) sts.

TOP OF SLEEVE

Rows 1–7 (12, 10, 13, 10, 17, 20, 14): Work even in Sc/dc Crunch pattern st.

Fasten off.

COLLAR

Row 1: Work 30 (33, 35, 40, 43, 46, 51, 56) Fsc, turn.

Rows 2–326 (326, 326, 336, 341, 344, 359, 359): Work even in sc ribbing pattern stitch.

Fasten off.

FINISHING

Block all pieces to schematic measurements.

Using locking mattress stitch technique, sew shoulder and side seams.

Set sleeves into armholes and sew into place.

Sew sleeve seams.

Pin center point of one long edge of Collar to center of back neckline; pin corners of same long edge of Collar to bottom front corners of garment; place pins to evenly distribute collar rows around front garment border; sew Collar in place.

Weave in ends.

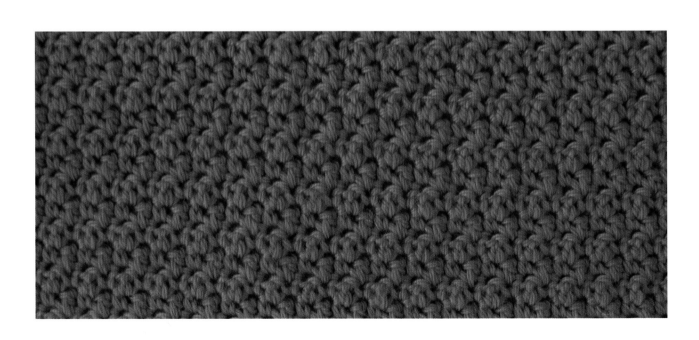

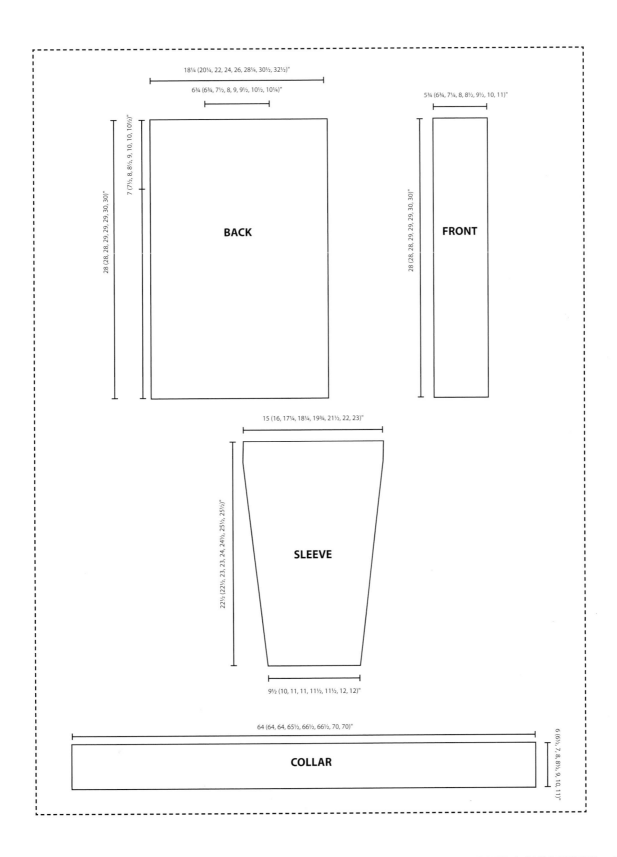

18¼ (20¼, 22, 24, 26, 28¼, 30½, 32½)"

6¾ (6¾, 7½, 8, 9, 9½, 10½, 10¼)"

7 (7½, 8, 8½, 9, 10, 10, 10½)"

28 (28, 28, 29, 29, 29, 30, 30)"

BACK

5¾ (6¾, 7¼, 8, 8½, 9½, 10, 11)"

28 (28, 28, 29, 29, 29, 30, 30)"

FRONT

15 (16, 17¼, 18¼, 19¾, 21½, 22, 23)"

22½ (22½, 23, 24, 24½, 25½, 25½)"

SLEEVE

9½ (10, 11, 11, 11½, 11½, 12, 12)"

64 (64, 64, 65½, 66½, 66½, 70, 70)"

6 (6½, 7, 8, 8½, 9, 10, 11)"

COLLAR

THREE-QUARTER SLEEVE CARDI

A FAB cardi is an essential piece for any wardrobe. We have given this enduring favorite design features such as a combination of lace and solid texture stitches and a longer length to flatter any body type. You can customize your cardi length by working fewer rows in the lace or body sections for a truly unique fit.

SKILL LEVEL: Intermediate
SIZES: S (M, L, XL, 2X, 3X, 4X, 5X)
Sample shown in size XL

FINISHED MEASUREMENTS

To Fit Bust: 32 (36, 40, 44, 48, 52, 56, 60) inches/81.5 (91.5, 101.5, 112, 122, 132, 142, 152.5) cm.
Finished Bust: 37 (40¾, 45½, 48¾, 52½, 57, 61, 65½) inches/94 (103.5, 115.5, 124, 133.5, 145, 155, 166.5) cm
Finished Length: 35 (35½, 36, 36½, 36.5, 36.5, 37, 37) inches/89 (90, 91.5, 92.5, 92.5, 92.5, 94, 94) cm

MATERIALS AND TOOLS

- Sample uses Knit Picks, Gloss Fingering (70% Merino Wool, 30% Silk; 1.75 ounces/50 g per skein = 220 yards/201 m): 10 (11, 12, 13, 14, 15, 16, 17) skeins in color Jade #24613 or 2200 (2420, 2640, 2860, 3080, 3300, 3520, 3740) yards/2010 (2211, 2412, 2613, 2814, 3015, 3216, 3417) m superfine weight yarn

- Crochet hook: 3.25mm (size D-3) or size to obtain gauge
- Yarn needle
- 3 (3, 3, 3, 4, 4, 4, 4) (7/8-inch/2.2 cm) buttons

BLOCKED GAUGES

Single crochet V-Stitch pattern: 50 sts = 7 inches/18 cm; 23 rows = 5 inches/12.5 cm

Papyrus pattern: 41 sts = 6¼ inches/16 cm; 13 rows = 5 inches/12.5 cm

Always take time to check your gauge.

GAUGE SWATCHES

Single crochet V-Stitch stitch swatch

Row 1: Work 50 Fsc, turn.

Rows 2–23: Work even in Sc V-St pattern st.

Papyrus stitch swatch

Row 1: Work 41 Fsc, turn.

Rows 2–13: Work even in papyrus pattern st.

STITCH GUIDE

Foundation single crochet (Fsc): Ch 2, insert hook in 2nd ch from hook, yo and draw up a loop, yo and draw through 1 loop (first "chain" made), yo and draw through 2 loops on hook (first sc made), *insert hook under 2 loops of the "chain" just made, yo and draw up a loop, yo and draw through 1 loop ("chain" made), yo and draw through 2 loops on hook (sc made); rep from * for indicated number of foundation sts.

Single crochet V-Stitch (Sc V-St): (Sc, ch 1, sc) in same st or sp.

Fan: (3 dc, ch 1, 3 dc) in same st.

Picot: (Sc, ch 3, sc) in same st or sp.

First double crochet (First-dc): Sc in first st, ch 2. Note: Use this stitch whenever the first stitch of a row is a dc.

First treble crochet (First-tr): Sc in first st, ch 3. Note: Use this stitch whenever the first stitch of a row is a tr.

PATTERN STITCHES

For Master Chart Key, see page 206.

Single crochet V-Stitch (Sc V-St) (worked on a multiple of 3 + 2 sts) Ⓐ

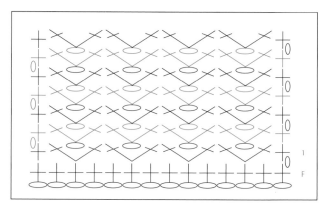

Ⓐ Single crochet V-Stitch stitch chart

Row 1: Ch 1, sc in first st, sk next st, *Sc V-St in next st, sk next 2 sts; rep from * across to last 3 sts, Sc V-St in next st, sk next st, sc in last st, turn.

Row 2: Ch 1, sc in first st, sk next st, *Sc V-St in next ch-1 sp, sk next 2 sts; rep from * across to last ch-1 sp, Sc V-St in last ch-1 sp, sk next st, sc in last st, turn.

Row 3: Rep row 2 for pattern.

Papyrus (multiple of 8 + 1 sts) Ⓑ

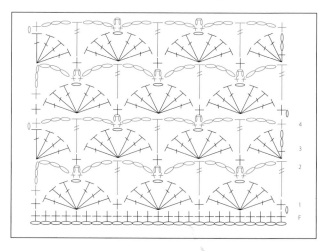

Ⓑ Papyrus stitch chart

Row 1: Ch 1, sc in first st, *sk next 3 sts, fan in next st, sk next 3 sts, sc in next st of picot; rep from * across, turn.

Row 2: First-tr, *ch 3, picot in ch-1 sp of next fan, ch 3, tr in next sc; rep from * across, turn.

Row 3: (First-dc, 3 dc) in first st, sc in ch-3 sp of next picot, *fan in next tr, sc in ch-3 sp of next picot; rep from * across to last st, 4 dc in last st, turn.

Row 4: Ch 1, sc in first st, ch 3, tr in next sc, *ch 3, picot in ch-1 sp of next fan, ch 3, tr in next sc; rep from * across to last 4 sts, ch 3, sk next 3 sts, sc in last st, turn.

Rep rows 1–4 for pattern.

SPECIAL TECHNIQUES

Locking mattress stitch (see Special Techniques, page 200)
Setting in sleeves (see Special Techniques, page 201)

Buttonhole: Hdc in each of next 6 sts, ch 4, drop loop from hook, insert hook in first buttonhole hdc made, place loop back on hook and draw through hdc, work 7 sc in ch-4 sp, sl st in same st as 6th buttonhole hdc.

NOTES

1. Upper Body is worked in Sc V-St pattern stitch from waist up to shoulder. Stitches are picked up across lower edge of Upper Body, and papyrus pattern stitch worked down to hem.

2. Sleeves are worked in Solid Stitch pattern from forearm up to sleeve cap. Stitches are picked up across lower edge of sleeve and papyrus pattern worked down to cuff.

3. Upper Body worked in one piece in Sc V-St pattern stitch for 2 inches (5 cm), then divided for armhole shaping.

4. Upper Body worked in one piece while still maintaining three separate pattern repeat sections (Back, Left Front, and Right Front).

5. Lower Body worked in one piece in papyrus pattern stitch.

6. Left Side and Right Side refer to left and right side as worn.

7. For the purpose of this pattern, all chain spaces count as 1 stitch.

8. If after a decrease the next stitch is a chain space, work one single crochet in pattern stitch in the place of that chain space then continue as instructed.

INSTRUCTIONS

UPPER BODY

Row 1: Work 264 (291, 324, 348, 375, 408, 435, 468) Fsc, turn.

Row 2 (RS): Ch 1, sc in first st, sk next st, [Sc V-St in next st, sk next 2 sts] 21 (23, 26, 28, 30, 33, 35, 38) times, Sc V-St in next st, sk next st, sc in next st, place marker between this sc and first sc of next section (Right Front Section worked); sc in next st, sk next st, [Sc V-St in next st, sk next 2 sts] 41 (46, 51, 55, 60, 65, 70, 75) times, Sc V-St in next st, sk next st, sc in next st, place marker between this sc and first sc of next section (Back Section worked); sc in next st, sk next st, [Sc V-St in next st, sk next 2 sts] 21 (23, 26, 28, 30, 33, 35, 38) times, Sc V-St in next st, sk next st, sc in next st (Left Front Section worked), turn.

Note: From here, work in pattern stitch as established, being mindful of beginnings and endings of sections.

Rows 3–41: Continue to work in Sc V-St pattern st as established for each section.

BEGIN ARMHOLE SHAPING

RIGHT FRONT

Work only across 68 (74, 83, 89, 95, 104, 110, 119) sts of Right Front Section.

Row 1 (RS): Ch 1, work in pattern st as established across first 61 (65, 74, 80, 84, 95, 101, 109) sts, sc in next st, turn, leaving last 6 (8, 8, 8, 10, 8, 8, 9) sts unworked—62 (66, 75, 81, 85, 96, 102, 110) sts.

Row 2 (WS): Ch 1, sc2tog, sc in next st, work in pattern st as established across, turn—61 (65, 74, 80, 84, 95, 101, 109) sts.

Row 3: Ch 1, work in pattern st as established to last 5 sts, sc in next st, sc2tog twice, turn—59 (63, 72, 78, 82, 93, 99, 107) sts.

Rows 4–5 (5, 9, 11, 13, 19, 23, 27): Rep last 2 rows 1 (1, 3, 4, 5, 8, 10, 12) times—56 (60, 63, 66, 67, 69, 69, 71) sts at end of last row.

Rows 6 (6, 10, 12, 14, 20, 24, 28)–26 (28, 30, 32, 34, 36, 40, 42): Work in pattern st as established.

BEGIN RIGHT FRONT NECKLINE SHAPING

Row 1 (RS): Ch 1, sl st in each of first 7 (8, 11, 15, 17, 20, 20, 22) sts, ch 1, sc in next st, work in pattern st across, turn—49 (52, 52, 51, 50, 49, 49, 49) sts.

Row 2 (WS): Ch 1, work in pattern st as established across to last 5 sts, sc in next st, sc2tog, turn, leaving last 2 sts unworked—46 (49, 49, 48, 47, 46, 46, 46) sts.

Row 3: Ch 1, sc2tog, sk next st, sc2tog, sc in next st, work in pattern st as established to end of row, turn—43 (46, 46, 45, 44, 43, 43, 43) sts.

Rows 4–7: Rep last 2 rows (twice)—31 (34, 34, 33, 32, 31, 31, 31) sts at end of last row.

Fasten off.

BACK

Worked across 128 (143, 158, 170, 185, 200, 215, 230) sts of Back Section.

With RS facing, skip first 6 (8, 8, 8, 10, 8, 8, 9) unworked sts of Back Section; join yarn with sl st in next st; first st of row 1 is worked in same st as joining.

Row 1 (RS): Ch 1, sc in first st, work in pattern st as established across next 114 (125, 140, 152, 163, 182, 197, 210) sts, sc in next st, turn, leaving last 6 (8, 8, 8, 10, 8, 8, 9) sts unworked—116 (127, 142, 154, 165, 184, 199, 212) sts.

Row 2 (WS): Ch 1, sc2tog, sc in next st, work in pattern st as established across to last 3 sts, sc in next st, sc2tog, turn—114 (125, 140, 152, 163, 182, 197, 210) sts.

Row 3: Ch 1, [sc2tog over next 2 sts] twice, sc in next st, work in pattern st as established across to last 5 sts, sc in next st, [sc2tog over next 2 sts] twice, turn—110 (121, 136, 148, 159, 178, 193, 206) sts.

Rows 4–5 (5, 9, 11, 13, 19, 23, 27): Rep last 2 rows 1 (1, 3, 4, 5, 8, 10, 12) times—104 (115, 118, 124, 129, 130, 133, 134) sts at end of last row.

Rows 6 (6, 10, 12, 14, 20, 24, 28)–26 (28, 30, 32, 34, 36, 30, 42): Work even in pattern st as established.

BEGIN BACK NECKLINE SHAPING
FIRST SIDE

Row 1 (RS): Ch 1, work in pattern st as established across first 39 (42, 42, 41, 40, 39, 39, 39) sts, sc in next st, turn, leaving last 64 (72, 75, 82, 88, 90, 93, 94) sts unworked—40 (43, 43, 42, 41, 40, 40, 40) sts.

Row 2 (WS): Ch 1, sc2tog, sk next st, sc2tog, sc in next st, work in pattern st as established across, turn—37 (40, 40, 39, 38, 37, 37, 37) sts.

Row 3: Ch 1, work in pattern st as established to last 6 sts, sc in next st, sc2tog, sk next st, sc2tog, turn—34 (37, 37, 36, 35, 34, 34, 34) sts.

Row 4: Rep row 2—31 (34, 34, 33, 32, 31, 31, 31) sts.

Row 5: Work even in pattern st as established.

Fasten off.

SECOND SIDE

Sk next 24 (29, 32, 40, 47, 50, 53, 54) unworked sts, join yarn with sl st in next st. First st of row 1 is worked in same st as joining.

Row 1 (RS): Ch 1, sc in first st, work in pattern st as established across, turn—40 (43, 43, 42, 41, 40, 40, 40) sts.

Row 2 (WS): Ch 1, work in pattern st as established to last 6 sts, sc in next st, sc2tog, sk next st, sc2tog, turn—37 (40, 40, 39, 38, 37, 37, 37) sts.

Row 3: Ch 1, sc2tog, sk next st, sc2tog, sc in next st, work in pattern st as established across, turn—34 (37, 37, 36, 35, 34, 34, 34) sts.

Row 4: Rep row 2—31 (34, 34, 33, 32, 31, 31, 31) sts.

Row 5: Work even in pattern st as established.

Fasten off.

LEFT FRONT

Worked across 68 (74, 83, 89, 95, 104, 110, 119) sts of Left Front Section.

With RS facing, skip first 6 (8, 8, 8, 10, 8, 8, 9) unworked sts of Left Front Section; join yarn with sl st in next st; first stitch of row 1 is worked in same sts as joining.

Row 1 (RS): Ch 1, sc in first st, work in pattern st as established across, turn—62 (66, 75, 81, 85, 96, 102, 110) sts.

Row 2 (WS): Ch 1, work in pattern st as established to last 3 sts, sc in next st, sc2tog, turn—61 (65, 74, 80, 84, 95, 101, 109) sts.

Row 3: Ch 1, [sc2tog over next 2 sts] twice, sc in next st, work in pattern st as established to end of row, turn—59 (63, 72, 78, 82, 93, 99, 107) sts.

Rows 4–5 (5, 9, 11, 13, 19, 23, 27): Rep last 2 rows 1 (1, 3, 4, 5, 8, 10, 12) times—56 (60, 63, 66, 67, 69, 69, 71) sts at end of last row.

Rows 6 (6, 10, 12, 14, 20, 24, 28)–26 (28, 30, 32, 34, 36, 30, 42): Work in pattern st as established.

BEGIN LEFT FRONT NECKLINE SHAPING

Row 1 (RS): Ch 1, work in pattern st as established across to last 8 (9, 12, 16, 18, 21, 21, 23) sts, sc in next st, turn, leaving last 7 (8, 11, 15, 17, 20, 20, 22) sts unworked—49 (52, 52, 51, 50, 49, 49, 49) sts.

Row 2 (WS): Ch 1, sc2tog, sk next st, sc2tog, sc in next st, work in pattern st as established across, turn—46 (49, 49, 48, 47, 46, 46, 46) sts.

Row 3: Ch 1, work in pattern st as established across to last 5 sts, sc in next st, sc2tog, turn, leaving last 2 sts unworked—43 (46, 46, 45, 44, 43, 43, 43) sts.

Rows 4–7: Rep last 2 rows (twice)—31 (34, 34, 33, 32, 31, 31, 31) sts at end of last row.

Fasten off.

LOWER BODY

With WS facing, join yarn with sl st in bottom corner st of Right Side. First st of set-up row is worked in same st as joining.

Set-up row (WS): Working across bottom of row 1 of Upper Body, ch 1, sc in each of first 10 (7, 5, 4, 13, 8, 19, 12) sts, [sc2tog, sc in each of next 9 (9, 10, 11, 10, 11, 10, 11) sts] 22 (25, 26, 26, 29, 30, 33, 34) times, sc2tog, sc in each of next 10 (7, 5, 4, 12, 8, 18, 12) sts, turn—241 (265, 297, 321, 345, 377, 401, 433) sts.

Rows 1–49 (49, 49, 49, 48, 47, 47, 46): Work even in papyrus pattern st.

Fasten off.

SLEEVE (MAKE 2)

UPPER SLEEVE

Row 1 (WS): Work 104 (113, 122, 131, 140, 149, 158, 167) Fsc, turn.

Rows 2–9: Work even in Sc V-St pattern st.

BEGIN SLEEVE CAP SHAPING

Row 1 (RS): Ch 1, sl st in first 6 (8, 8, 8, 10, 8, 8, 9) sts, ch 1, sc in first st, work in pattern st as established across to last 7 (9, 9, 9, 11, 9, 9, 10) sts, sc in next st, turn, leaving last 6 (8, 8, 8, 10, 8, 8, 9) sts unworked—92 (97, 106, 115, 120, 133, 142, 149) sts.

Row 2 (WS): Ch 1, sc2tog, sc in next st, work in pattern st as established across to last 3 sts, sc in next st, sc2tog, turn—90 (95, 104, 113, 118, 131, 140, 147) sts.

Row 3: Ch 1, [sc2tog over next 2 sts] twice, sc in next st, work in pattern st as established across to last 5 sts, sc in next st, [sc2tog over next 2 sts] twice, turn—86 (91, 100, 109, 114, 127, 136, 143) sts.

Rows 4–17 (17, 19, 19, 21, 21, 21, 21): Rep last 2 rows 7 (7, 8, 8, 9, 9, 9, 9) times—44 (49, 52, 61, 60, 73, 82, 89) sts at end of last row.

Row 18 (18, 20, 20, 22, 22, 22, 22): Ch 1, sl st in each of first 2 (2, 2, 3, 3, 4, 5, 6) sts, ch 1, sc2tog, sc in next st, work in pattern st as established across to last 4 (5, 5, 6, 5, 7, 7, 8) sts, sc in next st, sc2tog, turn, leaving last 1 (2, 2, 3, 2, 4, 4, 5) sts unworked—39 (43, 46, 53, 53, 63, 71, 76) sts.

Row 19 (19, 21, 21, 23, 23, 23, 23): Rep last row—34 (37, 40, 45, 46, 53, 60, 63) sts.

Row 20 (20, 22, 22, 24, 24, 24, 24): Ch 1, sl st in each for first 2 (2, 2, 3, 2, 4, 5, 5) sts, ch 1, sc2tog, sc in next st, work in pattern st as established across to last 4 (4, 5, 5, 5, 6, 7, 8) sts, sc in next st, sc2tog, turn, leaving last 1 (1, 2, 2, 2, 3, 4, 5) sts unworked—29 (32, 34, 38, 40, 44, 49, 51) sts.

Row 21 (21, 23, 23, 25, 25, 25, 25): Rep last row—24 (27, 28, 31, 34, 35, 38, 39) sts.

Fasten off.

LOWER SLEEVE

With WS facing, join yarn in bottom corner st of Upper Sleeve row 1. First st of set-up row is worked in same st as joining.

Set-up row (WS): Working across bottom of row 1 of Upper Sleeve, ch 1, sc in each of first 12 (10, 12, 10, 9, 8, 12, 11) sts, [sc2tog, sc in each of next 11 (11, 10, 10, 10, 10, 9, 9) sts] 6 (7, 8, 9, 10, 11, 12, 13) times, sc2tog, sc in each of next 12 (10, 12, 11, 9, 7, 12, 11) sts, turn—97 (105, 113, 121, 129, 137, 145, 153) sts.

Rows 1–29: Work even in papyrus pattern st.

Fasten off.

FINISHING

Block all pieces to schematic measurements.

Using locking mattress stitch technique, sew shoulder and side seams.

Set sleeves into armholes and sew in place.

Sew sleeve seams.

BUTTON BAND AND FRONT & NECKLINE BORDER

With RS facing, join yarn in bottom Right Front corner. Button Band and Border sts are worked in row-end sts.

Right Front Border: Ch 1, hdc evenly spaced across papyrus section.

Right Front Button Band: Working in each row-end st across Upper Body, hdc in each of next 32 (34, 36, 38, 34, 36, 40, 42) sts, make buttonhole, [hdc in each of next 4 sts, make buttonhole] 3 (3, 3, 3, 4, 4, 4, 4) times.

Neckline Border: 3 hdc in corner stitch, hdc evenly around neckline, 3 hdc in corner st.

Left Front Border: Hdc evenly spaced across papyrus section of Left Side.

Fasten off.

Sew buttons to Left Front edge opposite buttonholes.

Weave in ends.

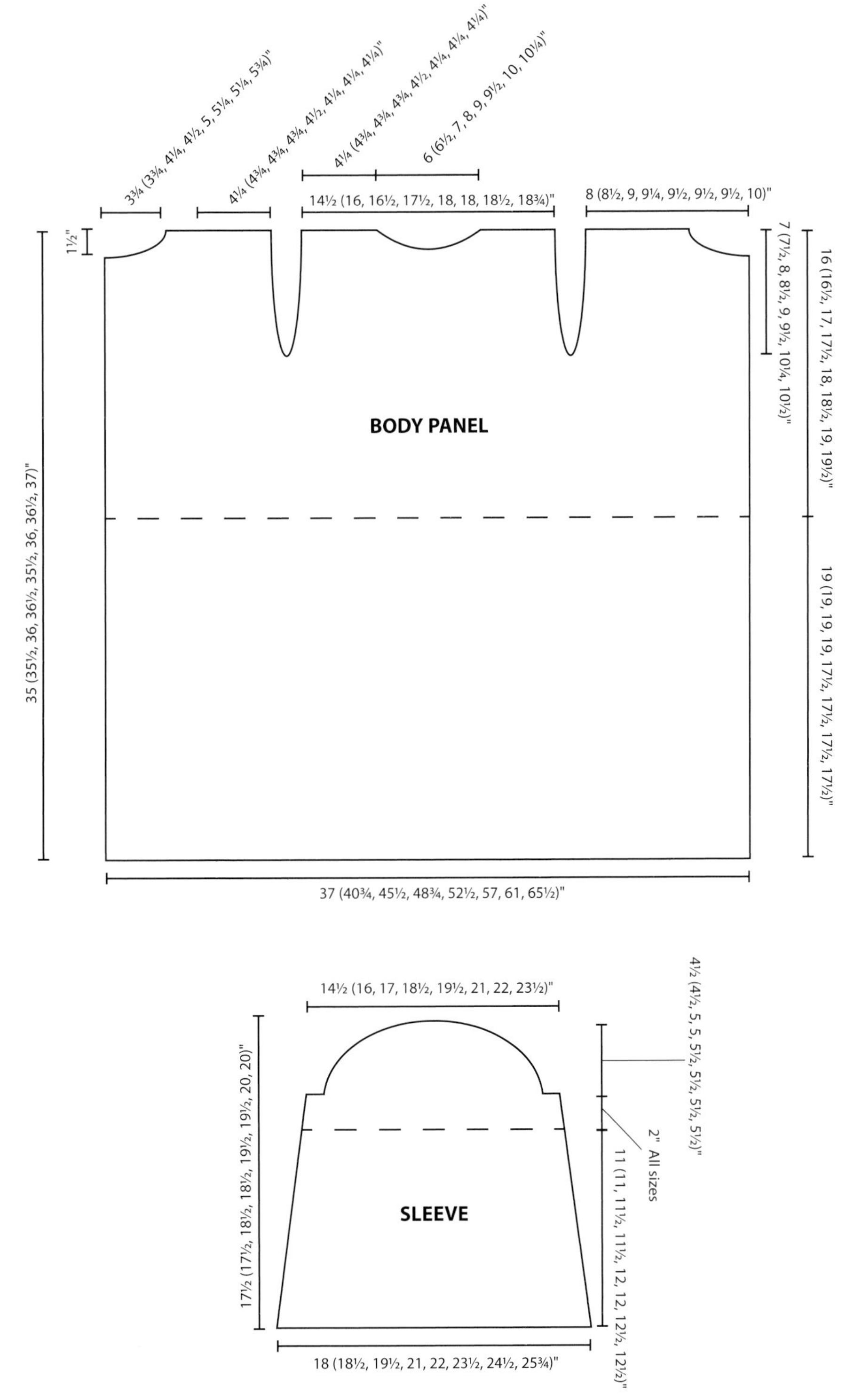
3¾ (3¾, 4¼, 4½, 5, 5¼, 5¼, 5¾)"
4¼ (4¾, 4¾, 4¾, 4½, 4¼, 4¼, 4¼)"
4¼ (4¾, 4¾, 4¾, 4½, 4¼, 4¼, 4¼)"
6 (6½, 7, 8, 9, 9½, 10, 10¼)"
14½ (16, 16½, 17½, 18, 18, 18½, 18¾)"
8 (8½, 9, 9¼, 9½, 9½, 9½, 10)"
1½"
7 (7½, 8, 8½, 9, 9½, 10¼, 10½)"
16 (16½, 17, 17½, 18, 18½, 19, 19½)"
BODY PANEL
35 (35½, 36, 36½, 35½, 36, 36½, 37)"
19 (19, 19, 19, 17½, 17½, 17½, 17½)"
37 (40¾, 45½, 48¾, 52½, 57, 61, 65½)"
14½ (16, 17, 18½, 19½, 21, 22, 23½)"
4½ (4½, 5, 5, 5½, 5½, 5½, 5½)"
2" All sizes
SLEEVE
17½ (17½, 18½, 18½, 19½, 19½, 20, 20)"
11 (11, 11½, 11½, 12, 12, 12½, 12½)"
18 (18½, 19½, 21, 22, 23½, 24½, 25¾)"

PONCHO TOP

We designed the stitch pattern and construction of this top to give you just the right amount of structure while still moving and draping beautifully on your body. This is one of those shapes that looks good on so many body types and keeps coming back around in fashion year after year.

SKILL LEVEL: Intermediate

SIZES: S/M (L/XL, 2X/3X, 4X/5X)

Sample shown in size L/XL

FINISHED MEASUREMENTS

To Fit Bust: 32-36 (40-44, 48-52, 56-60) inches/81.5-91.5 (101.5-112, 122-132, 142-152.5) cm

Main Body Width: 32½ (33½, 37, 38) inches/82.5 (85, 94, 96.5) cm

Finished Length: 28 (28½, 29, 29½) inches, 71 (72.5, 73.5, 75) cm

MATERIALS AND TOOLS

- Sample uses Mirasol, Nuna (40% Wool, 40% Silk, 20% Bamboo Viscose; 1.75 ounces/50 g = 191 yards/175 m): 14 (16, 18, 20) skeins in color French Navy #1018 or 2674 (3056, 3438, 3820) yards/2450 (2800, 3150, 3500) m of superfine weight yarn

- Crochet hooks: 2.75mm (size C-2) and 3.25mm (size D-3) or sizes to obtain gauge
- Yarn needle
- Stitch marker

BLOCKED GAUGES

Spike-V pattern with larger hook: 37 sts = 7¼ inches/18.5 cm; 22 rows = 6 inches/15 cm

Sc ribbing pattern with smaller hook: 30 sts = 5 inches/12.5 cm; 27 rows = 4¼ inches/11 cm

Always take time to check your gauge.

GAUGE SWATCHES

Spike-V stitch swatch

Foundation Row: Work 37 Fhdc, turn.

Rows 1 and 2: Ch 1, hdc in each st across, turn.

Rows 3–22: Work in Spike-V pattern st.

Sc ribbing stitch swatch

Row 1: Work 30 Fsc, turn.

Rows 2–27: Work in sc ribbing pattern st.

STITCH GUIDE

Foundation half double crochet (Fhdc): Ch 3, yo, insert hook in 3rd ch from hook, yo and draw up a loop, yo and draw through 1 loop (first "chain" made), yo and draw through all 3 loops on hook (first hdc made), *yo, insert hook under 2 loops of the "chain" just made, yo and draw up a loop, yo and draw through 1 loop ("chain" made), yo and draw through all 3 loops on hook (hdc made); rep from * for indicated number of foundation sts.

Hdc Spike: Yo, insert hook in indicated st, yo and draw up a loop even to the height of the working row.

Half double crochet through back loop only (hdc-tbl): Yo, insert hook in back loop of indicated st, yo and draw up a loop, yo and draw through 3 loops on hook.

Single crochet through back loop only (sc-tbl): Insert hook in back loop of indicated st, yo and draw up a loop, yo and draw through all 2 loops on hook.

PATTERN STITCHES

For Master Chart Key, see page 206.

Spike-V (worked on a multiple of 12 + 1 sts) Ⓐ

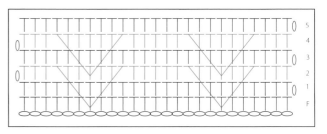

Ⓐ Spike-V stitch chart

Row 1 (RS): Ch 1, hdc in first st, *hdc in each of next 2 sts, sk next 3 sts, Hdc Spike in next st 2 rows below, hdc in 2nd skipped st, hdc in next skipped st, hdc in each of next 3 sts, Hdc Spike in same st as first Hdc Spike, hdc in each of next 3 sts; rep from * across, turn.

Row 2: Ch 1, hdc in each st across, turn.

Rep rows 1 and 2 for pattern.

Right Leaning Spike-V (worked on a multiple of 12 + 1 sts) Ⓑ

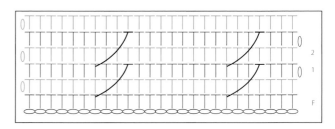

Ⓑ Right Leaning Spike-V stitch chart

Row 1 (RS): Ch 1, hdc in first st, *hdc in each of next 2 sts, sk next 3 sts, Hdc Spike in next st 2 rows below, hdc in 2nd skipped st, hdc in next skipped st, hdc in each of next 7 sts; rep from * across, turn.

Row 2: Ch 1, hdc in each st across, turn.

Rep rows 1 and 2 for pattern.

Left Leaning Spike-V (worked on a multiple of 12 + 1 sts)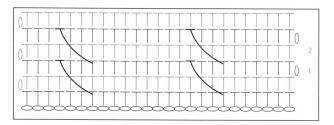

D Left Leaning Spike-V stitch chart

Row 1 (RS): Ch 1, hdc in first st, *hdc in each of next 8 sts, Hdc Spike in 3rd st to the right, hdc in each of next 3 sts; rep from * across, turn.

Row 2: Ch 1, hdc in each st across, turn.

Rep rows 1 and 2 for pattern.

Single crochet ribbing (sc ribbing) **D**

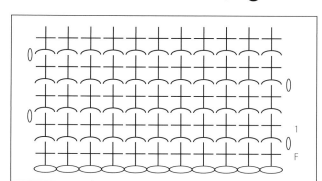

D Single crochet ribbing stitch chart

Row 1: Ch 1, sc in first st, sc-tbl in each st across to last st, sc in last st, turn.

Rep row 1 for pattern.

SPECIAL TECHNIQUES

Duplicate stitch (see Special Techniques, page 199)

Setting in a sleeve (see Special Techniques, page 201)

NOTES

1. When instructed to work in st 2 rows below, insert hook in indicated st in the row numbered 2 less than the row you are working. For example, if you are working row 5, a st "2 rows" below is in row 5 – 2 = row 3.

2. Left Side and Right Side refer to left and right side as worn.

3. When instructed to work in a pattern stitch "as established," work next row of pattern stitch and ensure that stitches line up as in previous rows.

INSTRUCTIONS

FRONT CENTER PANEL

Row 1 (WS): Work 85 (85, 97, 97) Fhdc, turn.

Rows 2 and 3: Ch 1, hdc in each st across, turn.

Rows 4–95 (97, 99, 101): Work even in Spike-V pattern st.

BEGIN FRONT NECKLINE SHAPING

FIRST SIDE

Row 1 (RS): Ch 1, work in pattern st across first 35 (33, 38, 37) sts, turn, leaving last 50 (52, 59, 60) sts unworked.

Row 2: Ch 1, hdc2tog, sk next st, hdc2tog, work in pattern st as established across, turn—32 (30, 35, 34) sts.

Row 3: Ch 1, work in pattern st as established across to last 5 sts, hdc2tog, sk next st, hdc2tog, turn—29 (27, 32, 31) sts.

Rows 4–7: Rep last 2 rows 2 more times—17 (15, 20, 19) sts at end of last row.

Row 8: Work even in pattern st as established.

Fasten off.

SECOND SIDE

With RS facing sk next 15 (19, 21, 23) unworked sts, join yarn in next st. First st of row 1 is worked in same st as joining.

Row 1 (RS): Ch 1, work in pattern st as established across, turn—35 (33, 38, 37) sts.

Row 2: Ch 1, work in pattern st as established across to last 5 sts, hdc2tog, sk next st, hdc2tog, turn—32 (30, 35, 34) sts.

Row 3: Ch 1, hdc2tog, sk next st, hdc2tog, work in pattern st as established across, turn—29 (27, 32, 31) sts.

Rows 4–7: Rep last 2 rows (twice)—17 (15, 20, 19) sts at end of last row.

Row 8: Work even in pattern st as established.

Fasten off.

LEFT FRONT PANEL

Row 1 (WS): Work 37 (49, 49, 61) Fhdc, turn.

Rows 2 and 3: Ch 1, hdc in each st across, turn.

Rows 4–103 (105, 107, 109): Work even in Right Leaning Spike-V pattern st.

Fasten off.

RIGHT FRONT PANEL

Row 1 (WS): Work 37 (49, 49, 61) Fhdc, turn.

Rows 2 and 3: Ch 1, hdc in each st across, turn.

Rows 4–103 (105, 107, 109): Work even in Left Leaning Spike-V pattern st.

Fasten off.

BACK CENTER PANEL

Row 1 (WS): Work 85 (85, 97, 97) Fhdc, turn.

Rows 2 and 3: Ch 1, hdc in each st across, turn.

Rows 4–97 (99, 101, 103): Work even in Spike-V pattern st.

BEGIN BACK NECKLINE SHAPING

FIRST SIDE

Row 1 (RS): Ch 1, work in pattern st across first 29 (27, 32, 31) sts, turn, leaving last 56 (58, 65, 66) sts unworked.

Row 2: Ch 1, hdc2tog, sk next st, hdc2tog, work in pattern st as established across, turn—26 (24, 29, 28) sts.

Row 3: Ch 1, work in pattern st as established across to last 5 sts, hdc2tog, sk next st, hdc2tog, turn—23 (21, 26, 25) sts.

Rows 4 and 5: Rep last 2 rows—17 (15, 20, 19) sts at end of last row.

Row 6: Work even in pattern st as established.

Fasten off.

SECOND SIDE

With RS facing, sk next 27 (31, 33, 35) unworked sts, join yarn in next st. First st of row 1 is worked in same st as joining.

Row 1 (RS): Ch 1, work even in pattern st as established across, turn—29 (27, 32, 31) sts.

Row 2: Ch 1, work in pattern st as established to last 5 sts, hdc2tog, sk next st, hdc2tog, turn—26 (24, 29, 28) sts.

Row 3: Ch 1, hdc2tog, sk next st, hdc2tog, work in pattern st as established across, turn—23 (21, 26, 25) sts.

Rows 4 and 5: Rep last 2 rows—17 (15, 20, 19) sts at end of last row.

Row 6: Work even in pattern st as established.

Fasten off.

RIGHT BACK PANEL

Work same as Left Front Panel.

LEFT BACK PANEL

Work same as Right Front Panel.

SLEEVE (MAKE 2)

Row 1: Work 66 (66, 72, 72) Fsc, turn.

Rows 2–51 (63, 70, 76): Work even in sc ribbing pattern st.

Fasten off.

FINISHING

Block all pieces to schematic measurements.

Using locking mattress st, sew shoulder seams.

Sew side seams leaving 5½ (5½, 6, 6) inches/14 (14,15, 15) cm opening for armholes.

Set sleeves into armholes and sew in place.

Sew sleeve seams.

COLLAR

Worked in the round.

With RS facing, join yarn in shoulder seam. First st of rnd 1 is worked in same st as joining.

Rnd 1: Ch 1, hdc evenly around neckline, do not join. Work in a spiral, marking beg of rnd and moving marker up as work progresses.

Rnd 2: Hdc-tbl of each st around.

Rep rnd 2 until piece measures 6 inches/15 cm deep.

Join with duplicate stitch.

Fold Collar in half lengthwise, and sew last rnd to inside of neckline.

Block collar to 10 (10½, 11, 11½) inches/25.5 (26.5, 28, 29) cm wide and 3 inches/7.5 cm deep.

Weave in ends.

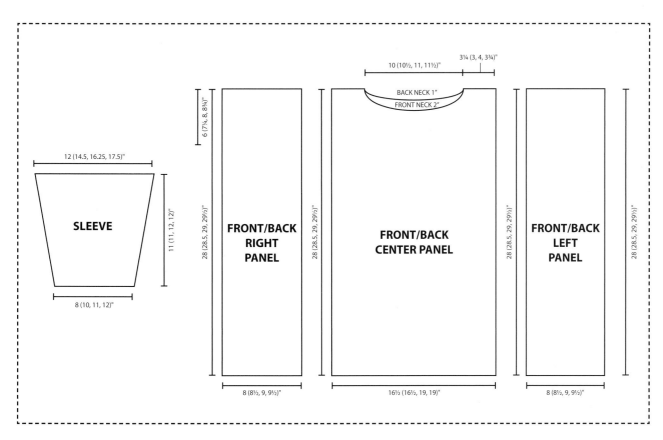

DRAPE FRONT CARDI

Cascading front panels and comfy slouchy sleeves make this the cardi of choice for everything from a day about town to working around the house to sitting quietly with your crochet projects.

We patterned this piece with a generous oversize fit through the body but added structure in the set-in sleeves to make it comfy and easy to wear and love. Once you make this and wear it, you will see why the drape front cardi has been a style favorite year after year.

SKILL LEVEL: Intermediate
SIZES: S (M, L, XL, 2X, 3X, 4X, 5X)
Sample shown in size large

FINISHED MEASUREMENTS

To Fit Bust: 32 (36, 40, 44, 48, 52, 56, 60) inches/81.5 (91.5, 101.5, 112, 122, 132, 142, 152.5) cm
Finished Bust: 34½ (40, 44, 48, 52, 55, 59, 63) inches/87.5, (101.5, 112, 122, 132, 139.5, 150, 160) cm
Finished Length: 25½ (26, 26½, 27, 27½, 28, 28½, 29) inches/65 (66, 67.5, 68.5, 70, 71, 72.5, 73.5) cm

MATERIALS AND TOOLS

- Sample uses Knit Picks, Capretta (80% Fine Merino Wool, 10% Cashmere, 10% Nylon; 1.75 ounces/50 g = 230 yards/210 m): 9 (10, 11, 12, 13, 14, 15, 16) skeins in color Pesto #25945 or 2070 (2300, 2530, 2760, 2990, 3220, 3450, 3680) yards/1890 (2100, 2310, 2520, 2730, 2940, 3150, 3360) m of superfine weight yarn

- Crochet hook: 3.5mm (size E-4) or size to obtain gauge
- Yarn needle

BLOCKED GAUGE

Gradient V-Stitch pattern: 38 sts = 6½ inches/16.5 cm; 24 rows = 8 inches/20.5 cm

Always take time to check your gauge.

GAUGE SWATCH

Gradient V-St stitch swatch

Foundation Row: Work 38 Fsc, turn.

Rows 1–12: Work even in Gradient V-St pattern st.

STITCH GUIDE

Foundation single crochet (Fsc): Ch 2, insert hook in 2nd ch from hook, yo and draw up a loop, yo and draw through 1 loop (first "chain" made), yo and draw through 2 loops on hook (first sc made), *insert hook under 2 loops of the "chain" just made, yo and draw up a loop, yo and draw through 1 loop ("chain" made), yo and draw through 2 loops on hook (sc made); rep from * for indicated number of foundation sts.

Double crochet V-Stitch (Dc-V St): (Dc, ch 1, dc) in next st.

Half double crochet V-Stitch (Hdc-V St): (Hdc, ch 1, hdc) in next st.

Single crochet V-Stitch (Sc V-St): (Sc, ch 2, sc) in next st.

First double crochet (First-dc): Sc in first st, ch 2. Note: Use this stitch whenever the first stitch of a row is a dc.

Double crochet 2 together (dc2tog): Yo, insert hook in next st and pull up a loop, insert hook in next st and pull up a loop, yo and draw through 3 loops on hook, yo and draw through 2 loops on hook.

Half double crochet 2 together (hdc2tog): Yo, insert hook in next st and pull up a loop, insert hook in next st and pull up a loop, yo and draw through all 4 loops on hook.

Single crochet 2 together (sc2tog): Insert hook in next st and pull up a loop, insert hook in next st and pull up a loop, yo and draw through all 3 loops on hook.

PATTERN STITCH

For Master Chart Key, see page 206.

Gradient V-Stitch (Gradient V-St) (worked on a multiple of 3 + 2 sts) Ⓐ

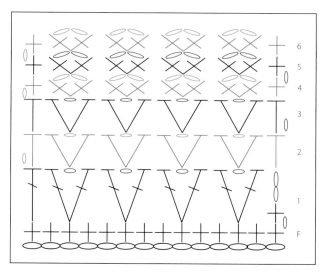

Ⓐ Gradient V-St stitch chart

Row 1: First-dc, sk next st, Dc-V in next st, *sk next 2 sts, Dc-V St in next st; repeat from * to last 2 sts, sk next st, dc in last st, turn.

Rows 2 and 3: Ch 1, hdc in first st, Hdc-V St in next ch-1 sp and in each ch-1 sp across to last st, hdc in last st, turn.

Rows 4–6: Ch 1, sc in first st, Sc V-St in next ch-1 sp and in each ch-1 sp across to last st, sc in last st, turn.

Rep rows 1–6 for pattern.

SPECIAL TECHNIQUES

Locking mattress stitch (see Special Techniques, page 200)

Setting in sleeves (see Special Techniques, page 201)

NOTES

1. For the purpose of this pattern, all chain spaces count as 1 stitch.

2. When instructed to "decrease X number of sts" use dc2tog, hdc2tog or sc2tog (see Stitch Guide) according to the pattern row you are working on. For example: if you are about to work a row of Dc-V stitches, you would dc2tog where the pattern reads "dec 1 st."

3. When instructed to "inc 1 st", work 2 dc, 2 hdc or 2 sc in first st according to the pattern row you are working on. For example: If you are about to work a row of Dc-V stitches, you would work 2 dc in first st where the pattern reads "inc 1 st."

4. If after a decrease the next st is a chain space, work one st in pattern st in the place of that chain space, then continue as instructed.

5. Left Side and Right Side refer to left and right side as worn.

A Note on Increasing

In this pattern, you will be instructed to increase or decrease "in pattern st as established." This means you should maintain the Gradient V-St pattern st as it has been worked up to this point in the pattern. There are two important properties of the Gradient V-St pattern st that you will need to maintain:

1. The Gradient V-St pattern has a 6-row repeat. Ensure that this 6-row repeat continues.

2. The Gradient V-St pattern has a pattern repeat in multiples of 3 + 2 stitches. Once you have increased a total of 3 stitches on each side of your established pattern, you will have enough increase stitches to begin working pattern repeats of the Gradient V-St pattern on the next row.

INSTRUCTIONS

BACK PANEL

Foundation Row: Work 101 (116, 128, 140, 152, 161, 173, 185) Fsc, turn.

Rows 1–54: Work even in Gradient V-St pattern st.

ARMHOLE SHAPING

Row 1: Ch 1, sl st in first 5 (5, 6, 7, 5, 7, 8, 8) sts, ch 1, First-dc in next st, work in pattern st as established across to last 6 (6, 7, 8, 6, 8, 9, 9) sts, dc in next st, turn, leaving last 5 (5, 6, 7, 5, 7, 8, 8) sts unworked—91 (106, 116, 126, 142, 147, 157, 169) sts.

Row 2: Ch 1, hdc2tog, ch 1, hdc in next ch-1 sp, work in pattern st as established to last ch sp, hdc in last ch sp, ch 1, hdc2tog—89 (104, 114, 124, 140, 145, 155, 167) sts.

Row 3: Ch 1, [hdc2tog over next 2 sts] twice, ch 1, hdc in next ch-1 sp, work in pattern st as established across to last 2 ch-1 sps, hdc in next ch-1 sp, ch 1, (hdc2tog) twice, turn—85 (100, 110, 120, 136, 141, 151, 163) sts.

SIZES M (L, XL, 2X, 3X, 4X, 5X)

Row 4: Working in pattern st as established, dec 1 st at beginning and end of row—98 (108, 118, 134, 139, 149, 161) sts.

Row 5: Working in pattern st as established, dec 2 sts at beginning and end of row—94 (104, 114, 130, 135, 145, 157) sts.

SIZES L (XL, 2X, 3X, 4X, 5X)

Rows 6–7 (9, 13, 15, 17, 21): Rep last 2 rows 1 (2, 4, 5, 6, 8) times—98 (102, 106, 105, 109, 109) sts at end of last row.

ALL SIZES

Rows 4 (6, 8, 10, 14, 16, 18, 22)–23 (24, 26, 27, 29, 30, 32, 33): Work even in pattern st as established.

LEFT FRONT PANEL

Foundation Row: Work 101 (116, 128, 140, 152, 161, 173 185) Fsc, turn.

Rows 1–54: Work even in Gradient V-St pattern st.

ARMHOLE SHAPING

Row 1 (RS): Ch 1, sl st in first 5 (5, 6, 7, 5, 7, 8, 8) sts, ch 1, First-dc in next st, work in pattern st as established across, turn—96 (111, 122, 133, 147, 154, 165, 177) sts.

Row 2 (WS): Ch 1, work in pattern st as established across to last ch-1 sp, hdc in last ch-1 sp, ch 1, hdc2tog, turn—95 (110, 121, 132, 146, 153, 164, 176) sts.

Row 3: Ch 1, [hdc2tog over last 2 sts] twice, ch 1, hdc in next ch-1 sp, work in pattern st as established across, turn—93 (108, 119, 130, 144, 151, 162, 174) sts.

SIZES M (L, XL, 2X, 3X, 4X, 5X)

Row 4 (WS): Working in pattern st as established, decrease 1 st at end of row—107 (118, 129, 143, 150, 161, 173) sts.

Row 5: Working in pattern st as established, decrease 2 sts at beginning of row—105 (116, 127, 141, 148, 159, 171) sts.

SIZES L (XL, 2X, 3X, 4X, 5X)

Rows 6–7 (9, 13, 15, 17, 21): Rep last 2 rows 1 (2, 4, 5, 6, 8) times—113 (121, 129, 133, 141, 147) sts.

ALL SIZES

Rows 4 (6, 8, 10, 14, 16, 18, 22)–23 (24, 26, 27, 29, 30, 32, 33): Work even in pattern st as established.

RIGHT FRONT PANEL

Foundation Row: Work 101 (116, 128, 140, 152, 161, 173 185) Fsc, turn.

Rows 1–54: Work even in Gradient V-St pattern st.

ARMHOLE SHAPING

Row 1 (RS): Ch 1, work in pattern st as established across to last 6 (6, 7, 8, 6, 8, 9, 9) sts, dc in next st, turn, leaving last 5 (5, 6, 7, 5, 7, 8, 8) sts unworked—96 (111, 122, 133, 147, 154, 165, 177) sts.

Row 2 (WS): Ch 1, hdc2tog, ch 1, hdc in next ch-1 sp, work in pattern st as established across, turn—95 (110, 121, 132, 146, 153, 164, 176) sts.

Row 3: Ch 1, work in pattern st as established across to last 2 ch-1 sps, hdc in next ch-1 sp, ch 1, (hdc2tog) twice, turn—93 (108, 119, 130, 144, 151, 162, 174) sts.

SIZES M (L, XL, 2X, 3X, 4X, 5X)

Row 4 (WS): Working in pattern st as established, dec 1 st at beginning of row—107 (118, 129, 143, 150, 161, 173) sts.

Row 5: Working in pattern st as established, dec 2 sts at end of row—105 (116, 127, 141, 148, 159, 171) sts.

SIZES L (XL, 2X, 3X, 4X, 5X)

Rows 6–7 (9, 13, 15, 17, 21): Rep last 2 rows 1 (2, 4, 5, 6, 8) times—113 (121, 129, 133, 141, 147) sts.

ALL SIZES

Rows 4 (6, 8, 10, 14, 16, 18, 22)–23 (24, 26, 27, 29, 30, 32, 33): Work even in pattern st as established.

SLEEVE (MAKE 2)

CUFF

Foundation Row: Work 59 (62, 65, 68, 71, 74, 77, 80) Fsc, turn.

Rows 1–3: Work even in Gradient V-St pattern st.

BEGIN SLEEVE INCREASES

Row 4: Ch 1, inc 1 in first st, work in pattern st as established across to last st, inc 1 in last st, turn—61 (64, 67, 70, 73, 76, 79, 82) sts.

Rows 5 and 6: Work even in pattern st as established.

Rows 7–24 (42, 63, 51, 48, 42, 39, 33): Rep last 3 rows 6 (12, 19, 15, 14, 12, 11, 9) times—73 (88, 105, 100, 101, 100, 101, 100) sts.

SIZES S (M) ONLY

Row 25 (43): Rep row 4—75 (90) sts.

Rows 26 (44)–28 (46): Work even in pattern st as established.

Rows 29 (47)–60 (62): Rep last 4 rows 8 (4) times—91 (98) sts at end of last row.

SIZES XL (2X, 3X, 4X, 5X) ONLY

Row 52 (49, 43, 40, 34): Rep row 4—102 (103, 102, 103, 102) sts.

Row 53 (50, 44, 41, 35): Work even in pattern st as established.

Rows 54 (51, 45, 42, 36)–63 (66, 68, 71, 71): Rep last 2 rows 5 (8, 12, 15, 18) times—112 (119, 126, 133, 138) sts.

ALL SIZES

Rows 61 (63, 64, 64, 67, 69, 72, 72)–66 (68, 69, 69, 72, 74, 77, 77): Work even in pattern st as established.

BEGIN SLEEVE CAP SHAPING

Row 1: Ch 1, sl st in next 6 sts, ch 1, work in pattern st as established across to last 6 sts, turn, leaving last 6 sts unworked—79 (86, 93, 100, 107, 114, 121, 126) sts.

Rows 2–5 (3, 9, 6, 13, 10, 8, 5): Ch 1, sk first st, dec 1 over next 2 sts, work in pattern st to last 3 sts, dec 1 in next 2 sts, turn, leaving last st unworked—67 (78, 61, 70, 59, 78, 93, 110) sts at end of last row.

Rows 6 (4, 10, 7, 14, 11, 9, 6)–10 (10, 13, 13, 16, 16, 16, 16): Ch 1, sk first st, sl st in next st, ch 1, dec 1 in next 2 sts, work in pattern st to last 4 sts, dec 1 in next 2 sts, turn, leaving last 2 sts unworked—37 (36, 37, 38, 41, 42, 45, 44) sts.

Row 11 (11, 14, 14, 17, 17, 17, 17): Ch 1, sk first st, sl st in next 2 sts, ch 1, work in pattern st as established across to last 4 sts, dec 1 in next 2 sts, turn, leaving last 2 sts unworked—31 (30, 31, 32, 35, 36, 39, 38) sts.

Row 12 (12, 15, 15, 18, 18, 18, 18): Rep last row—25 (24, 25, 26, 29, 30, 31, 32) sts.

Fasten off.

FINISHING

Block all pieces to finished measurements.

Using locking mattress stitch, sew shoulder and side seams.

Set sleeves into armholes and sew in place.

Sew sleeve seams.

TOP BORDER

With RS facing, join yarn in corner of Front panel.

Row 1: Work in row 1 of pattern st as established evenly across tops of Front and Back panels.

Rows 2–18: Work even in pattern st as established.

Fasten off.

Block Top Border to width of Front and Back panels and 6 inches/15 cm long.

Weave in ends.

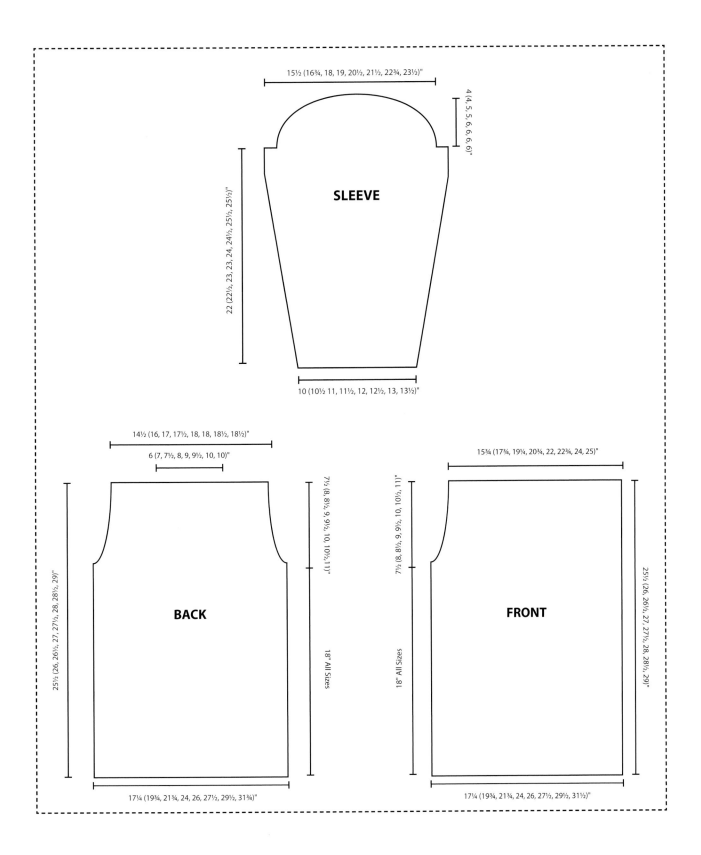

SLEEVE

15½ (16¾, 18, 19, 20½, 21½, 22¾, 23½)"

4 (4, 5, 5, 6, 6, 6, 6)"

22 (22½, 23, 23, 24, 24½, 25½, 25½)"

10 (10½ 11, 11½, 12, 12½, 13, 13½)"

BACK

14½ (16, 17, 17½, 18, 18, 18½, 18½)"

6 (7, 7½, 8, 9, 9½, 10, 10)"

7½ (8, 8½, 9, 9½, 10, 10½, 11)"

18" All Sizes

25½ (26, 26½, 27, 27½, 28, 28½, 29)"

17¼ (19¾, 21¾, 24, 26, 27½, 29½, 31¾)"

FRONT

15¾ (17¾, 19¼, 20¾, 22, 22¾, 24, 25)"

7½ (8, 8½, 9, 9½, 10, 10½, 11)"

18" All Sizes

25½ (26, 26½, 27, 27½, 28, 28½, 29)"

17¼ (19¾, 21¾, 24, 26, 27½, 29½, 31½)"

TWO-WAY TOP

I've always loved clever fashion that retains its functionality and stylish looks, and I like to think we have achieved that combination with this design. The generous fit in the body tapers through the Dolman sleeves to the ribbed cuff, while the upper and lower body shaping tapers to two borders—one wider, one narrower. But which way is up? The neckline and hemline are interchangeable, so you can wear this piece either end up for two distinctly different styles.

SKILL LEVEL: Advanced

SIZES: S (M, L, XL, 2X, 3X, 4X, 5X)
Sample shown in size XL

FINISHED MEASUREMENTS

To Fit Bust: 32 (36, 40, 44, 48, 52, 56, 60) inches/81.5 (91.5, 101.5, 112, 122, 132, 142, 152.5) cm

Finished Length: 28 (28, 29, 29, 29, 29, 30, 30) inches/71 (71, 73.5, 73.5, 73.5, 73.5, 76, 76) cm

MATERIALS AND TOOLS

◾ Sample uses Knit Picks, Gloss Fingering (70% Merino Wool, 30% Silk; 3.5 ounces/100 g per skein = 220 yards/201 m): 10 (11, 12, 13, 14, 15, 16, 17) skeins in color Winter Night #24617 or 2200 (2420, 2640, 2860, 3080, 3300, 3520, 3740) yards/2010 (2211, 2412, 2613, 2814, 3015, 3216, 3417) m of superfine weight yarn

◾ Crochet hook: 3.5mm (size E-4) or size to obtain gauge
◾ Yarn needle
◾ Stitch markers
◾ Pins

BLOCKED GAUGES

Basket Weave cables pattern: 41 sts = 7½ inches/19 cm; 24 rows = 5½ inches/14 cm

Sc ribbing pattern: 30 sts = 5 inches/12.5 cm; 28 rows = 4½ inches/11.5 cm

Always take time to check your gauge.

STITCH GUIDE

Foundation half double crochet (Fhdc): Ch 3, yo, insert hook in 3rd ch from hook, yo and draw up a loop, yo and draw through 1 loop (first "chain" made), yo and draw through all 3 loops on hook (first hdc made), *yo, insert hook under 2 loops of the "chain" just made, yo and draw up a loop, yo and draw through 1 loop ("chain" made), yo and draw through all 3 loops on hook (hdc made); rep from * for indicated number of foundation sts.

Front Post double crochet (FPdc): Yo, insert hook from front to back and then to front again around post of designated st, yo and draw up loop, [yo and draw through 2 loops on hook] twice.

Front Post treble crochet (FPtr): Yo (twice), insert hook from front to back and then to front again around post of designated st, yo and draw up a loop, [yo and draw through 2 loops on hook] 3 times.

Front Post double treble crochet (FPdtr): Yo (3 times), insert hook from front to back and then to front again around post of designated st, yo and draw up a loop, [yo and draw through 2 loops on hook] 4 times.

3-over-3 FPdtr left cross cable (worked over 7 sts): Skip next 4 sts, FPdtr around the post of each of next 3 sts 2 rows below; hdc in last skipped st; working in front of FPdtr just made, FPdtr around the post of each of first 3 skipped sts 2 rows below.

3-over-3 FPdtr right cross cable (worked over 7 sts): Skip next 4 sts, FPdtr around the post of each of next 3 sts 2 rows below; hdc in last skipped st; working behind FPdtr just made, FPdtr around the post of each of first 3 skipped sts 2 rows below.

Single crochet through back loop only (sc-tbl): Insert hook in back loop of indicated st, yo and draw up a loop, yo and draw through 2 loops on hook.

Half double crochet 2 together (hdc2tog): Yo, insert hook in next st and pull up a loop, insert hook in next st and pull up a loop, yo and draw through all 4 loops on hook.

PATTERN STITCHES

For Master Chart Key, see page 206.

Basket Weave Cables (work on a multiple of 10 + 1 sts) Ⓐ

Row 1: Ch 1, hdc in each st across, turn.

Row 2: Ch 1, sc in first st and in each st across, turn.

Row 3 (RS): Ch 1, hdc in first st, [FPdc around the post of next st 2 rows below] 3 times, hdc in each of next 3 sts, *work 3-over-3 FPdtr left cross cable, hdc in each of next 3 sts; rep from * across to last 4 sts, [FPdc around next st 2 rows below] 3 times, hdc in last st, turn.

Row 4: Rep row 2.

Row 5: Ch 1, hdc in first 2 sts, [FPtr around the post of previous st 2 rows below] 3 times, hdc in next st, [FPtr around the post of next FPdtr 2 rows below] 3 times, *hdc in each of next 3 sts, [FPtr around the post of previous st 2 rows below] 3 times, hdc in next st, sk next st, [FPtr around the post of next st 2 rows below] 3 times; rep from * across to last 2 sts, (hdc in next st) twice, turn.

Row 6: Rep row 2.

Row 7: Ch 1, hdc in first 2 sts, work 3-over-3 FPdtr right cross cable, *hdc in each of next 3 sts, work 3-over-3 FPdtr right cross cable; rep from * across to last 2 sts, hdc in each of next 2 sts, turn.

Row 8: Rep row 2.

Row 9: Ch 1, hdc in first st, *[FPtr around the post of next FPdtr 2 rows below] 3 times, hdc in each of next 3 sts, [FPtr around the post of previous FPdtr, 2 rows below] 3 times, hdc in next st; rep from * across, turn.

Rep rows 2–9 for pattern.

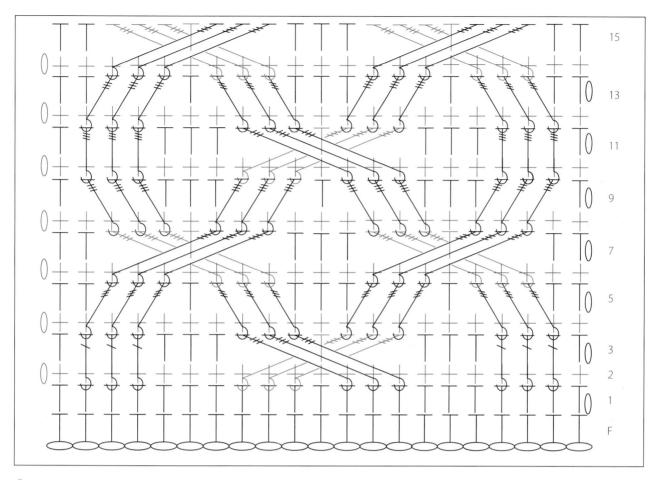

A Basket Weave Cables stitch chart

Single crochet ribbing (sc ribbing) (worked on any number of sts) **B**

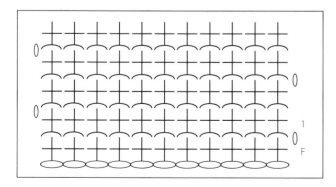

B Single crochet ribbing stitch chart

Row 1: Ch 1, sc in both loops of first st, sc-tbl in each st across to last st, sc in both loops of last st, turn.

Rep row 1 for pattern.

SPECIAL TECHNIQUE

Locking mattress stitch (see Special Techniques, page 200)

NOTES

1. When instructed to work in st 2 rows below, insert hook in indicated stitch in the row numbered 2 less than the row you are working. For example, if you are working row 5, a stitch "2 rows" below is in row 5 – 2 = row 3.

2. When instructed to work in side of stitch, insert hook from front to back into the indicated stitch between the 2 vertical strands of yarn directly below the first wrap, catching 2 side strands of yarn.

3. When instructed to work in a pattern stitch "as established," work the next row of pattern stitch and ensure that the stitches line up as in previous rows.

4. When instructed to "decrease X number of sts," use hdc2tog or sc2tog (see Stitch Guide) according to the pattern row you are working on. For example, if you are about to work a row of hdc stitches, you would hdc2tog where the pattern reads "decrease 1 st."

5. When instructed to "inc X number of sts," work 2 hdc or 2 sc in first st according to the pattern row you are working on. For example, if you are about to work a row of hdc stitches, and the pattern reads "increase 1 st," you would work 2 hdc in first st.

6. Always skip stitch in current row behind each post stitch worked.

A Note on Increasing:

In all remaining sections, you will be instructed to increase "in pattern stitch as established." This means you should maintain the Basket Weave Cables Stitch Pattern as it has been worked up to this point in the pattern. There are two important properties of the Basket Weave Cables Stitch Pattern that you will need to maintain:

1. The Basket Weave Cables Stitch Pattern has an 8-row repeat. From here on, ensure that this 8-row repeat continues.

2. The Basket Weave Cables Stitch Pattern has a pattern repeat in multiples of 10 + 1 stitches. Once you have increased a total of 10 sts on each side of your established pattern, you will have enough increase stitches to begin working pattern repeats of Basket Weave Cables Stitch Pattern on the next RS row.

INSTRUCTIONS

BODY PANEL (MAKE 2)

NARROW YOKE RIBBING

Row 1: Work 18 Fsc, turn.

Rows 2–115 (126, 138, 149, 161, 172, 183, 194): Work even in sc ribbing.

Do not fasten off. At end of last row, rotate work ¼ turn to the right for working in row-end sts of ribbing.

MAIN BODY

Row 1: Ch 1, hdc in each of first 5 (6, 4, 6, 4, 10, 14, 12) sts, [hdc2tog, sc in each of next 6 sts] 13 (14, 16, 17, 19, 10, 11, 12) times, hdc2tog, sc in each of next 4 (6, 4, 5, 3, 10, 13, 12) sts, turn—101 (111, 121, 131, 141, 161, 171, 181) hdc.

Rows 2–9: Work rows 2–9 of Basket Weave Cables pattern st.

BEGIN FIRST HALF BODY SHAPING

Row 1: Ch 1, inc 1 st in first st, work in pattern st as established across to last st, inc 1 st in last st, turn—103 (113, 123, 133, 143, 163, 173, 183) sts.

Rows 2–3 (4, 6, 9, 10, 20, 21, 26): Rep last row 2 (3, 5, 8, 9, 19, 20, 25) times—107 (119, 133, 149, 161, 201, 213, 233) sts.

Row 4 (5, 7, 10, 11, 21, 22, 27): Ch 1, inc 1 st in each of first 2 sts, work in pattern st as established to last 2 sts, inc 1 st in each of last sts, turn—111 (123, 137, 153, 165, 205, 217, 237) sts.

SIZES S (M, L, XL, 2X, 3X, 4X) ONLY

Rows 5 (6, 8, 11, 12, 22, 23)–26: Rep last row 22 (21, 19, 16, 15, 5, 4) times—199 (207, 213, 217, 225, 225, 233) sts at end of last row.

SLEEVE

Rows 1–22 (22, 26, 26, 26, 26, 30, 30): Work even in pattern st as established.

BEGIN SECOND HALF BODY SHAPING

Row 1: Ch 1, [dec 1 st over next 2 sts] twice, work in pattern st as established to last 2 sts, [dec 1 st over next 2 sts] twice, turn—195 (203, 209, 213, 221, 221, 229, 233) sts.

Rows 2–13 (16, 16, 13, 12, 10, 10, 9): Rep last row 12 (15, 15, 12, 11, 9, 9, 8) times—147 (143, 149, 165, 177, 185, 193, 201) sts.

Row 14 (17, 17, 14, 13, 11, 11, 10): Ch 1, [dec 1 st over next 2 sts] 3 (3, 1, 1, 1, 1, 1, 1) times, work in pattern st as established to last 6 (6, 2, 2, 2, 2, 2, 2) sts, [dec 1 st over next 2 sts] 3 (3, 1, 1, 1, 1, 1, 1) times, turn—141 (137 (147, 163, 175, 183, 191, 199) sts.

Rows 15 (18, 18, 15, 14, 12, 12, 11)–18: Rep last row 4 (1, 1, 4, 5, 7, 7, 8) times—117 (131, 145, 155, 165, 169, 177, 183) sts.

Fasten off.

WIDE YOKE RIBBING (MAKE 2)

Row 1: Work 48 Fsc, turn.

Rows 2–96 (107, 119, 128, 136, 140, 146, 152): Work in sc ribbing pattern st.

Fasten off.

CUFF RIBBING (MAKE 2)

Row 1: Work 15 Fsc, turn.

Rows 2–56 (56, 67, 67, 67, 67, 79, 79): Work in sc ribbing pattern st.

Fasten off.

FINISHING

Block all pieces to schematic measurements.

Using locking mattress stitch, sew Front to Back across side seams above and below Cuffs.

Sew last row of Second Yoke Ribbing to first row of Second Yoke Ribbing.

Sew last row of Cuff Ribbing to first row of Cuff Ribbing.

Pin first Wide Yoke Ribbing panel in place evenly along edge of Second Half of Body; sew Wide Yoke Ribbing in place. Rep for second Wide Yoke Ribbing panel.

Pin Cuff Ribbing in place evenly around sleeve opening and sew in place.

Weave in ends.

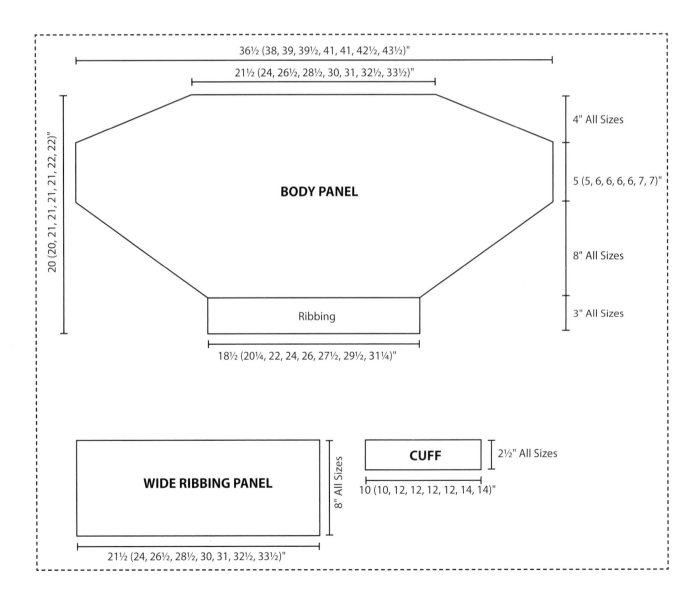

36½ (38, 39, 39½, 41, 41, 42½, 43½)"

21½ (24, 26½, 28½, 30, 31, 32½, 33½)"

4" All Sizes

BODY PANEL

5 (5, 6, 6, 6, 6, 7, 7)"

8" All Sizes

20 (20, 21, 21, 21, 21, 22, 22)"

Ribbing

3" All Sizes

18½ (20¼, 22, 24, 26, 27½, 29½, 31¼)"

WIDE RIBBING PANEL

8" All Sizes

CUFF

2½" All Sizes

10 (10, 12, 12, 12, 12, 14, 14)"

21½ (24, 26½, 28½, 30, 31, 32½, 33½)"

DRESSES
& SKIRT

OFF-THE-SHOULDER DRESS

Chic, elegant, and flattering on so many body types, we designed this piece so you can give yourself a slightly customized fit by blocking your finished piece to follow your body in all the right places and just flow right over others. Wear the neckline folded down and off the shoulders or up and draped around your neckline, depending on your style mood.

SKILL LEVEL: Beginner
SIZES: S (M, L, XL, 2X, 3X, 4X, 5X)
Sample shown in size small

FINISHED MEASUREMENTS

To Fit Bust: 32 (36, 40, 44, 48, 52, 56, 60) inches/81.5 (91.5, 101.5, 112, 122, 132, 142, 152.5) cm
Finished Bust: 34½ (38½, 43½, 48, 51, 55, 59½, 63½) inches/87.5 (98, 110.5, 122, 129.5, 139.5, 151, 161.5) cm
Finished Hip: 36 (40, 45, 49½, 54½, 58½, 63, 67) inches/91.5 (101.5, 114.5, 125.5, 138.5, 148.5, 160, 170) cm

MATERIALS AND TOOLS

- Sample uses Malabrigo Sock yarn (100% Superwash Merino; 3.5 ounces/100 g = 440 yards/402 m): 6 (7, 7, 8, 9, 9, 10, 11) skeins in color Violetta Africana #808 or 2640 (3080, 3080, 3520, 3960, 3960, 4400, 4840) yards/2412 (2814, 2814, 3216, 3618, 3618, 4020, 4422) m of superfine weight yarn

- Crochet hooks: 3.25mm (size D-3) and 4.0mm (size G-6) or sizes to obtain gauge
- Crochet hooks: 3.5mm (size E-4) and 3.75mm (size F-5) (for Collar only)
- Yarn needle

BLOCKED GAUGES

Single crochet V-Stitch pattern with largest hook: 38 sts = 5¼ inches/13.5 cm; 22 rows = 4½ inches/11.5 cm

Sc ribbing pattern with smallest hook, 28 sts = 4¼ inches/11 cm; 30 rows 4 inches/10 cm

Always take time to check your gauge.

GAUGE SWATCHES

Single crochet V-Stitch stitch swatch

Row 1 (WS): With largest hook, work 38 Fsc, turn.

Rows 2–22: Work even in Sc V-St pattern st.

Sc ribbing stitch swatch

Row 1: With smallest hook, work 28 Fsc, turn.

Rows 2–30: Work even in sc ribbing pattern st.

STITCH GUIDE

Foundation single crochet (Fsc): Ch 2, insert hook in 2nd ch from hook, yo and draw up a loop, yo and draw through 1 loop (first "chain" made), yo and draw through 2 loops on hook (first sc made), *insert hook under 2 loops of the "chain" just made, yo and draw up a loop, yo and draw through 1 loop ("chain" made), yo and draw through 2 loops on hook (sc made); rep from * for indicated number of foundation sts.

Single crochet through back loop only (sc-tbl): Insert hook in back loop of indicated st, yo and draw up a loop, yo and draw through 2 loops on hook.

Single crochet V-Stitch (Sc V-St): (Sc, ch 1, sc) in same st or sp.

PATTERN STITCHES

For Master Chart Key, see page 206.

Single crochet V-Stitch (Sc V-St) (worked on a multiple of 3 + 2 sts) Ⓐ

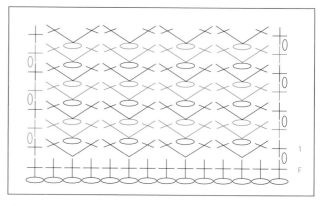

Ⓐ Single crochet V-Stitch stitch chart

Row 1: Ch 1, sc in first st, sk next st, *Sc V-St in next st, sk next 2 sts; rep from * across to last 3 sts, Sc V-St in next st, sk next st, sc in last st, turn.

Row 2: Ch 1, sc in first st, sk next st, *Sc V-St in next ch-1 sp, sk next 2 sts; rep from * across to last ch-1 sp, Sc V-St in last ch-1 sp, sk next st, sc in last st, turn.

Rep row 2 for pattern.

Single crochet V (Sc-V pattern) worked in turned rounds (worked on a multiple of 3 sts)

Row 1: Ch 1, sk first st, *Sc-V pattern in next ch-1 sp, sk next 2 sts; rep from * around, join with sl st in first sc, turn.

Rep row 1 for pattern.

Single crochet ribbing (sc ribbing)

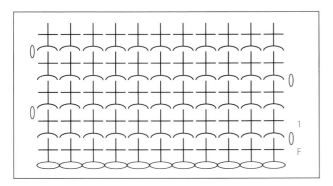

B Single crochet ribbing stitch chart

Row 1: Ch 1, sc in both loops of first st, sc-tbl in each st across to last st, sc in both loops of last st, turn.
Rep row 1 for pattern.

SPECIAL TECHNIQUE
Locking mattress stitch (see Special Techniques, page 200)

NOTES
1. Left Side and Right Side refer to left and right side as worn.
2. For the purpose of this pattern, all chain spaces count as 1 stitch.
3. When instructed to work in a pattern stitch "as established," work the next row of pattern stitch and ensure that the stitches line up as in previous rows.
4. Collar is worked in turned rounds. Turned rounds are worked back and forth like rows but joined with a slip stitch like rounds before turning.
5. Ribbing section is worked first from side to side, then stitches for main body are worked in side of ribbing rows.
6. Ribbing section is worked with smallest hook; Main Body is worked with largest hook.

7. If after a decrease the next stitch is a chain space, work one single crochet in the place of that chain space, then continue as instructed.

A Note on Increasing
In this pattern, you will be instructed to increase or decrease "in pattern stitch as established." This means you should maintain the Sc-V pattern stitch as it has been worked up to this point in the pattern. There is one important property of the Sc-V pattern stitch that you will need to maintain:

The Sc-V pattern stitch has a pattern rep in multiples of 3 + 2 stitches. Once you have increased a total of 3 stitches on each side of your established pattern, you will have enough increase stitches to begin working pattern repeats of the Sc-V pattern stitch on the next row.

INSTRUCTIONS

BODY PANEL (MAKE 2)

HEM RIBBING
Row 1: With smallest hook, work 20 Fsc, turn.
Rows 2–135 (150, 169, 185, 204, 219, 235, 250): Work in sc ribbing pattern st.
Do not fasten off. At end of last row, rotate work ¼ turn to the right for working in row-end sts of ribbing.

MAIN BODY
Set-up row (RS): With largest hook, ch 1, working in row-end sts across side of ribbing, sc in each of first 26 (29, 26, 24, 23, 25, 26, 26) sts, [sc2tog, sc in each of next 25 (28, 27, 25, 24, 26, 24, 26) sts] 3 (3, 4, 5, 6, 6, 7, 7) times, sc2tog, sc in each of next 26 (29, 25, 24, 23, 24, 25, 26) sts, turn—131 (146, 164, 179, 197, 212, 227, 242) sts.
Rows 1–30: Work even in Sc-V pattern st.

BEGIN WAIST SHAPING

Row 31: Ch 1, sc in first st, sc2tog, sc in next st, work in pattern st as established across to last 4 sts, sc in next st, sc2tog, sc in last st, turn—129 (144, 162, 177, 195, 210, 225, 240) sts.

Rows 32–34: Work even in pattern st as established.

Rows 35–42 (42, 42, 42, 54, 54, 54, 54): Rep last 4 rows 2 (2, 2, 2, 5, 5, 5, 5) times—125 (140, 158, 173, 185, 200, 215, 230) sts at end of last row.

Rows 43 (43, 43, 43, 55, 55, 55, 55)–104 (100, 100, 102, 98, 94, 96, 94): Work even in pattern st as established.

BEGIN BODY RAGLAN SHAPING

Row 1: Ch 1, sl st in first 6 (5, 4, 7, 7, 7, 7, 7) sts, ch 1, sc in next st, work in pattern st as established across to last 7 (6, 5, 8, 8, 8, 8, 8) sts, sc in next st, turn, leaving last 6 (5, 4, 7, 7, 7, 7, 7) sts unworked—113 (130, 150, 159, 171, 186, 201, 216) sts.

Row 2: Ch 1, sc in first st, sc2tog, sc in next st, work in pattern st as established to last 4 sts, sc in next st, sc2tog, sc in last st, turn—111 (128, 148, 157, 169, 184, 199, 214) sts.

SIZES S (M, L, XL, 2X, 3X, 4X) ONLY

Rows 3–18 (20, 22, 22, 20, 16, 12): Rep last row 16 (18, 20, 20, 18, 14, 10) times—79 (92, 108, 117, 133, 156, 179) sts at end of last row.

SIZES S (M) ONLY

Row 19 (21): Ch 1, sc in first st, sc2tog, sc in next st, work in pattern st as established across to end of row, turn—78 (91) sts.

SIZES L (XL, 2X, 3X, 4X, 5X) ONLY

Row 23 (23, 21, 17, 13, 3): Ch 1, sc in first st, [sc2tog] 2 times, sc in next st, work in pattern st as established to last 4 sts, sc in next st, sc2tog, sc in last st, turn—105 (114, 130, 153, 176, 211) sts.

ALL SIZES

Rows 20 (22, 24, 24, 22, 18, 14, 4)–24 (28, 30, 32, 34, 38, 40, 42): Rep last row 5 (7, 7, 9, 13, 21, 27, 39) times—73 (84, 84, 87, 91, 90, 95, 94) sts at end of last row.

Fasten off.

SLEEVE (MAKE 2)

CUFF RIBBING

With 3.25mm/D-3 hook:

Row 1: 14 Fsc, turn.

Rows 2–53 (59, 62, 68, 71, 74, 80, 80): Work even in sc ribbing pattern st.

Do not fasten off. At end of last row, rotate work ¼ turn to the right for working in row-end sts of ribbing.

MAIN SLEEVE

Set-up row (RS): With largest hook, ch 1, working in row-end sts across side of ribbing, sc in each row-end st across, turn—53 (59, 62, 68, 71, 74, 80, 80) sts.

Row 1: Work even in Sc-V pattern stitch, turn.

Row 2: Ch 1, 2 sc in first st, work in pattern st as established across to last st, 2 sc in last st, turn—55 (61, 64, 70, 73, 76, 82, 82) sts.

Rows 3–5: Work even in pattern st as established.

Rows 6–49 (41, 69, 81, 53, 37, 9, 9): Rep last 4 rows 11 (9, 16, 19, 12, 8, 1, 1) times—77 (79, 96, 108, 97, 92, 84, 84) sts at end of last row.

Row 50 (42, 70, 82, 54, 38, 10, 10): Rep row 2—79 (81, 98, 110, 99, 94, 86, 86) sts.

Rows 51 (43, 71, 83, 55, 39, 11, 11)–54 (46, 74, 84, 56, 40, 12, 12): Work even in pattern st as established.

Rows 55 (47, 75, 85, 57, 41, 13, 13)–94 (96, 99, 99, 104, 106, 111, 111): Rep last 5 (5, 5, 3, 3, 3, 3, 3) rows 8 (10, 5, 5, 16, 22, 33, 33) times—95 (101, 108, 120, 131, 138, 152, 152) sts at end of last row.

Rows 95 (97, 100, 100, 105, 107, 112, 112)–98 (100, 103, 103, 108, 110, 115, 115): Work even in pattern st as established.

BEGIN SLEEVE RAGLAN SHAPING

Row 1: Ch 1, sl st in first 6 (5, 4, 7, 7, 7, 7, 7) sts, sc in next st, work in pattern st as established across to last 7 (6, 5, 8, 8, 8, 8, 8) sts, sc in next st, turn, leaving last 6 (5, 4, 7, 7, 7, 7, 7) sts unworked—83 (91, 100, 106, 117, 124, 138, 138) sts.

Row 2: Ch 1, sc in first st, sc2tog, sc in next st, work in pattern st as established across to last 4 sts, sc in next st, sc2tog, sc in last st, turn—81 (89, 98, 104, 115, 122, 136, 136) sts.

Row 3: Work even in pattern st as established.

Rows 4–23 (27, 29, 29, 29, 35, 29, 39): Rep last 2 rows 10 (12, 13, 13, 13, 16, 13, 18) times—61 (65, 72, 78, 89, 90, 110, 100) sts at end of last row.

Row 24 (28, 30, 30, 30, 36, 30, 40): Rep row 2—59 (63, 70, 76, 87, 88, 108, 98) sts.

SIZES XL (2X, 3X, 4X, 5X) ONLY

Rows 31 (31, 37, 31, 41)–32 (34, 38, 40, 42): Rep last row 2 (4, 2, 10, 2) times—72 (79, 84, 88, 94) sts at end of last row.

ALL SIZES

Fasten off.

FINISHING

Block all pieces to finished dimensions.

Sew raglan edges of sleeves to raglan edges of body panels.

Sew side and sleeve seams.

COLLAR

Collar is worked in Sc-V pattern stitch in turned rnds.

With RS facing, using smallest hook, join yarn in right corner st of Back Panel. First st of row 1 is worked in same st as joining.

Set-up rnd: Ch 1, sc in first st, ch 1, sk next st, sc in next st, *sc in next st, ch 1, sk next st, sc in next st; rep from * around neck opening, join with sl st in first sc, turn.

Rnds 1–12: Work in Sc-V pattern stitch.

Rnds 13–15: With 3.5mm/E–4 hook, work in Sc-V pattern stitch.

Rnds 16–36: With 3.75mm/F-5 hook, work in Sc-V pattern stitch.

Fasten off.

Block collar to finished dimensions.

Weave in ends.

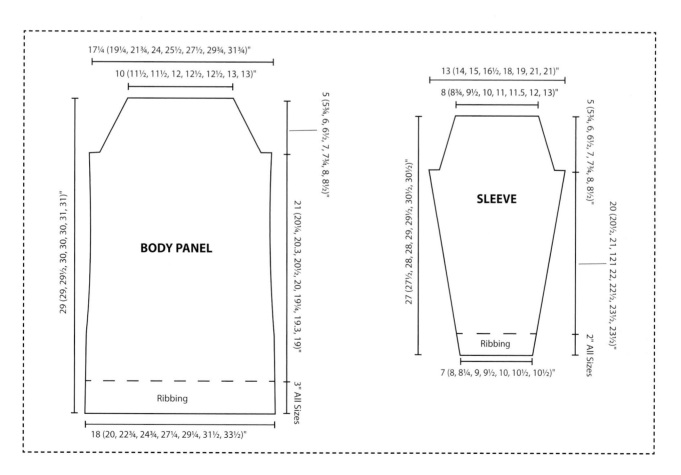

BODY PANEL

17¼ (19¼, 21¾, 24, 25½, 27½, 29¾, 31¾)"

10 (11½, 11½, 12, 12½, 12½, 13, 13)"

5 (5¾, 6, 6½, 7, 7¾, 8, 8½)"

29 (29, 29½, 30, 30, 30, 31, 31)"

21 (20¼, 20.3, 20½, 20, 19¼, 19.3, 19)"

3" All Sizes

Ribbing

18 (20, 22¾, 24¾, 27¼, 29¼, 31½, 33½)"

SLEEVE

13 (14, 15, 16½, 18, 19, 21, 21)"

8 (8¾, 9½, 10, 11, 11.5, 12, 13)"

5 (5¾, 6, 6½, 7, 7¾, 8, 8½)"

27 (27½, 28, 28, 29, 29½, 30½, 30½)"

20 (20½, 21, 121 22, 22½, 23½, 23½)"

2" All Sizes

Ribbing

7 (8, 8¼, 9, 9½, 10, 10½, 10½)"

CABLES AND LACE TUNIC

We're adding a dash of elegance to the après-ski style with a tunic featuring flowing lace cascading down from an elegantly cabled yoke and fitted shoulders. Wear this as a layering piece for a special occasion, a fun day about town, or while sitting by a glowing fire with a steaming mug of cocoa.

SKILL LEVEL: Intermediate

SIZES: S (M, L, XL, 2X, 3X, 4X, 5X)

Sample shown in size small

FINISHED MEASUREMENTS

To Fit Bust: 32 (36, 40, 44, 48, 52, 56, 60) inches/81.5 (91.5, 101.5, 112, 122, 132, 142, 152.5) cm

Finished Bust: 35½ (40, 42, 46, 50, 54, 58, 62½) inches/90, (101.5, 106.5, 117, 127, 137, 147.5, 159) cm

Finished Length: 36 (36½, 37½, 38¼, 39, 40, 41, 41¾) inches/91.5 (92.5, 95, 97, 99, 101.5, 104, 106) cm

MATERIALS AND TOOLS

▨ Sample uses Knit Picks Stroll Sock (75% Superwash Merino Wool, 25% Nylon; 1.75 ounces/50 g = 231 yards/211 m): 8 (9, 10, 11, 12, 12, 13, 14) skeins in color Dove Heather #25023 or 1848 (2079, 2310, 2541, 2772, 2772, 3003, 3234) yards/1688 (1899, 2110, 2321, 2532, 2532, 2743, 2954) m of superfine weight yarn

▨ Crochet hooks: 3.25mm (size D-3) and 3.5mm (size E-4) or sizes to obtain gauge

▨ Yarn needle

▨ Stitch markers

▨ Pins

BLOCKED GAUGES

Main Body lace pattern: With larger hook, 29 sts = 5 inches/12.5 cm; 15 rows = 5¾ inches/14.5 cm

Yoke cable pattern: With larger hook, 31 sts = 5 inches/12.5 cm; 28 rows = 5¾ inches/14.5 cm

Sc ribbing pattern: With smaller hook, 32 sts = 5 inches/12.5 cm; 29 rows = 4¼ inches/11 cm

Woven hdc pattern: With larger hook, 16 sts = 4 inches/10 cm; 10 rows = 2 inches/5 cm

Always take time to check your gauge.

STITCH GUIDE

Foundation single crochet (Fsc): Ch 2, insert hook in 2nd ch from hook, yo and draw up a loop, yo and draw through 1 loop (first "chain" made), yo and draw through 2 loops on hook (first sc made), *insert hook under 2 loops of the "chain" just made, yo and draw up a loop, yo and draw through 1 loop ("chain" made), yo and draw through 2 loops on hook (sc made); rep from * for indicated number of foundation sts.

Foundation half double crochet (Fhdc): Ch 1, yo, insert hook in 3rd ch from hook, yo and draw up a loop, yo and draw through 1 loop (first "chain" made), yo and draw through all 3 loops on hook (first hdc made), *yo, insert hook under 2 loops of the "chain" just made, yo and draw up a loop, yo and draw through 1 loop ("chain" made), yo and draw through all 3 loops on hook (hdc made); rep from * for indicated number of foundation sts.

First double crochet (First-dc): Sc in first st, ch 2. Note: Use this stitch whenever the first stitch of a row is a dc.

Double crochet V-stitch (Dc-V St): (Dc, ch 1, dc) in same st or sp.

3-dc fan: 3 dc in same st or sp.

Front Post double crochet (FPdc): Yo, insert hook from front to back and then to front again around post of designated st, yo and draw up loop, [yo and draw through 2 loops on hook] twice.

Front Post treble crochet (FPtr): Yo (twice), insert hook from front to back and then to front again around post of designated st, yo and draw up a loop, [yo and draw through 2 loops on hook] 3 times.

Front Post double treble crochet (FPdtr): Yo (3 times), insert hook from front to back and then to front again around post of designated st, yo and draw up a loop, [yo and draw through 2 loops on hook] 4 times.

2-1-2 FPtr left cross (worked over 5 sts): Skip next 3 sts, FPtr around each of next 2 sts 2 rows below; working behind FPtr just made, hdc in 3rd skipped stitch; work in front of FPtr just made, FPtr around each of first 2 skipped stitches 2 rows below.

4-over-4 FPdtr left cross (worked over 8 sts): Skip next 4 sts, FPdtr around each of next 4 sts 2 rows below; working in front of FPdtr just made, FPdtr around each of first 4 skipped stitches 2 rows below.

4-1-4 FPdtr left cross (worked over 9 sts): Skip next 5 stitches, FPdtr around each of next 4 stitches 2 rows below; working behind FPdtr just made, hdc in 4th skipped stitch; working in front of FPdtr just made, FPdtr around each of first 4 skipped stitches 2 rows below.

PATTERN STITCHES

For Master Chart Key, see page 206.

Main Body lace (work on a multiple of 6 + 1 sts) Ⓐ

Row 1: Ch 1, sc in first st, *ch 2, sk next 2 sts, 3-dc fan in next st, ch 2, sk next 2 sts, sc in next st; rep from * across, turn.

Row 2: (First-dc, dc) in first st, ch 1, sc in 2nd dc of next 3-dc fan, *ch 1, Dc-V St in next sc, ch 1, sc in 2nd dc of next 3-dc fan; rep from * across to last st, ch 1, 2 dc in last st, turn.

Row 3: Ch 1, sc in first st, ch 2, 3-dc fan in next sc, ch 2, *sc in ch-1 sp of next Dc-V St, ch 2, 3-dc fan in next sc; rep from * across to last 2 sts, ch 2, sk next st, sc in last st, turn.

Rep rows 2 and 3 for pattern.

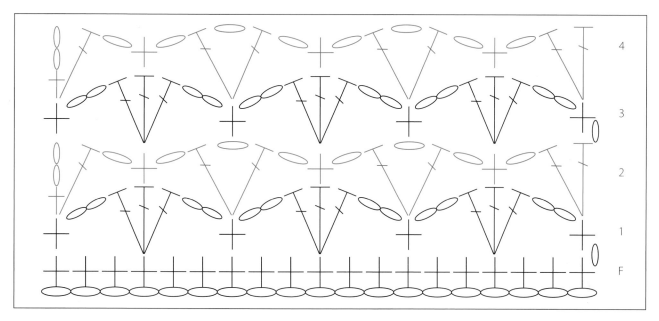

A Main Body lace stitch chart

Yoke cable **B**

Row 1: Ch 1, sc in each st across, turn.

Row 2 (RS): Ch 1, hdc in each of first 11 sts, FPdc in each of next 4 sts, hdc in next st, FPdc in each of next 4 sts, hdc in each of last 11 sts, turn.

Row 3: Rep row 1.

Row 4: Ch 1, hdc in each of first 11 sts, work 4-1-4 FPdtr left cross, hdc in each of last 11 sts, turn.

Row 5: Rep row 1.

Row 6: Ch 1, hdc in each of first 9 sts, (FPtr around post st 2 rows below) 4 times, hdc in each of next 5 sts, (FPtr around post st 2 rows below) 4 times, hdc in each of last 9 sts, turn.

Row 7: Rep row 1.

Row 8: Ch 1, hdc in each of first 7 sts, (FPtr around post st 2 rows below) 4 times, hdc in each of next 2 sts, work 2-1-2 FPtr left cross, hdc in each of next 2 sts, (FPtr around post st 2 rows below) 4 times, hdc in each of last 7 sts, turn.

Row 9: Rep row 1.

Row 10: Ch 1, hdc in each of first 6 sts, (FPdc around post st 2 rows below) 4 times, hdc in each of next 3 sts, (FPdc around next st 2 rows below) twice, hdc in next st, (FPdc around next st 2 rows below) twice, hdc in each of next 3 sts, (FPdc around post st 2 rows below) 4 times, hdc in each of last 6 sts, turn.

Row 11: Rep row 1.

Row 12: Ch 1, hdc in each of first 2 sts, work 4-over-4 FPdtr left cross, hdc in each of next 3 sts, work 2-1-2 FPtr left cross, hdc in each of next 3 sts, work 4-over-4 FPdtr left cross, hdc in each of last 2 sts, turn.

Row 13: Rep row 1.

Row 14: Ch 1, hdc in each of first 2 sts, (FPdc around next post st 2 rows below) 8 times, hdc in each of next 3 sts, (FPdc around next st 2 rows below) twice, hdc in next st, (FPdc around next st 2 rows below) twice, hdc in each of next 3 sts, (FPdc around next post st 2 rows below) 8 times, hdc in each of last 2 sts, turn.

Row 15: Rep row 1.

Row 16: Ch 1, hdc in each of first 2 sts, work 4-over-4 FPdtr left cross, hdc in each of next 3 sts, work 2-1-2 FPtr left cross, hdc in each of next 3 sts, work 4-over-4 FPdtr left cross, hdc in each of last 2 sts, turn.

Row 17: Rep row 1.

Row 18: Ch 1, hdc in each of first 2 sts, (FPdc around next post st 2 rows below) 8 times, hdc in each of next 3 sts, (FPdc around next st 2 rows below) twice, hdc in next st, (FPdc around next st 2 rows below) twice, hdc in each of next 3 sts, (FPdc around next post st 2 rows below) 8 times, hdc in each of last 2 sts, turn.

Row 19: Rep row 1.

Row 20: Ch 1, hdc in each of first 2 sts, work 4-over-4 FPdtr left cross, hdc in each of next 3 sts, work 2-1-2 FPtr left cross, hdc in each of next 3 sts, work 4-over-4 FPdtr left cross, hdc in each of last 2 sts, turn.

Row 21: Rep row 1.

Row 22: Ch 1, hdc in each of first 7 sts, (FPdc around post st 2 rows below) 4 times, hdc in each of next 2 sts, (FPdc around next st 2 rows below) twice, hdc in next st, (FPdc around next st 2 rows below) twice, hdc in each of next 2 sts, (FPdc around post st 2 rows below) 4 times, hdc in each of last 7 sts, turn.

Row 23: Rep row 1.

Row 24: Ch 1, hdc in each of first 9 sts, (FPtr around post st 2 rows below) 4 times, work 2-1-2 FPtr left cross, (FPtr around post st 2 rows below) 4 times, hdc in each of last 9 sts, turn.

Row 25: Rep row 1.

Row 26: Ch 1, hdc in each of first 11 sts, (FPdtr around post st 2 rows below) 4 times, hdc in next st, (FPdtr around post st 2 rows below) 4 times, hdc in each of last 11 sts, turn.

Row 27: Rep row 1.

Row 28: Ch 1, hdc in each of first 11 sts, work 4-1-4 FPdtr left cross, hdc in each of last 11, turn.

SPECIAL TECHNIQUE

Locking mattress stitch (see Special Techniques, page 200)

NOTES

1. When instructed to work in a pattern stitch "as established," work the next row of pattern stitch and ensure that the stitches line up as in previous rows.

2. Yoke is worked from side to side.

3. Body and Sleeve sections are made from the top down.

4. If after a decrease the next stitch is a chain space, work one stitch in pattern stitch in the place of that chain space, then continue as instructed.

5. Always skip stitch in current row behind each post stitch worked.

A Note on Increasing

In this pattern, you will be instructed to increase or decrease "in pattern stitch as established." This means you should maintain the Main Body lace pattern stitch as it has been worked up to this point in the pattern. There are two important properties of the Main Body lace pattern stitch that you will need to maintain:

1. The Main Body lace pattern stitch has a 2-row repeat. Ensure that this 2-row rep continues.

2. The Main Body lace pattern stitch has a pattern rep in multiples of 6 + 1 stitches. Once you have increased a total of 6 stitches on each side of your established pattern, you will have enough increase stitches to begin working pattern repeats of the Main Body lace pattern stitch on the next row.

INSTRUCTIONS

YOKE

Row 1: Work 31 Fhdc, turn.

Row 2: Ch 1, sc in each st across, turn.

Row 3: Ch 1, hdc in each of first 11 sts, FPdc in each of next 4 sts 2 rows below, hdc in next st, FPdc in each of next 4 sts 2 rows below, hdc in each of next 11 sts, turn.

Row 4: Rep row 2.

Row 5: Ch 1, hdc in each of first 11 sts, work 4-1-4 FPdtr left cross, hdc in each of next 11 sts, turn.

Rows 6–201 (229, 257, 285, 313, 337, 369, 397): Work even in Yoke Cable pattern.

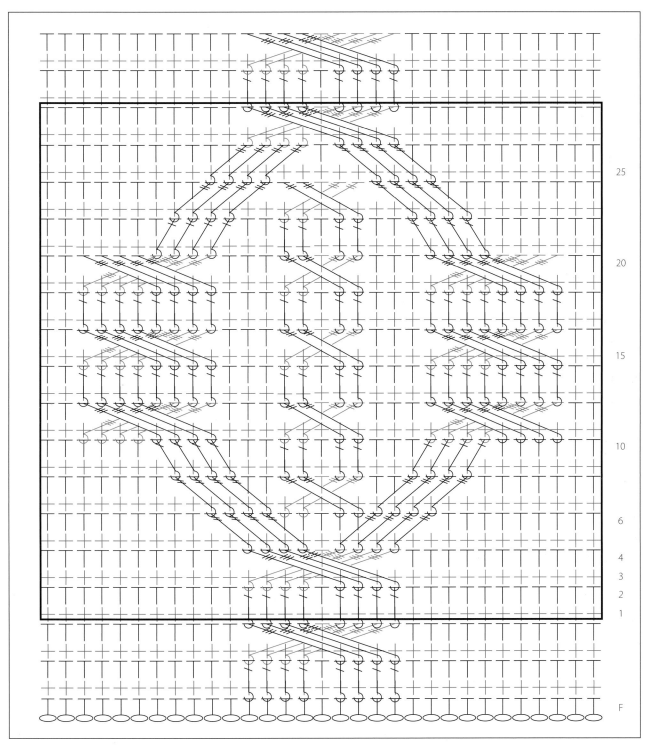

B Yoke cable stitch chart

Rows 202 (230, 258, 286, 314, 338, 370, 398)–205 (233, 261, 289, 317, 345, 373, 401): Rep rows 2–5.

Fasten off.

BODY PANEL (MAKE 2)

Foundation Row: Work 103 (115, 121, 133, 145, 157, 169, 181) Fsc, turn.

Rows 1–10: Work even in Main Body lace pattern st.

Row 11: Ch 1, 2 sc in first st, work in pattern st as established across to last st, 2 sc in last st, turn—17 (19, 20, 22, 24, 26, 28, 30) pattern reps; with 2 sc at each end.

Rows 12 and 13: Work even in pattern st as established.

Row 14: (First-dc, dc) in first st, work in pattern st as established across to last st, 2 dc in last st, turn—17 (19, 20, 22, 24, 26, 28, 30) pattern reps; 4 dc at each end.

Rows 15 and 16: Work even in pattern st as established.

Rows 17–22: Rep rows 11–16—17 (19, 20, 22, 24, 26, 28, 30) pattern reps; 6 dc at each end.

Rows 23–26: Rep rows 11–14—17 (19, 20, 22, 24, 26, 28, 30) pattern reps; 8 dc at each end.

Row 27: Ch 1, sc in first st, ch 2, sk next 2 sts, 3-dc fan in next st, ch 2, sk next 2 sts, sc in next dc, ch 2, 3-dc fan in next sc, *ch 2, sc in ch-1 sp of next Dc-V St, ch 2, 3-dc fan in next sc; rep from * across to last sc, ch 2, sk next dc, sc in next sc, ch 2, sk next 2 sts, 3-dc fan in next st, ch 2, sk next 2 sts, sc in last dc, turn—19 (21, 22, 24, 26, 28, 30, 32) pattern reps; 1 sc at each end.

Row 28: Work even in pattern st as established.

Rows 29–37: Rep rows 11–19—19 (21, 22, 24, 26, 28, 30, 32) pattern reps; 4 sc at each end.

Rows 38–73 (73, 74, 76, 76, 76, 77, 77): Work even in pattern st as established.

Fasten off.

SLEEVE (MAKE 2)

Foundation Row: Work 79 (85, 91, 91, 97, 103, 115, 121) Fsc, turn.

Rows 1–10: Work even in Main Body lace pattern st—13 (14, 15, 15, 16, 17, 19, 20) pattern reps.

Row 11: Ch 1, dec 1 in first 2 sts, work in pattern st as established across to last 2 sts, dec 1 in last 2 sts, turn.

Row 12: Work even in pattern st as established.

Rows 13–16 (16, 16, 16, 22, 28, 34, 40): Rep last 2 rows 2 (2, 2, 2, 5, 8, 11, 14) times—12 (13, 14, 14, 14, 14, 15, 15) pattern reps.

Rows 17 (17, 17, 17, 23, 29, 35, 41)–46 (46, 47, 47, 48, 48, 50, 50): Work even in pattern st as established.

Fasten off.

FINISHING

Block all pieces to schematic measurements.

Sew ends of Yoke together. This seam will be the Center Back of Yoke.

Sew Body Panel sides and Sleeve seams.

Place markers 1¼ (1½, 1½, 1¾, 2, 2, 2¼, 2½) inches/3.2 (3.8, 3.8, 4.5, 5, 5, 5.5, 6.5) cm in from side on top edge of the Body Panel.

Place markers 1¼ (1½, 1½, 1¾, 2, 2, 2¼, 2½) inches/3.2 (3.8, 3.8, 4.5, 5, 5, 5.5, 6.5) cm in from seams on top edge of Sleeves; match up Body Panel seam with Sleeve seam, and sew top edge of Body to top edge of Sleeve bet markers. Rep for other side.

With RS together, sew top edge of Body/Sleeves to bottom edge of Yoke, easing in fullness.

SHOULDERS

Working in the round:

Join yarn with sl st in seam at Center Back on top edge of Yoke.

Rnd 1: Ch 1, working in row-end sts, [hdc in each of next 13 (15, 17, 19, 22, 26, 26, 28) sts, pm] 5 (7, 9, 11, 5, 6, 5, 5) times, [hdc in each of next 14 (16, 18, 20, 23, 27, 27, 29) sts, pm] 10 (8, 6, 4, 9, 7, 9, 9) times—205 (233, 261, 289, 317, 345, 373, 401) sts.

Rnd 2: *Hdc in each st around to 2 sts before marker, hdc2tog; rep from * around—190 (218, 246, 274, 303, 332, 359, 387) sts.

Rnd 3: Hdc in each st around.

Rnds 4–15 (17, 19, 21, 25, 29, 31, 33): Rep last 2 rnds 6 (7, 8, 9, 11, 13, 14, 15) times—100 (113, 126, 139, 149, 163, 163, 177) sts.

Rnd 16 (18, 20, 22, 26, 30, 32, 34): Rep row 2—85 (98, 111, 124, 135, 150, 149, 163) sts.

Fasten off.

Note: Additional repeats of last 2 rounds may be worked for a smaller neck opening.

Weave in ends.

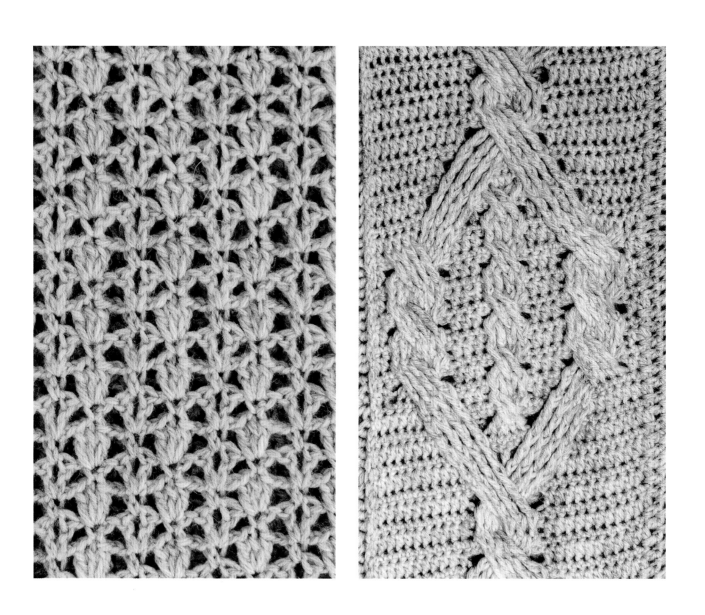

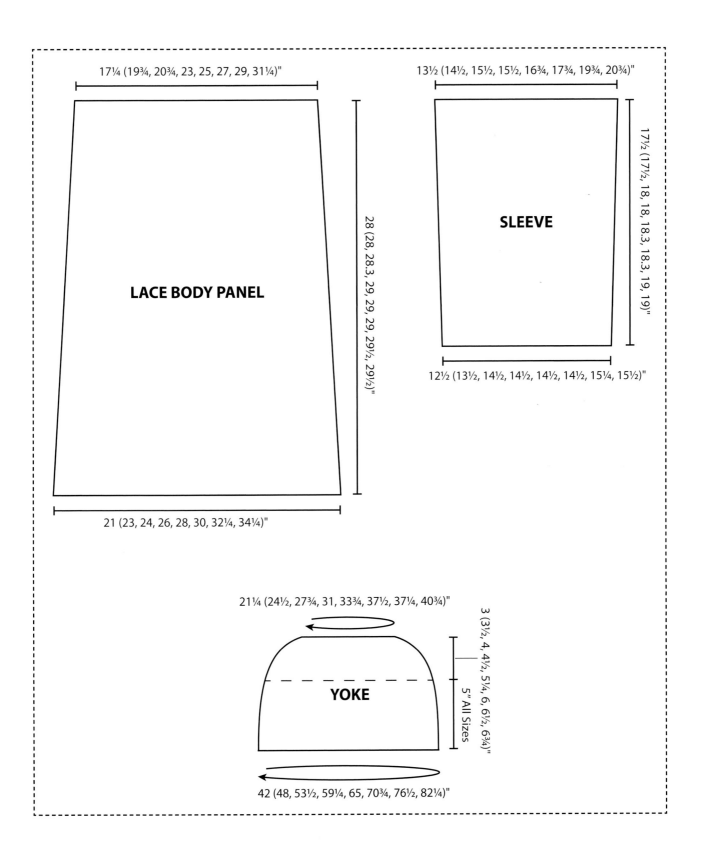

17¼ (19¾, 20¾, 23, 25, 27, 29, 31¼)"

LACE BODY PANEL

28 (28, 28.3, 29, 29, 29, 29½, 29½)"

21 (23, 24, 26, 28, 30, 32¼, 34¼)"

13½ (14½, 15½, 15½, 16¾, 17¾, 19¾, 20¾)"

SLEEVE

17½ (17½, 18, 18, 18.3, 18.3, 19, 19)"

12½ (13½, 14½, 14½, 14½, 14½, 15¼, 15½)"

21¼ (24½, 27¾, 31, 33¾, 37½, 37¼, 40¾)"

YOKE

3 (3½, 4, 4½, 5¼, 6, 6½, 6¾)"

5" All Sizes

42 (48, 53½, 59¼, 65, 70¾, 76½, 82¼)"

COWL NECK SWEATER DRESS

This sweater dress has the comfy feel of a chunky, wooly sweater dress with the light flow and easy movement of lightweight yarn. The graphic cables that border the bottom hem and the giant cables on the cowl neckline make this a true statement piece.

SKILL LEVEL: Intermediate

SIZES: S (M, L, XL, 2X, 3X, 4X, 5X)

Sample shown in size small

FINISHED MEASUREMENTS

To Fit Bust: 32 (36, 40, 44, 48, 52, 56, 60) inches/81.5 (91.5, 101.5, 112, 122, 132, 142, 152.5) cm

Finished Bust: 36 (40, 44, 48, 52, 56, 60, 64) inches/91.5, (101.5, 112, 122, 132, 142, 152.5, 162.5) cm

Finished Length: 32 (32, 32½, 33, 33, 33, 33½, 33½) inches/81.5 (81.5, 82.5, 84, 84, 84, 85, 85) cm

MATERIALS AND TOOLS

- Sample uses Lion Brand LB Collection, Superwash Merino (100% Superwash Merino Wool; 3.5 ounces/100 g = 306 yards/280 m): 7 (8, 9, 10, 10, 11, 12, 13) skeins in color Ivory #480-098 or 2142 (2448, 2754, 3060, 3060, 3366, 3672, 3978) yards/1960 (2240, 2520, 2800, 2800, 3080, 3360, 3640) m of lightweight yarn

- Crochet hooks: 3.75mm (size F-5) and 4.0mm (size G-6) or sizes to obtain gauge
- Yarn needle
- Pins

BLOCKED GAUGES

Sc linen stitch variation 1 with larger hook: 29 sts = 5 inches/12.5 cm; 23 rows = 4¾ inches/12 cm

Sc ribbing pattern with smaller hook: 26 sts = 5 inches/12.5 cm; 22 rows = 4 inches/10 cm

Cable points pattern with larger hook: 25 sts = 5½ inches/14 cm; 25 rows = 6 inches/15 cm

Giant cable pattern with larger hook: 25 sts = 5¼ inches/13.5 cm; 49 rows = 10¾ inches/27.5 cm

Always take time to check your gauge.

GAUGE SWATCHES

Sc linen stitch variation 1 stitch swatch

Row 1: With larger hook, work 29 Fsc, turn.

Rows 2–23: Work even in sc linen st var 1 pattern st.

Sc ribbing stitch swatch

Row 1: With smaller hook, work 26 Fsc, turn.

Rows 2–22: Work even in sc ribbing pattern st.

STITCH GUIDE

Foundation single crochet (Fsc): Ch 2, insert hook in 2nd ch from hook, yo and draw up a loop, yo and draw through 1 loop (first "chain" made), yo and draw through 2 loops on hook (first sc made), *insert hook under 2 loops of the "chain" just made, yo and draw up a loop, yo and draw through 1 loop ("chain" made), yo and draw through 2 loops on hook (sc made); rep from * for indicated number of foundation sts.

Foundation half double crochet (Fhdc): Ch 3, yo, insert hook in 3rd ch from hook, yo and draw up a loop, yo and draw through 1 loop (first "chain" made), yo and draw through all 3 loops on hook (first hdc made), *yo, insert hook under 2 loops of the "chain" just made, yo and draw up a loop, yo and draw through 1 loop ("chain" made), yo and draw through all 3 loops on hook (hdc made); rep from * for indicated number of foundation sts.

Front Post double crochet (FPdc): Yo, insert hook from front to back and then to front again around post of designated st, yo and draw up loop, [yo and draw through 2 loops on hook] twice.

Front Post treble crochet (FPtr): Yo (twice), insert hook from front to back and then to front again around post of designated st, yo and draw up a loop, [yo and draw through 2 loops on hook] 3 times.

Front Post treble Point (FPtr Point): Yo (twice), insert hook from front to back to front again around next post st 2 rows below, yo and draw up a loop, yo and draw through 2 loops on hook (3 loops on hook), sk next st, yo, insert hook from front to back to front again around next designated post st 2 rows below, yo and draw up a loop, yo and draw through 2 loops on hook (4 loops on hook), yo and draw through 3 loops, yo and draw through 2 loops.

2-over-2 FPtr left cross cable (worked over 5 sts): Sk next 3 sts, FPtr around each of next 2 sts 2 rows below; working behind FPtr just made, hdc in 3rd skipped st; working in front of FPtr just made, FPtr around each of first 2 skipped sts 2 rows below.

Front Post quadruple treble crochet (FPqtr): Yo (6 times), insert hook from front to back to front again around next post st 2 rows below, yo and draw up a loop, (yo and draw through 2 loops on hook) 7 times.

6-over-6 FPqtr left cross cable (worked over 13 sts): Sk next 7 sts, FPqtr around the post of each of next 6 post sts 2 rows below; working behind FPqtr just made, hdc in 7th skipped st; working in front of FPqtr just made, FPqtr around the post of each of 6 skipped post sts 2 rows below.

Single crochet through back loop only (sc-tbl): Insert hook in back loop of indicated st, yo and draw up a loop, yo and draw through 2 loops on hook.

PATTERN STITCHES

For Master Chart Key, see page 206.

Cable points (worked on a multiple of 8 + 1 sts) Ⓐ

Row 1: Ch 1, hdc in each st across, turn.

Row 2: Ch 1, sc in each st across, turn.

Row 3 (RS): Ch 1, hdc in first st, *[FPdc around the post of next st 2 rows below] twice, hdc in each of next 3 sts, [FPdc around the post of next st 2 rows below] twice, hdc in next st; rep from * across, turn.

Row 4: Rep row 2.

Row 5: Ch 1, hdc in first st, *hdc in next st, [FPdc around the post of previous st 2 rows below] twice, hdc in next st, sk next st, [FPdc around the post of next st 2 rows below] twice, hdc in each of next 2 sts; rep from * across, turn.

Row 6: Rep row 2.

Row 7: Ch 1, hdc in first st, *hdc in next st, work 2-over-2 FPtr left cross cable, hdc in each of next 2 sts; rep from * across, turn.

Row 8: Rep row 2.

Row 9: Ch 1, hdc in first st, *sk next st, [FPdc around the post of next st 2 rows below] twice, hdc in each of next 3 sts, [FPdc around the post of previous st 2 rows below] twice, hdc in next st; rep from * across, turn.

Rows 10–16: Rep rows 2–8.

Row 17: Ch 1, hdc in first st, *hdc in next st, [FPdc around the post of next st 2 rows below] twice, hdc in next st, [FPdc around the post of next st 2 rows below] twice, hdc in each of next 2 sts; rep from * across, turn.

Row 18: Rep row 2.

Row 19: Ch 1, hdc in first st, *hdc in each of next 2 sts, FPtr around the post of previous st 2 rows below, work FPtr Point, sk next st, FPtr around the post of next st 2 rows below, hdc in each of next 3 sts; rep from * across, turn.

Row 20: Rep row 2.

Row 21: Ch 1, hdc in first st, *hdc in each of next 3 sts, work FPtr Point, hdc in each of next 4 sts; rep from * across, turn.

Row 22: Rep row 2.

Row 23: Ch 1, hdc in first st, *hdc in each of next 3 sts, FPdc around next st 2 rows below, hdc around each of next 4 sts; rep from * across, turn.

Row 24: Rep row 2.

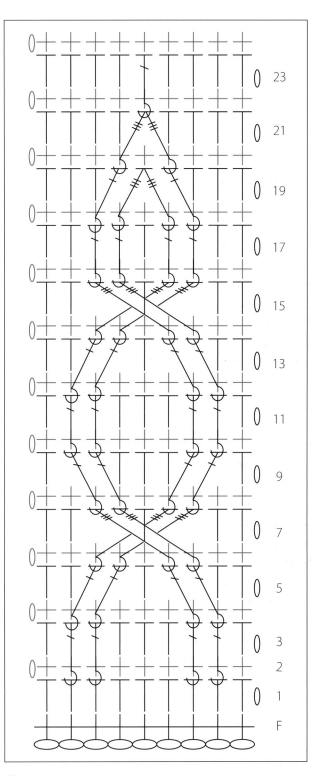

A Cable points stitch chart

Single crochet linen stitch variation 1 (sc linen st var 1) (multiple of 2+1 sts) Ⓑ

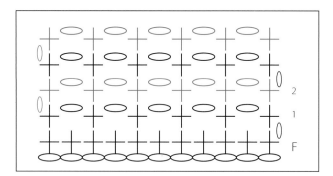

Ⓑ Single crochet linen stitch variation 1 stitch chart

Row 1: Ch 1, sc in first st, *ch 1, sk next st, sc in next st; rep from * across, turn.

Row 2: Ch 1, sc in first st, *ch 1, sk next ch-1 sp, sc in next st; rep from * across, turn.

Rep row 2 for pattern st.

Single crochet ribbing (sc ribbing) Ⓒ

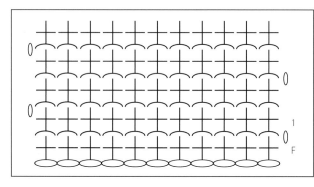

Ⓒ Single crochet ribbing stitch chart

Row 1: Ch 1, sc in both loops of first st, sc-tbl in each st across to last st, sc in both loops of last st, turn.

Rep row 1 for pattern st.

SPECIAL TECHNIQUE

Locking mattress stitch (see Special Techniques, page 200)

Setting in a sleeve (see Special Techniques, page 201)

NOTES

1. When instructed to work in st 2 rows below, insert hook in indicated stitch in the row numbered 2 less than the row you are working. For example, if you are working row 5, a stitch "2 rows" below is in row 5 – 2 = row 3.

2. Left Side and Right Side refer to left and right side as worn.

3. When instructed to work in a pattern stitch "as established," work the next row of pattern stitch and ensure that the stitches line up as in previous rows.

4. For the purpose of this pattern, all chain spaces count as 1 stitch.

5. When instructed to work in side of stitch, insert hook from front to back into the indicated stitch between the 2 vertical strands of yarn directly below the first wrap catching 2 side strands of yarn.

6. Always skip stitch in current row behind each post stitch worked.

INSTRUCTIONS

FRONT BODY PANEL

BOTTOM BORDER

Foundation Row: With larger hook, work 83 Fsc, turn.

Row 1: Ch 1, hdc in each of first 1 (2, 3, 2, 1, 1, 1, 1) sts, work row 1 of cable points pattern st, hdc in each of last 1 (2, 3, 2, 1, 1, 1, 1) sts, turn.

Row 2: Ch 1, sc in each st across, turn.

Rows 3–24: Work cable points pattern st as established, maintaining additional sts at beg and end of row as indicated in row 1.

MAIN BODY

Row 1 (RS): Ch 1, sc in each of first 10 (12, 1, 8, 8, 4, 17, 15) sts, [2 sc in next st, sc in each of next 2 (2, 3, 2, 3, 3, 2, 2) sts] 21 (23, 25, 31, 27, 31, 35, 39) times, 2 sc in next st, sc in each of next 9 (11, 1, 7, 6, 2, 16, 14) sts, turn—105 (117, 129, 141, 151, 163, 175, 187) sts.

Rows 2–106 (106, 108, 111, 111, 111, 113, 113): Work in sc linen st var 1 pattern st.

BEGIN FRONT NECKLINE SHAPING

FIRST SIDE

Row 1: Ch 1, work in pattern st as established across 43 (49, 52, 58, 60, 65, 69, 75) sts, sc in next st, turn, leaving rem 61 (67, 76, 82, 90, 97, 105, 111) sts unworked—44 (50, 53, 59, 61, 66, 70, 76) sts.

Row 2: Ch 1, sc in first st, sc2tog, sc in next st, work in pattern st as established across, turn—43 (49, 52, 58, 60, 65, 69, 75) sts.

Row 3: Ch 1, work in pattern st as established across to last 5 sts, sc in next st, sk next st, sc2tog, sc in last st, turn—41 (47, 50, 56, 58, 63, 67, 73) sts.

Row 4: Work even in pattern st as established.

Row 5: Ch 1, work in pattern st as established across to last 4 sts, sc in next st, sc2tog, sc in last st, turn—40 (46, 49, 55, 57, 62, 66, 72) sts.

Row 6: Ch 1, sc in first st, sc2tog, sk next st, sc in next st, work in pattern st as established across, turn—38 (44, 47, 53, 55, 60, 64, 70) sts.

Row 7: Work even in pattern st as established.

Rows 8–19: Rep last 6 rows (twice)—26 (32, 35, 41, 43, 48, 52, 58) sts at end of last row.

Row 20: Work even in pattern st as established. Fasten off.

SECOND SIDE

Sk next 17 (17, 23, 23, 29, 31, 35, 35) unworked center sts, join yarn with sl st in next st; first st of row 1 is worked in same st as joining.

Row 1: Ch 1, sc in first st, work in pattern st as established across, turn—44 (50, 53, 59, 61, 66, 70, 76) sts.

Row 2: Ch 1, work in pattern st as established across to last 4 sts, sc in next st, sc2tog, sc in last st, turn—43 (49, 52, 58, 60, 65, 69, 75) sts.

Row 3: Ch 1, sc in first st, sc2tog, sk next st, sc in next st, work in pattern st as established across, turn—41 (47, 50, 56, 58, 63, 67, 73) sts.

Row 4: Work even in pattern st as established.

Row 5: Ch 1, sc in first st, sc2tog, sc in next st, work in pattern st as established across, turn—40 (46, 49, 55, 57, 62, 66, 72) sts.

Row 6: Ch 1, work in pattern st as established across to last 5 sts, sc in next st, sk next st, sc2tog, sc in last st, turn—38 (44, 47, 53, 55, 60, 64, 70) sts.

Row 7: Work even in pattern st as established.

Rows 8–19: Rep last 6 rows (twice)—26 (32, 35, 41, 43, 48, 52, 58) sts at end of last row.

Row 20: Work even in pattern st as established. Fasten off.

BACK BODY PANEL

BOTTOM BORDER

Work same as Front Bottom Border.

MAIN BODY

Row 1 (RS): Ch 1, sc in each of first 10 (12, 1, 8, 8, 4, 17, 15) sts, [sc 2 in next st, sc 2 (2, 3, 2, 3, 3, 2, 2)] 21 (23, 25, 31, 27, 31, 35, 39) times, 2 sc in next st, sc in each of next 9 (11, 1, 7, 6, 2, 16, 14) sts, turn—105 (117, 129, 141, 151, 163, 175, 187) sts.

Rows 2–121 (121, 123, 126, 126, 126, 128, 128): Work even in sc linen st var 1 pattern stitch.

BEGIN BACK NECKLINE SHAPING

FIRST SIDE

Row 1: Ch 1, work in pattern st as established across first 37 (43, 46, 52, 54, 59, 63, 69) sts, sc in next st, turn, leaving rem 67 (73, 82, 88, 96, 103, 111, 117) sts unworked—38 (44, 47, 53, 55, 60, 64, 70) sts.

Row 2: Ch 1, sc in first st, [sc2tog over next 2 sts] twice, sk next st, sc in next st, work in pattern st as established across, turn—35 (41, 44, 50, 52, 57, 61, 67) sts.

Row 3: Ch 1, work in pattern st as established across to last 7 sts, sc in next st, sk next st, [sc2tog over next 2 sts] twice, sc in last st, turn—32 (38, 41, 47, 49, 54, 58, 64) sts.

Rows 4 and 5: Rep last 2 rows—26 (32, 35, 41, 43, 48, 52, 58) sts at end of last row.

Fasten off.

Skip next 29 (29, 35, 35, 41, 43, 47, 47) unworked center sts, join yarn with sl st in next st; first st of row 1 is worked in same st as joining.

Row 1: Ch 1, sc in first st, work in pattern st as established across, turn—38 (44, 47, 53, 55, 60, 64, 70) sts.

Row 2: Ch 1, work in pattern st as established across to last 7 sts, sc in next st, sk next st, [sc2tog over next 2 sts] twice, sc in last st, turn—35 (41, 44, 50, 52, 57, 61, 67) sts.

Row 3: Ch 1, sc in first st, [sc2tog over next 2 sts] twice, sk next st, sc in next st, work in pattern st as established across, turn—32 (38, 41, 47, 49, 54, 58, 64) sts.

Rows 4 and 5: Rep last 2 rows—26 (32, 35, 41, 43, 48, 52, 58) sts at end of last row.

Fasten off.

SLEEVE (MAKE 2)

FOREARM RIBBING

Row 1: With smaller hook, work 37 Fsc, turn.

Rows 2–40 (40, 43, 47, 47, 52, 56, 59): Work even in sc ribbing pattern st.

Do not fasten off. At end of last row, rotate work ¼ turn to the right for working in row-end sts of ribbing.

Set-up row: With larger hook, ch 1, working in row-end sts across side of ribbing, 2 sc in first st, [2 sc in next st, sc in next st] 19 (19, 21, 23, 23, 25, 27, 29) times, 2 (2, 0, 0, 0, 2, 2, 0) sc in last st, turn—61 (61, 65, 71, 71, 79, 85, 89) sts.

Rows 1 and 2: Work even in sc linen st var 1 pattern st.

BEGIN SLEEVE SHAPING

Row 1: Ch 1, 2 sc in first st, work in pattern st as established across to last st, 2 sc in last st, turn—63 (63, 67, 73, 73, 81, 87, 91) sts.

Row 2: Work even in pattern st as established.

Rows 3–14 (32, 34, 34, 46, 40, 36, 36): Rep last 2 rows 6 (15, 16, 16, 22, 19, 17, 17) times—75 (93, 99, 105, 117, 119, 121, 125) sts at end of last row.

Row 15 (33, 35, 35, 47, 41, 37, 37): Ch 1, 2 sc in first st, work in pattern st as established across to last st, 2 sc in last st, turn—77 (95, 101, 107, 119, 121, 123, 127) sts.

Rows 16 (34, 36, 36, 48, 42, 38, 38)–17 (35, 37, 37, 49, 43, 39, 39): Work even in pattern st as established.

SIZES S (M, L, XL, 3X, 4X, 5X) ONLY

Rows 18 (36, 38, 38, 44, 40, 40)–41 (41, 43, 43, 46, 48, 48): Rep last 3 rows 8 (2, 2, 2, 1, 3, 3) more times—93 (99, 105, 111, 123, 129, 133) sts at end of last row.

ALL SIZES

Rows 42 (42, 44, 44, 47, 47, 49, 49)–49 (49, 51, 51, 54, 54, 56, 56): Work in pattern st as established.

Fasten off.

COWL

Foundation Row: With larger hook, work 49 Fsc, turn.

Row 1: Ch 1, hdc in each st across, turn.

Row 2: Ch 1, sc in each st across, turn.

Row 3 (RS): Ch 1, hdc in each of first 13 sts, [FPdc around the post of next st 2 rows below] 6 times, hdc in each of next 11 sts, [FPdc around the post of next st 2 rows below] 6 times, hdc in each of last 13 sts, turn.

Rows 4 and 5: Rep rows 2 and 3.

Row 6: Rep row 2.

Row 7: Ch 1, hdc in each of first 14 sts, [FPdc around the post of next st 2 rows below] 6 times, hdc in each of next 9 sts, [FPdc around the post of next st 2 rows below] 6 times, hdc in each of last 14 sts, turn.

Row 8: Rep row 2.

Row 9: Ch 1, hdc in each of first 15 sts, [FPdc around the post of next st 2 rows below] 6 times, hdc in each of next 7 sts, [FPdc around the post of next st 2 rows below] 6 times, hdc in each of last 15 sts, turn.

Row 10: Rep row 2.

Row 11: Ch 1, hdc in each of first 16 sts, [FPdc around the post of next st 2 rows below] 6 times, hdc in each of next 5 sts, [FPdc around the post of next st 2 rows below] 6 times, hdc in each of last 16 sts, turn.

Row 12: Rep row 2.

Row 13: Ch 1, hdc in each of first 17 sts, [FPdc around the post of next st 2 rows below] 6 times, hdc in each of next 3 sts, [FPdc around the post of next st 2 rows below] 6 times, hdc in each of last 17 sts, turn.

Row 14: Rep row 2.

Row 15: Ch 1, hdc in each of first 18 sts, [FPdc around the post of next st 2 rows below] 6 times, hdc in next st, [FPdc around the post of next st 2 rows below] 6 times, hdc in each of last 18 sts, turn.

Row 16: Rep row 2.

Row 17: Rep row 15.

Row 18: Rep row 2.

Row 19: Rep row 13.

Row 20: Rep row 2.

Row 21: Rep row 11.

Row 22: Rep row 2.

Row 23: Rep row 9.

Row 24: Rep row 2.

Row 25: Rep row 7.

Row 26: Rep row 2.

Row 27: Rep row 5.

Row 28: Rep row 2.

Row 29: Rep row 3.

Row 30: Rep row 2.

Rows 31–142: Rep rows 3–30 (4 times).

Fasten off.

FINISHING

Block all pieces to schematic measurements.

Using locking mattress stitch technique, sew shoulder and side seams.

Fold Sleeves in half lengthwise. Matching fold to shoulder seams, sew top of each Sleeve in place on side of Front and Back. Sew side and underarm seams.

Sew ends of Cowl together. This seam will be the Center Back of Cowl.

With WS facing, pin Center Back of Cowl to center of back neckline; place pins to evenly distribute Cowl rows around neckline; sew Cowl in place.

Weave in ends.

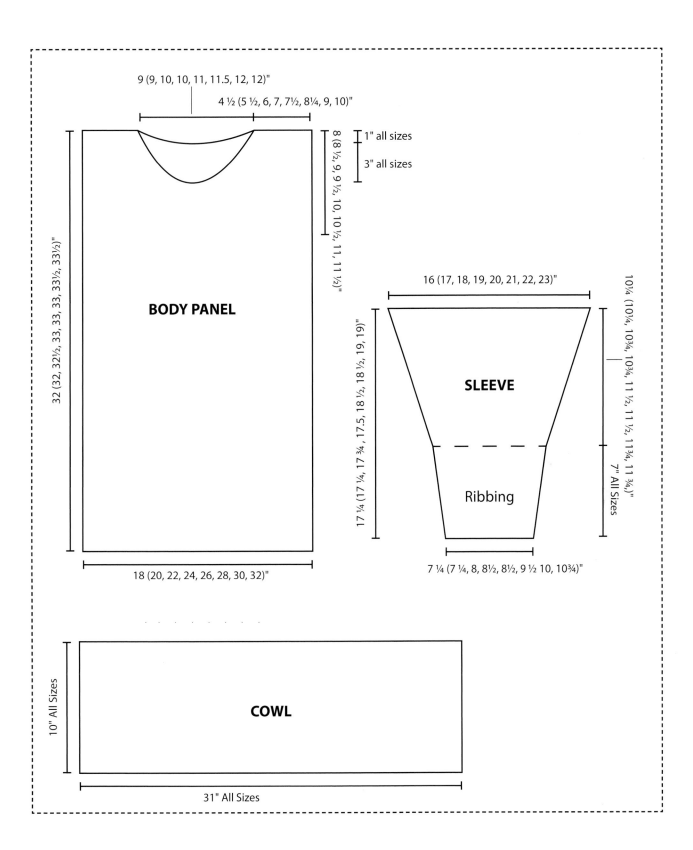

9 (9, 10, 10, 11, 11.5, 12, 12)"

4 ½ (5 ½, 6, 7, 7½, 8¼, 9, 10)"

1" all sizes

3" all sizes

8 (8½, 9, 9 ½, 10, 10 ½, 11, 11 ½)"

BODY PANEL

32 (32, 32½, 33, 33, 33, 33½, 33½)"

18 (20, 22, 24, 26, 28, 30, 32)"

16 (17, 18, 19, 20, 21, 22, 23)"

10¼ (10¼, 10¾, 10¾, 11 ½, 11 ½, 11¾, 11 ¾,)"

SLEEVE

17 ¼ (17 ¼, 17 ¾, 17.5, 18 ½, 18 ½, 19, 19)"

7" All Sizes

Ribbing

7 ¼ (7 ¼, 8, 8½, 8½, 9 ½ 10, 10¾)"

10" All Sizes

COWL

31" All Sizes

MOTIF MAXI SKIRT

Made from the top down using join-as-you-go construction, this pattern combines delicate lace with mesmerizing motifs to create a maxi skirt that is light and lacy with a style that is graceful and timeless.

Layer this skirt over a coordinating or contrasting lining or leggings to really make your intricate, eye-catching, lace handiwork shine.

SKILL LEVEL: Advanced

SIZES: S (M, L, XL, 2X, 3X, 4X, 5X)
Sample shown in size small

FINISHED MEASUREMENTS

To Fit Waist: 25-26 (28-30, 32-34, 36-38, 40-42, 44-45, 46-47, 49-50) inches/63.5-66 (71-76, 81.5-86.5, 91.5-96.5, 101.5-106.5, 112-114.5, 117-119.5, 124.5-127) cm

Finished Waist: 30 (34, 38, 42, 46, 49, 51, 54) inches/76 (86.5, 96.5, 106.5, 117, 124.5, 129.5, 137) cm

To Fit Hip: 35-36 (38-40, 42-44, 46-48, 52-53, 54-55, 56-57, 61-62) inches/89-91.5 (96.5-101.5, 106.5-112, 117-122, 132-134.5, 137-139.5, 142-145, 155-157.5) cm.

Finished Hip: 40 (45, 50, 55, 59½, 59½, 64½, 69½) inches/101.5 (114.5, 127, 139.5, 151, 151, 164, 176.5) cm

Fourth motif round: 80 (90, 100, 110, 120, 120, 130, 140) inches/203 (228.5, 254, 279.5, 305, 305, 330, 355.5) cm.

Finished Length: 37½ inches/95 cm

MATERIALS AND TOOLS

- Sample shown in Knit Picks Curio size 10 crochet thread (100% Cotton; 3.5 ounces/100 g = 721 yards/659 m): 4 (5, 6, 6, 7, 7, 7, 8) balls in color Chocolate #26256 or 2884 (3605, 4326, 4326, 5047, 5047, 5047, 5768) yards/2636 (3295, 3954, 3954, 4613, 4613, 4613, 5272) m of size 10 crochet thread

- Crochet hooks: 1.9mm (size 5) and 1.65mm (size 7) steel crochet hooks or sizes to obtain gauge
- Stitch markers
- Yarn needle
- ¾-inch-wide/2 cm elastic, 1 inch/2.5 cm longer than waist measurement

BLOCKED GAUGES

Motif with smaller hook: 5-inch/12.5 cm square

Solid pattern with larger hook: 41 sts = 5¼ inches/13.5 cm; 19 rows = 4 inches/10 cm

Always take time to check your gauge.

STITCH GUIDE

Slip ring: Wrap yarn in ring around index finger, ensuring the yarn tail falls behind working yarn. Grip the ring and tail firmly between middle finger and thumb. Insert hook through center of ring, yo (with working yarn) and draw up loop, work sts of first rnd in ring. After the first rnd of sts has been worked, pull gently, but firmly, on yarn tail to tighten ring.

Foundation single crochet (Fsc): Ch 2, insert hook in 2nd ch from hook, yo and draw up a loop, yo and draw through 1 loop (first "chain" made), yo and draw through 2 loops on hook (first sc made), *insert hook under 2 loops of the "chain" just made, yo and draw up a loop, yo and draw through 1 loop ("chain" made), yo and draw through 2 loops on hook (sc made); rep from * for indicated number of foundation sts.

First double crochet (First-dc): Sc in first st, ch 2. Note: Use this stitch whenever the first stitch of a row is a dc.

Double crochet 3 together (dc3tog): [Yo, insert hook in next st and draw up a loop, yo and draw through 2 loops on hook] 3 times, yo and draw through all 4 loops on hook.

First dc3tog: Sc in first st, ch 1, [yo, insert hook in next st and draw up a loop, yo and draw through 2 loops on hook] twice, yo, draw through all 3 loops on hook. Note: Use this stitch whenever the first stitch of a row is a dc3tog.

PATTERN STITCHES

For Master Chart Key, see page 206.

First Motif

Make slip ring (see Stitch Guide).

Rnd 1: Work 8 hdc in slip ring, join with sl st—8 hdc.

Rnd 2: (First-dc, dc) in first st, ch 1, *2 dc in next st, ch 1; rep from * around, join with sl st in first st—8 ch-1 sps.

Rnd 3: (First-dc, dc) in first st, 2 dc in next st, ch 2, sk next ch-1 sp, *(2 dc in next st) twice, ch 2, sk next ch-1 sp; rep from * around, join with sl st in first st—8 ch-2 sps.

Rnd 4: First dc in first st, *dc2tog over next 2 sts, dc in next st, ch 3, sc in next ch-2 sp, ch 3**, dc in next st; rep from * around, ending last rep at **, join with sl st in first st—16 ch-3 sps.

Rnd 5: First dc3tog in first 3 sts, *(ch 3, sc) in each of next 2 ch-3 sps, ch 3**, dc3tog over next 3 dc; rep from * around, ending last rep at **, join with sl st in first dc3tog —24 ch-3 sps.

Rnd 6: Sl st in next ch-3 sp, ch 1, sc in same sp, (ch 4, sc) in each of next 2 ch-3 sps, ch 4, dc in next dc3tog, *(ch 4, sc) in each of next 6 ch-3 sps, ch 4**, dc in next dc3tog; rep from * around, ending last rep at **, join with sl st in first sc—28 ch-4 sps.

Rnd 7: Sl st in next ch-4 sp, ch 1, sc in same sp, ch 4, sc in next ch-4 sp, ch 4, sk next ch-4 sp, sc in next dc, *sk next ch-4 sp, (ch 4, sc) in each of next 5 ch-3 sps, ch 4, sk next ch-4 sp , sc in next dc; rep from * around, sk next ch-4 sp, (ch 4, sc) in each of next 3 ch-3 sps, ch 4, join with sl st in first sc—24 ch-4 sps.

Rnd 8: Sl st in next ch-4 sp, ch 1, sc in same sp, ch 5, sc in next ch-4 sp, ch 3, *(3 dc, ch 3, 3 dc) in next sc, ch 3, sc in next ch-4 sp**, (ch 5, sc) in each of next 5 ch-4 sps, ch 3; rep from * around, ending last rep at **, (ch 5, sc) in each of next 3 ch-4 sps, ch 5, join with sl st in first sc.

Rnd 9: Sl st in next ch-5 sp, ch 1, sc in same sp, ch 5, sc in next ch-3 sp, *ch 3, (3 dc, ch 3, 3 dc) in next ch-3 sp, ch 3, sc in next ch-3 sp, ch 5, [sc in next ch-5 sp, (3 dc, ch 3, 3 dc) in next ch-5 sp] twice**, sc in next ch-5 sp, ch 5, sc in next ch-3 sp; rep from * around, ending last rep at **, join with sl st in first sc.

Rnd 10: Sl st in next ch-5 sp, (First-dc, 2 dc, ch 3, 3 dc) in same sp, *sc in next ch-3 sp, ch 3, (3 dc, ch 3, 3 dc) in next ch-3 sp, ch 3, sc in next ch-3 sp, (3 dc, ch 3, 3 dc) in next ch-5 sp, sc in next ch-1 sp, (3 dc, ch 3, 3 dc) in next sc, sc in next ch-1 sp**, (3 dc, ch 3, 3 dc) in next ch-5 sp; rep from * around, ending last rep at **, join with sl st in first st. Fasten off.

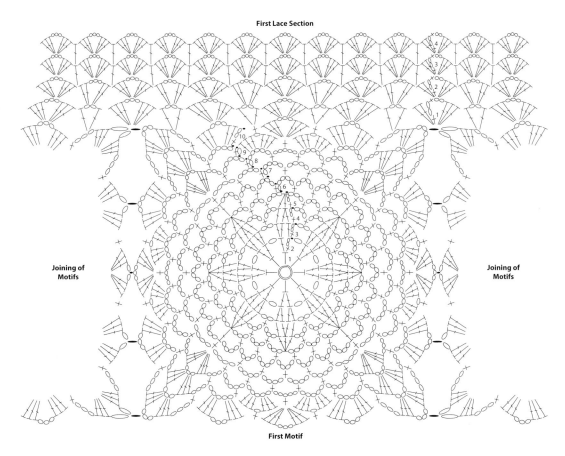

First Lace Section

Joining of Motifs

Joining of Motifs

First Motif

First Motif with joins to Second and Successive Motifs and Motif joins to first lace section

Second and Successive Motifs

Work same as First Motif through rnd 9. Then, join each motif to previous motif(s) and to Upper Body or previous Lace Section where applicable, while completing last rnd. Hold previous motif with RS facing you and ch-3 spaces matching. For each ch-3 sp to be joined, work ch-3 join instead of ch-3 sp.

Solid Pattern Stitch (worked on a multiple of 4 + 1 sts)

Row 1: (First-dc, dc) in first st, sk next st, sc in next st, *sk next st, 3 dc in next st, sk next st, sc in next st; rep from * across to last 2 sts, sk next st, 2 dc in last st, turn.

Row 2: Ch 1, sc in first st, *sk next st, 3 dc in next sc, sk next st, sc in next st; rep from * across, turn.

Rep rows 1 and 2 for pattern.

Panel

Rnd 1: *2 dc in next st, sk next st, sc in next st, [sk next st, 3 dc in next st, sk next st, sc in next st] 14 (16, 18, 20, 22, 23, 24, 26) times, sk next st, 2 dc in next st.

Rnd 2: Sc in next st, [sk next st, 3 dc in next sc, sk next st, sc in next dc] 15 (17, 19, 21, 23, 24, 25, 27) times

Rep rnds 1 and 2 for pattern.

Second Lace Section

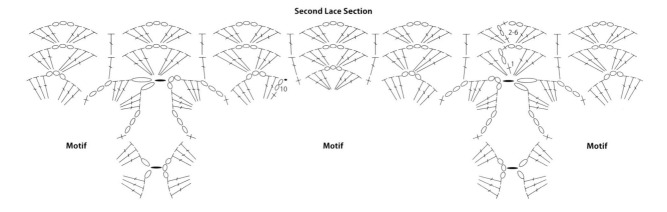

Motif   Motif   Motif

Motif joins to second lace section

SPECIAL TECHNIQUES

Join with duplicate stitch (see Special Techniques, page 199)

Ch-3 join: Work (ch 1, sl st in corresponding st or sp, ch 1) instead of ch-3 sp of motif.

NOTES

1. Join the last stitch of each round of Upper Skirt with a slip stitch in the first stitch of the same round. When beginning the next round, work the first stitch in the same stitch as the joining slip stitch. If first stitch of a round is a dc, work First-dc (see Stitch Guide).

2. Unless otherwise stated, when instructions indicate to place marker (pm), place stitch marker in stitch just made. In following rows, move marker up to corresponding stitch in current row.

3. Work motifs using join-as-you-go assembly.

4. When instructed to work in a pattern stitch "as established," work the next row of pattern stitch and ensure that the stitches line up as in previous rows.

INSTRUCTIONS

WAISTBAND

Foundation Row: With larger hook, work 237 (265, 297, 329, 361, 385, 401, 421) Fsc, turn.

Rows 1–13: Work in Solid pattern st.

Row 14: Work in Solid pattern st, join for working in the rnd with sl st in first st made, do not turn.

Do not fasten off.

UPPER SKIRT

Work now progresses in rnds.

Place marker in first st of each rnd, and move marker up as work progresses.

Set-up rnd (RS): Ch 1, hdc in each of first 19 (14, 16, 18, 20, 48, 50, 21) sts, [2 hdc in next st, hdc in each of next 19 (16, 18, 20, 22, 47, 49, 20) sts] 10 (14, 14, 14, 14, 6, 6, 18) times, 2 hdc in next st, hdc in each of next 17 (12, 14, 16, 18, 48, 50, 21) sts—248 (280, 312, 344, 376, 392, 408, 440) sts.

Note: In addition to placing a marker at beg of each rnd, place markers to mark first and last sts of Panels. When pattern says to work "to start of Panel," work to this marker and work "Panel" between these markers.

Rnd 1: First-dc, pm, work Panel rnd 1, *dc in next st, pm, work Panel rnd 1; rep from * around, join with sl st in first dc.

Rnd 2: Ch 1, sc in first st, work Panel rnd 2, *sc in next st, work Panel rnd 2; rep from * around, join with sl st in first sc.

Rnd 3: (First-dc, dc) in first st, pm in First-dc, work Panel rnd 1, *3 dc in next st, pm in center dc of 3-dc group just made, work Panel rnd 1; rep from * around, dc once more in first worked st, join with sl st in first dc—256 (288, 320, 352, 384, 400, 416, 448) sts.

Rnd 4: Ch 1, sc in first st, sc in next st, work Panel rnd 2, *sc in each of next 3 sts, work Panel rnd 2; rep from * around, sc in next st, join with sl st in first sc.

Rnd 5: First-dc in first st, 2 dc in next st, work Panel rnd 1, *2 dc in next st, dc in next st, pm, 2 dc in next st, work Panel rnd 1; rep from * around, 2 dc in last st, join with sl st in first dc—264 (296, 328, 360, 392, 408, 424, 456) sts.

Rnd 6: Ch 1, sc in first 3 sts, work Panel rnd 2, *sc in each of next 7 sts, work Panel rnd 2; rep from * around, sc in each of last 2 sts, join with sl st in first sc.

Rnd 7: First-dc in first st, 2 dc in next st, dc in next st, work Panel rnd 1, *dc in next st, 2 dc in next st, dc in next st, 2 dc in next st, dc in next st, work Panel rnd 1; rep from * around, dc in next st, 2 dc in next st, join with sl st in first dc—272 (304, 336, 368, 400, 416, 432, 464) sts.

Rnd 8: Ch 1, sc in first st and in each st to start of Panel, work Panel rnd 2, *sc in each st to start of Panel, work Panel rnd 2; rep from * around, sc in each st to end of round, join with sl st in first sc.

Rnd 9: First-dc in first st, 2 dc in next st, dc in each st to start of Panel, work Panel rnd 1, *dc in each st to one st before marker, 2 dc in st before marker**, dc in next st, 2 dc in next st, dc in each st to start of Panel, work Panel rnd 1; rep from * around, ending last rep at **, join with sl st in first dc—280 (312, 344, 376, 408, 424, 440, 472) sts.

Rnds 10–17 (19, 21, 23, 23, 19, 25, 27): Rep last 2 rnds 4, (5, 6, 7, 7, 5, 8, 9) times—312 (352, 392, 432, 464, 464, 504, 544) sts.

Rnd 18 (20, 22, 24, 24, 20, 26, 28): Rep rnd 8.

Rnd 19 (21, 23, 25, 25, 21, 27, 29): First-dc in first st, dc in each st to start of Panel, work Panel rnd 1, *dc in each st to start of Panel, work Panel rnd 1; rep from * around, dc in each st to beg of rnd, join with sl st in first dc—312 (352, 392, 432, 464, 464, 504, 544) sts.

Rnds 20 (22, 24, 24, 20, 26, 28, 30)–51: Rep last 2 rows 16 (15, 14, 14, 16, 13, 12, 11) times.

Rnd 52: Rep rnd 8.

Fasten off.

Remove all but first marker.

MOTIF SECTION 1

With smaller hook, make and join 8 (9, 10, 11, 12, 12, 13, 14) Motifs in a circle around bottom of Upper Skirt, joining to Upper Skirt and to previous Motif of current section while completing last rnd.

1. Starting at remaining marker, place 7 (8, 9, 10, 11, 11, 12, 13) additional markers at 5-inch/12.5 cm intervals around bottom edge of Upper Skirt.

2. When joining to the bottom edge of Upper Skirt, work corner ch-3 joins into the marked sts, space other ch-3 joins evenly between the corner joins. Work the first corner ch-3 join of a motif on lower edge of Upper Skirt into the same marked stitch as the last corner join of the previous motif.

FIRST LACE SECTION

With smaller hook, join yarn in junction bet 2 motifs on bottom edge of Motif Section 1.

Rnd 1: (First-dc, 2 dc) in same sp as joining, *(dc, ch 2, dc) in next ch-3 sp, [(3 dc, ch 3, 3 dc) in next ch-3 sp, (dc, ch 2, dc) in next sc] twice, (3 dc, ch 3, 3 dc) in next ch-3 sp, (dc, ch 2, dc) in next ch-3 sp**, (3 dc, ch 3, 3 dc) in junction bet next 2 motifs; rep from * around, ending last rep at **, 3 dc in same sp as First-dc, ch 2, sc in first dc instead of last ch-3 sp.

Rnd 2: (First-dc, 2 dc) in first sp, *(2 dc, ch 3, 2 dc) in next ch-2 sp**, (3 dc, ch 3, 3 dc) in next ch-3 sp; rep from * around, ending last rep at **, 3 dc in same sp as First- dc, ch 2, sc in first dc instead of last ch-3 sp.

Rnd 3: (First-dc, 2 dc) in first sp, *dc in sp bet current shell and next shell**, (3 dc, ch 3, 3 dc) in next ch-3 sp; rep from * around, ending last rep at **, 3 dc in same sp as First-dc, ch 2, sc in first dc instead of last ch-3 sp.

Rnd 4: (First-dc, 2 dc) in first sp, *sk next 3 sts, dc in next dc**, (3 dc, ch 3, 3 dc) in next ch-3 sp; rep from * around, ending last rep at **, 3 dc in same sp as First-dc, ch 2, sc in first dc instead of last ch-3 sp.

Rnds 5 and 6: Rep row 4.

MOTIF SECTION 2

With smaller hook, make and join 16 (18, 20, 22, 24, 24, 26, 28) Motifs in a circle around bottom of First Lace Section, joining to First Lace Section and to previous Motif of current section while completing last rnd.

1. Starting at last space made in rnd 6 of Lace Section, place 15 (17, 19, 21, 23, 23, 25, 27) additional markers in every 4th ch-3 space around rnd 6 of Lace Section.

2. When joining Motifs to rnd 6 of Lace Section, work corner ch-3 joins into the marked spaces, work other ch-3 joins into ch-3 spaces between the corner joins. Work the first corner ch-3 join of Motif into first placed marker.

MOTIF SECTION 3

With smaller hook, make and join 16 (18, 20, 22, 24, 24, 26, 28) Motifs in a circle around bottom of Motif Section 2, joining to Motif Section 2 and to previous Motif of current section while completing last rnd.

SECOND LACE SECTION

With smaller hook, join yarn in junction bet 2 motifs on bottom edge of Motif Section 3.

Rnd 1: (First-dc, 2 dc) in same sp as joining, *dc in next ch-3 sp, [(3 dc, ch 3, 3 dc) in next ch-3 sp, dc in next sc] twice, (3 dc, ch 3, 3 dc) in next ch-3 sp, dc in next ch-3 sp**, (3 dc, ch 3, 3 dc) in junction bet next 2 motifs; rep from * around, ending last rep at **, 3 dc in same sp as First-dc, ch 2, sc in first dc instead of last ch-3 sp.

Rnd 2: (First-dc, 2 dc) in first sp, *sk next 3 sts, dc in next dc**, (3 dc, ch 3, 3 dc) in next ch-3 sp; rep from * around, ending last rep at **, 3 dc in same sp as First-dc, ch 2, sc in first dc instead of last ch-3 sp.

Rnds 3–6: Rep rnd 2.
Fasten off.

MOTIF SECTION 4

Work same as Motif Section 2.

FINISHING

Block to finished measurements.
Weave in ends.

WAISTBAND

Measure waist of wearer. Cut a length of elastic 1 inch/2.5 cm longer (for overlap) than waist measurement. Place the elastic on the inside of the waistband, and fold the band over the elastic for sewing. Sew the waistband in place, making sure that the stitches do not show on the outside. After seam is complete, pull ends of elastic through opening in waistband; overlap the ends of the elastic and sew them together securely. Use locking mattress stitch to secure remaining waistband opening.

VESTS
& TANKS

HIKING VEST

To the mountains, the park, or just to hang around your own backyard, we designed this sturdy zip-front vest to keep up with you regardless of where your adventure leads you.

Folded single crochet ribbing creates the collar and borders the armhole and hemline for a comfortable fit that moves with you and can be blocked to provide a more customized fit.

Add a zipper closure to the hidden internal pocket to keep your treasures (or car keys) from getting lost along the trail (or somewhere between aisles 5 and 9 at the grocery store).

SKILL LEVEL: Beginner
SIZES: S (M, L, XL, 2X, 3X, 4X, 5X)
Sample shown in size small

FINISHED MEASUREMENTS

To Fit Bust: 32 (36, 40, 44, 48, 52, 56, 60) inches/81.5 (91.5, 101.5, 112, 122, 132, 142, 152.5) cm
Finished Bust: 36 (40, 44, 48, 52, 56, 60, 64) inches/ 91.5 (101.5, 112, 122, 132, 142, 152.5, 162.5) cm
Finished Length: 27 (27, 27½, 28, 28, 28, 28½, 28½) inches/68.5 (68.5, 70, 71, 71, 71, 72.5, 72.5) cm

MATERIALS AND TOOLS

- Sample uses Mango Moon, Bulu (100% Merino Wool; 1.75 ounces/50 g = 150 yards/137 m): 10 (11, 12, 14, 15, 16, 17, 18) hanks in color Jasper #5104 or 1500 (1650, 1800, 2100, 2250, 2400, 2550, 2700/1370 (1507, 1644, 1918, 2055, 2192, 2329, 2466) m of superfine weight yarn

- Crochet hooks: 2.75mm (size C-2) and 3.5mm (E-4) or sizes to obtain gauge
- Yarn needle
- Two-way separating zipper: 30 (30, 30½, 31, 31, 31, 31½, 31½) inches/76 (76, 77.5, 79, 79, 79, 80, 80) cm long

BLOCKED GAUGES

Sc linen st pattern with larger hook: 39 sts = 6 inches/15 cm; 26 rows = 4¾ inches/12 cm

Sc ribbing pattern with smaller hook: 36 sts = 6 inches/15 cm; 28 rows = 4½ inches/11.5 cm

Always take time to check your gauge.

GAUGE SWATCHES

Single crochet linen stitch swatch

Row 1: With larger hook, work 39 Fsc, turn.

Rows 2–26: Work even in sc linen st pattern st.

Sc ribbing stitch swatch

Row 1: With smaller hook, work 36 Fsc, turn.

Rows 2–28: Work even in sc ribbing pattern st.

STITCH GUIDE

Foundation single crochet (Fsc): Ch 2, insert hook in 2nd ch from hook, yo and draw up a loop, yo and draw through 1 loop (first "chain" made), yo and draw through 2 loops on hook (first sc made), * insert hook under 2 loops of the "chain" just made, yo and draw up a loop, yo and draw through 1 loop ("chain" made), yo and draw through 2 loops on hook (sc made); rep from * for indicated number of foundation sts.

Single crochet through back loop only (sc-tbl): Insert hook in back loop of indicated stitch, yo and draw up a loop, yo and draw through 2 loops on hook.

PATTERN STITCHES

For Master Chart Key, see page 206.

Single crochet linen stitch (sc linen st) (work on an odd number of sts) A

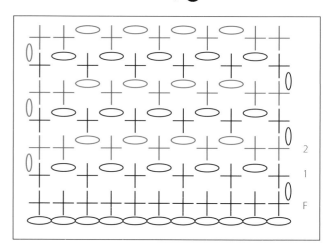

A Single crochet linen stitch chart

Row 1: Ch 1, sc in first st, *ch 1, sk next st, sc in next st; rep from * across, turn.

Row 2: Ch 1, sc in first st, *sc in next ch-1 sp, ch 1, sk next sc; rep from * to last ch-1 sp, sc in last ch-1 sp, sc in last st, turn.

Row 3: Ch 1, sc in first st, *ch 1, sk next st, sc in next ch-1 sp; rep from * to last 2 sts, ch 1, sk next st, sc in last st, turn. Repeat rows 2 and 3 for pattern.

Single crochet ribbing (sc ribbing) (any number of sts) B

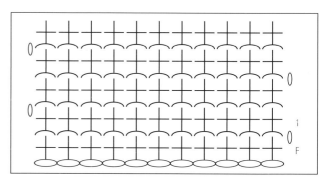

B Single crochet ribbing stitch chart

Row 1: Ch 1, sc in both loops of first st, sc-tbl of each st across to last st, sc in both loops of last st, turn.

Repeat row 1 for pattern.

SPECIAL TECHNIQUES

Locking mattress stitch (see Special Techniques, page 200)

Custom zipper creation (see Special Techniques, pages 198–199)

NOTES

To prevent color pooling when using variegated and hand-dyed yarns such as Bulu, alternate balls of yarn every other row. Carry your yarn up the side of the garment by twisting the unused strand under the working yarn; this will prevent gaps or loose ends.

INSTRUCTIONS

BACK PANEL

RIBBING BORDER

Row 1: With smaller hook, work 24 Fsc, turn.

Rows 2–112 (125, 137 150, 162, 175, 187, 200): Work in sc ribbing pattern st. Do not fasten off. At end of last row, rotate work ¼ turn to the right for working in row-end sts of ribbing.

MAIN BODY

Row 1: With larger hook, working in row-end st of ribbing, ch 1, sc in each of first 18 (18, 19, 18, 21, 21, 20, 19) row-end sts, [2 sc in next row-end st, sc in each of next 18 (17, 19, 18, 19, 18, 20, 19) row-end sts] 4 (5, 5, 6, 6, 7, 7, 8) times, 2 sc in next st, sc in each of next 17 (16, 17, 17, 20, 20, 19, 20) row-end sts, turn—117 (131, 143, 157, 169, 183, 195, 209) sts.

Rows 2–100 (96, 96, 96, 94, 90, 90, 88): Work even in sc linen st pattern.

ARMHOLE SHAPING

Row 1 (RS): Ch 1, sl st in first 6 (5, 6, 7, 8, 9, 10, 11) sts, ch 1, sc2tog, work in pattern st as established to last 8 (7, 8, 9, 10, 11, 12, 13) sts, sc2tog, turn, leaving last 6 (5, 6, 7, 8, 9, 10, 11) sts unworked—103 (119, 129, 141, 151, 163, 173, 185) sts.

Row 2: Ch 1, sc2tog, work in pattern st as established to last 2 sts, sc2tog, turn—101 (117, 127, 139, 149, 161, 171, 183) sts.

Row 3: Ch 1, sk first st, sc2tog, work in pattern st as established to last 3 sts, sc2tog, turn, leaving last st unworked—97 (113, 123, 135, 145, 157, 167, 179) sts.

SIZES M (L, XL, 2X, 3X, 4X, 5X) ONLY

Rows 4–5 (7, 9, 11, 15, 17, 21): Rep last 2 rows 1 (2, 3, 4, 6, 7, 9) times—107 (111, 117, 121, 121, 125, 125) sts at end of last row.

ALL SIZES

Rows 4 (6, 8, 10, 12, 16, 18, 22)–5 (7, 9, 11, 13, 17, 19, 23): Rep row 2 of shaping (twice)—93 (103, 107, 113, 117, 117, 121, 121) sts.

Rows 6 (8, 10, 12, 14, 18, 20, 24)–38 (41, 44, 46, 49, 52, 55, 57): Work even in pattern st as established.

Fasten off.

LEFT FRONT PANEL

RIBBING BORDER

Row 1: With smaller hook, work 24 Fsc, turn.

Rows 2–56 (62, 70, 76, 81, 87, 95, 100): Work in sc ribbing pattern st.

At end of last row, rotate work ¼ turn to the right for working in row-end sts of ribbing.

MAIN BODY

Row 1 (RS): With larger hooking, working in row-end st of ribbing, ch 1, sc in each of first 13 (15, 17, 18, 15, 18, 18, 16) row-end sts, [2 sc in next row-end st, sc in each of next 13 (15, 17, 18, 15, 16, 18, 16) row-end sts] 2 (2, 2, 2, 3, 3, 3, 4) times, 2 sc in next st, sc in each of next 14 (14, 16, 19, 17, 17, 19, 15) row-end sts, turn—59 (65, 73, 79, 85, 91, 99, 105) sts.

Rows 2–100 (96, 96, 96, 94, 90, 90, 88): Work even in sc linen st pattern.

ARMHOLE SHAPING

Row 1 (RS): Ch 1, sl st in first 6 (5, 6, 7, 8, 9, 10, 11) sts, ch 1, sc2tog, work in pattern st as established across, turn—52 (59, 66, 71, 76, 81, 88, 93) sts.

Row 2 (WS): Ch 1, work in pattern st as established across to last 2 sts, sc2tog, turn—51 (58, 65, 70, 75, 80, 87, 92) sts.

Row 3: Ch 1, sk first st, sc2tog, work in pattern st as established across, turn—49 (56, 63, 68, 73, 78, 85, 90) sts.

SIZES M (L, XL, 2X, 3X, 4X, 5X) ONLY

Rows 4–5 (7, 9, 11, 15, 17, 21): Rep last 2 rows 1 (2, 3, 4, 6, 7, 9) times—53 (57, 59, 61, 60, 64, 63) sts at end of last row.

ALL SIZES

Row 4 (6, 8, 10, 12, 16, 18, 22): Rep row 2—48 (52, 56, 58, 60, 59, 63, 62) sts.

Row 5 (7, 9, 11, 13, 17, 19, 23): Ch 1, sc2tog, work in pattern st as established across, turn—47 (51, 55, 57, 59, 58, 62, 61) sts.

Rows 6 (8, 10, 12, 14, 18, 20, 24)–26 (30, 32, 34, 38, 40, 44, 46): Work even in pattern st as established.

NECKLINE SHAPING

Row 1 (RS): Ch 1, work in pattern st as established across to last 9 (8, 10, 10, 11, 11, 14, 14) sts, sc2tog, turn, leaving last 7 (6, 8, 8, 9, 9, 12, 12) sts unworked—39 (44, 46, 48, 49, 48, 49, 48) sts.

Row 2 (WS): Ch 1, sk first st, hdc2tog, sc2tog, work in pattern st as established across, turn—36 (41, 43, 45, 46, 45, 46, 45) sts.

Row 3: Ch 1, work in pattern st as established to last 3 sts, sc2tog, turn, leaving last st unworked—34 (39, 41, 43, 44, 43, 44, 43) sts.

Rows 4–7 (7, 7, 7, 9, 9, 9, 9): Rep last 2 rows 2 (2, 2, 2, 3, 3, 3, 3) times—24 (29, 31, 33, 29, 28, 29, 28) sts at end of last row.

SIZES L (XL) ONLY

Row 8 (8) (WS): Rep row 2—28 (30) sts.

SIZE L ONLY

Row 9 (RS): Ch 1, work in pattern st as established across to last 2 sts, sc2tog, turn—27 sts.

SIZE 4X ONLY

Row 10 (WS): Ch 1, sc2tog, work in pattern st as established across, turn—28 sts.

SIZES S (M, L, XL, 2X, 3X) ONLY

Rows 8 (8, 10, 9, 10, 10)–12 (11, 12, 12, 11, 12): Work even in pattern st as established.

Fasten off.

SIZES 4X (5X) ONLY

Row 11 (11): Work even in pattern st as established.
Fasten off.

RIGHT FRONT PANEL

Work same as Left Front to Armhole Shaping.

ARMHOLE SHAPING

Row 1 (RS): Ch 1, work in pattern st as established across to last 8 (7, 8, 9, 10, 11, 12, 13) sts, sc2tog, turn, leaving last 6 (5, 6, 7, 8, 9, 10, 11) sts unworked—52 (59, 66, 71, 76, 81, 88, 93) sts.

Row 2 (WS): Ch 1, sc2tog, work in pattern st as established across, turn—51 (58, 65, 70, 75, 80, 87, 92) sts.

Row 3: Ch 1, work in pattern st as established across to last 3 sts, sc2tog, turn, leaving last st unworked—49 (56, 63, 68, 73, 78, 85, 90) sts.

SIZES M (L, XL, 2X, 3X, 4X, 5X) ONLY

Rows 4–5 (7, 9, 11, 15, 17, 21): Rep last 2 rows 1 (2, 3, 4, 6, 7, 9) times—53 (57, 59, 61, 60, 64, 63) sts at end of last row.

ALL SIZES

Row 4 (6, 8, 10, 12, 16, 18, 22): Rep row 2—48 (52, 56, 58, 60, 59, 63, 62) sts.

Row 5 (7, 9, 11, 13, 17, 19, 23): Ch 1, work in pattern st as established across to last 2 sts, sc2tog, turn—47 (51, 55, 57, 59, 58, 62, 61) sts.

Rows 6 (8, 10, 12, 14, 18, 20, 24)–26 (30, 32, 34, 38, 40, 44, 46): Work even in pattern st as established.

NECKLINE SHAPING

Row 1 (RS): Ch 1, sl st in first 7 (6, 8, 8, 9, 9, 12, 12) sts, ch 1, sc2tog, work in pattern st as established across, turn—39 (44, 46, 48, 49, 48, 49, 48) sts.

Row 2 (WS): Ch 1, work in pattern st as established across to last 5 sts, sk next st, sc2tog, hdc2tog, turn—36 (41, 43, 45, 46, 45, 46, 45) sts.

Row 3: Ch 1, sk first st, sc2tog, work in pattern st as established across, turn—34 (39, 41, 43, 44, 43, 44, 43) sts.

Rows 4–7 (7, 7, 7, 9, 9, 9, 9): Rep last 2 rows 2 (2, 2, 2, 3, 3, 3, 3) times—24 (29, 31, 33, 29, 28, 29, 28) sts.

SIZES L (XL) ONLY

Row 8 (8) (WS): Rep row 2—28 (30) sts.

SIZE L ONLY

Row 9 (RS): Ch 1, sc2tog, work in pattern st as established across, turn—27 sts.

SIZE 4X ONLY

Row 10 (WS): Ch 1, work in pattern st as established across to last 2 sts, sc2tog, turn—28 sts.

SIZES S (M, L, XL, 2X, 3X) ONLY

Rows 8 (8, 10, 9, 10, 10)–12 (11, 12, 12, 11, 12): Work even in pattern st as established.

Fasten off.

SIZES 4X (5X) ONLY

Row 11 (11): Work even in pattern st as established.

Fasten off.

ARMHOLE BORDER RIBBING

Row 1: With smaller hook, work 12 Fsc, turn.

Rows 2–100 (106, 112, 118, 124, 131, 137, 143): Work even in sc ribbing pattern st.

Fasten off.

COLLAR

Row 1: With smaller hook, work 36 Fsc, turn.

Rows 2–93 (93, 106, 106, 120, 126, 132, 132): Work even in sc ribbing pattern st.

Fasten off.

POCKET

Row 1: With larger hook, work 33 Fsc, turn.

Rows 2–27: Work even in sc linen st pattern.

Row 28: Ch 1, sc in each st and sp across.

Fasten off, leaving a long sewing length.

FINISHING

Block pieces to schematic measurements.

Sew shoulder and side seams.

Sew one long edge of Armhole Border Ribbing to armhole. Fold Armhole Border Ribbing in half lengthwise, and sew second long edge to inside of armhole. Rep with second Armhole Border.

Sew one long edge of Collar to neckline. Fold Collar in half lengthwise and sew second long edge to inside of neckline.

Fold bottom hem Ribbing Border in half lengthwise and sew to inside edge of garment.

Sew Pocket to Right Front inside of vest, ½ inch (1.3 cm) in from front edge and 1 inch (2.5 cm) above ribbing.

Sew zipper into front of garment.

Weave in ends.

HIKING VEST SCHEMATIC

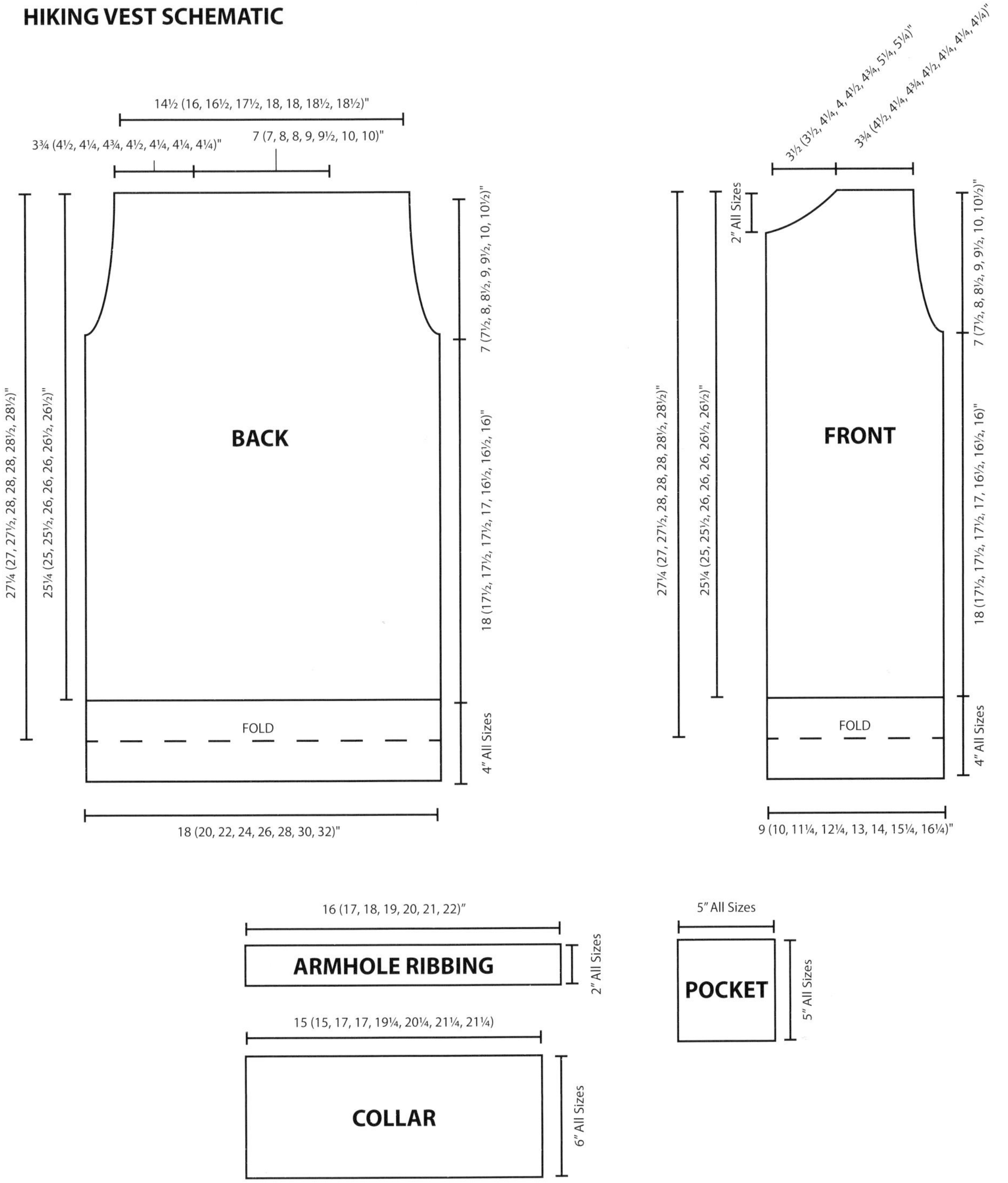
14½ (16, 16½, 17½, 18, 18, 18½, 18½)"
3¾ (4½, 4¼, 4¾, 4½, 4¼, 4¼, 4¼)"
7 (7, 8, 8, 9, 9½, 10, 10)"
27¼ (27, 27½, 28, 28, 28, 28½, 28½)"
25¼ (25, 25½, 26, 26, 26, 26½, 26½)"
7 (7½, 8, 8½, 9, 9½, 10, 10½)"
18 (17½, 17½, 17½, 17, 16½, 16½, 16)"
4" All Sizes
BACK
FOLD
18 (20, 22, 24, 26, 28, 30, 32)"
3½ (3½, 4¼, 4, 4½, 4¾, 5¼, 5¼)"
3¾ (4½, 4¼, 4¾, 4½, 4¼, 4¼, 4¼)"
2" All Sizes
27¼ (27, 27½, 28, 28, 28, 28½, 28½)"
25¼ (25, 25½, 26, 26, 26, 26½, 26½)"
7 (7½, 8, 8½, 9, 9½, 10, 10½)"
18 (17½, 17½, 17½, 17, 16½, 16½, 16)"
4" All Sizes
FRONT
FOLD
9 (10, 11¼, 12¼, 13, 14, 15¼, 16¼)"
16 (17, 18, 19, 20, 21, 22)"
ARMHOLE RIBBING
2" All Sizes
15 (15, 17, 17, 19¼, 20¼, 21¼, 21¼)
COLLAR
6" All Sizes
5" All Sizes
POCKET
5" All Sizes

CROSS FRONT VEST

The classic vest is given an upgrade with a bold graphic color stripe and flattering front cross shaping. Express your colorful style as boisterous or as subdued as you like with endless color combinations or even a beautiful solid hue. You could even use up those odds and ends of your favorite yarns to make the colors go wild and create a truly unique piece for your wardrobe.

SKILL LEVEL: Intermediate
SIZES: S (M, L, XL, 2X, 3X, 4X, 5X)
Sample shown in size small

FINISHED MEASUREMENTS

To Fit Bust: 32 (36, 40, 44, 48, 52, 56, 60) inches/81.5 (91.5, 101.5, 112, 122, 132, 142, 152.5) cm
Finished Bust: 34 (38, 42, 46, 50, 54½, 58, 62) inches/86.5 (96.5, 106.5, 117, 127, 138.5, 147.5, 157.5) cm

MATERIALS AND TOOLS

▪ Sample uses Cascade 220 Superwash Sport (100% Superwash Merino Wool; 1.75 ounces/50 g = 136.5 yards/125 m): 4 (5, 5, 6, 6, 7, 7) skeins Charcoal #900 (A); 4 (5, 5, 6, 6, 6, 7, 7) skeins in Silver Gray #1946 (B) or 1092 (1365, 1365, 1638, 1638, 1638, 1911, 1911) yards/1000 (1250, 1250, 1500, 1500, 1500, 1750, 1750) m of lightweight yarn

▪ Crochet hook: 3.75mm (size F-5) or size to obtain gauge
▪ Yarn needle
▪ Two 1½-inch/3.8 cm buttons

37 sts = 6½ inches/16.5 cm; 27 rows x 5¼ inches/13.5 cm in pattern stitch

Always take time to check your gauge.

STITCH GUIDE

Foundation half double crochet (Fhdc): Ch 3, yo, insert hook in 3rd ch from hook, yo and draw up a loop, yo and draw through 1 loop (first "chain" made), yo and draw through all 3 loops on hook (first hdc made), *yo, insert hook under 2 loops of the "chain" just made, yo and draw up a loop, yo and draw through 1 loop ("chain" made), yo and draw through all 3 loops on hook (hdc made); rep from * for indicated number of foundation sts.

Half double crochet 2 together (hdc2tog): Yo, insert hook in next st and pull up a loop, insert hook in next st and pull up a loop, yo and draw through all 4 loops on hook.

PATTERN STITCHES

For Master Chart Key, see page 206.

Single crochet linen stitch (sc linen st) (worked on an odd number of sts) Ⓐ

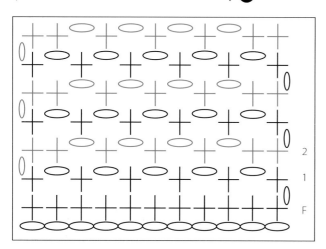

Ⓐ **Single crochet linen stitch chart**

Row 1: Ch 1, sc in first st, *ch 1, sk next st, sc in next st; rep from * across, turn.

Row 2: Ch 1, sc in first st, *sc in next ch-1 sp, ch 1, sk next sc; rep from * across to last ch-1 sp, sc in last ch-1 sp, sc in last st, turn.

Row 3: Ch 1, sc in first st, *ch 1, sk next st, sc in next ch-1 sp; rep from * across to last 2 sts, ch 1, sk next st, sc in last st, turn.

Rep rows 2 and 3 for pattern.

Single crochet linen stitch (sc linen st) with color changes (worked on an odd number of sts)

Rows 1–8: Change color every row.

Rows 9–26: Change color every other row and carry yarn up side of work.

SPECIAL TECHNIQUES

Color change at end of row (see Special Techniques, page 198)

Carry yarn up side of work (see Special Techniques, page 198)

Locking mattress stitch (see Special Techniques, page 200)

NOTES

1. When instructed to work in a pattern stitch "as established," work the next row of pattern stitch and ensure that the stitches line up as in previous rows.

2. Left Side and Right Side refer to left and right side as worn.

INSTRUCTIONS

BACK PANEL

Row 1: With A, work 97 (109, 121, 131, 143, 155, 165, 177) Fhdc, turn.

Row 2 (RS): Ch 1, sc in first st, *ch 1, sk next st, sc in next st; rep from * across, turn. Fasten off A. Join B.

Row 3: With B, ch 1, sc in first st, *sc in next ch-1 sp, ch 1, sk next sc; rep from * across to last ch-1 sp, sc in last ch-1 sp, sc in last st, turn. Fasten off B. Join A.

Rows 4–9: Rep last 2 rows.

Row 10: With A, ch 1, sc in first st, *ch 1, sk next st, sc in next st; rep from * across, turn.

Row 11: Ch 1, sc in first st, *sc in next ch-1 sp, ch 1, sk next sc; rep from * across to last ch-1 sp, sc in last ch-1 sp, sc in last st, turn. Drop A to WS to be picked up later. Join B.

Rows 12 and 13: With B, rep rows 10 and 11.

Rep rows 10–13 for pattern.

Rows 14–88 (85, 85, 84, 82, 79, 80, 78): Work even in pattern st as established.

Note: Maintain color changes as established; that is, continue to change colors every 2 rows while working remainder of pattern.

BEGIN ARMHOLE SHAPING

Row 1: Sl st in first 5 (6, 10, 10, 15, 18, 18, 23) sts, ch 1, work in pattern st as established to last 5 (6, 10, 10, 15, 18, 18, 23) sts, turn leaving last 5 (6, 10, 10, 15, 18, 18, 23) sts unworked—87 (97, 101, 111, 113, 119, 129, 131) sts.

Row 2: Ch 1, hdc2tog, work in pattern st as established to last 2 sts, hdc2tog, turn—85 (95, 99, 109, 111, 117, 127, 129) sts.

Rows 3–5 (5, 5, 8, 7, 10, 14, 15): Rep row 2—79 (89, 93, 97, 101, 101, 103, 103) sts.

Rows 6 (6, 6, 9, 8, 11, 15, 16)–36 (39, 41, 44, 46, 49, 52, 54): Work even in pattern st and color changes as established.

BEGIN BACK NECKLINE SHAPING

FIRST SIDE

Row 1: Ch 1, work in pattern st as established across first 30 (34, 35, 36, 37, 37, 37, 37) sts, hdc2tog, turn, leaving remaining sts unworked—31 (35, 36, 37, 38, 38, 38, 38) sts.

Row 2: Ch 1, sk first st, sl st in next 1 (2, 2, 3, 4, 4, 4, 4) sts, ch 1, hdc2tog, work in pattern st as established across, turn—28 (31, 32, 32, 32, 32, 32, 32) sts.

Row 3: Ch 1, work in pattern st as established across to last 4 (4, 5, 5, 5, 5, 5, 5) sts, hdc2tog, turn, leaving last 2 (2, 3, 3, 3, 3, 3, 3) sts unworked—25 (28, 28, 28, 28, 28, 28, 28) sts.

Row 4: Sl st in first st, ch 1, hdc2tog, work in pattern st as established across, turn—23 (26, 26, 26, 26, 26, 26, 26) sts.

Row 5: Work even in pattern st as established.

Fasten off.

SECOND SIDE

With First Side on your right-hand side, sk next 15 (16, 18, 20, 22, 22, 24, 24) unworked sts; join yarn in next unworked st; first st of row 1 is worked in same st as joining.

Row 1: Ch 1, hdc2tog, work in pattern st as established across, turn—31 (35, 36, 37, 38, 38, 38, 38) sts.

Row 2: Ch 1, work in pattern st as established to last 4 (5, 5, 6, 7, 7, 7, 7) sts, hdc2tog, turn, leaving last 2 (3, 3, 4, 5, 5, 5, 5) sts unworked—28 (31, 32, 32, 32, 32, 32, 32) sts.

Row 3: Ch 1, sk first st, sl st in next 1 (1, 2, 2, 2, 2, 2, 2) sts, ch 1, sc2tog, work in pattern st as established across, turn—25 (28, 28, 28, 28, 28, 28, 28) sts.

Row 4: Ch 1, work in pattern st as established to last 3 sts, hdc2tog, turn, leaving last st unworked—23 (26, 26, 26, 26, 26, 26, 26) sts.

Row 5: Ch 1, work even in pattern st as established.

Fasten off.

LEFT FRONT PANEL

Row 1: With A, work 75 (87, 97, 109, 121, 131, 143, 155) Fhdc, turn.

Work same as Back through row 13.

Rows 14–62 (60, 60, 58, 56, 54, 54, 52): Work even in pattern st as established.

Note: Maintain color changes as established; that is, continue to change colors every 2 rows while working remaining pattern rows.

BEGIN FRONT NECKLINE SHAPING

Row 1 (WS): Ch 1, hdc2tog, sk next st, work in pattern st as established across, turn—73 (85, 95, 107, 119, 129, 141, 153) sts.

Row 2 (RS): Work even in pattern st as established.

Rows 3–26: Maintaining color sequence as established, rep rows 1 and 2 (12 times)—49 (61, 71, 83, 95, 105, 117, 129) sts.

BEGIN ARMHOLE SHAPING AND CONTINUE FRONT NECKLINE SHAPING

Row 1 (WS): Ch 1, hdc2tog, sk next st, work in pattern st as established to last 5 (6, 10, 10, 15, 18, 18, 23) sts, turn, leaving last 5 (6, 10, 10, 15, 18, 18, 23) sts unworked—42 (53, 59, 71, 78, 85, 97, 104) sts.

Row 2 (RS): Ch 1, hdc2tog, work in pattern st as established across, turn—41 (52, 58, 70, 77, 84, 96, 103) sts.

Row 3: Ch 1, hdc2tog, sk next st, work in pattern st as established to last 2 sts, hdc2tog, turn—38 (49, 55, 67, 74, 81, 93, 100) sts.

Rows 4–5 (5, 5, 7, 7, 9, 13, 15): Maintaining color sequence as established, rep rows 2 and 3 (1 [1, 1, 2, 2, 3, 5, 6] times)—34 (45, 51, 59, 66, 69, 73, 76) sts.

SIZES XL (3X, 4X) ONLY

Row 8 (10, 14): Rep row 2—58 (68, 72) sts.

SIZES S (M, L, 2X, 5X) ONLY

Row 6 (6, 6, 8, 16) (RS): Work even in pattern st as established.

CONTINUE FRONT NECKLINE SHAPING

SIZES S (M, L, XL, 2X, 3X, 4X) ONLY

Row 1 (WS): Ch 1, hdc2tog, sk next st, work in pattern st as established across, turn—32 (43, 49, 56, 64, 66, 70) sts.

Row 2 (RS): Work even in pattern st as established.

SIZES S (M, L, XL, 2X, 3X) ONLY

Rows 3–10 (10, 10, 8, 8, 6): Maintaining color sequence as established, rep rows 1 and 2 (4 [4, 4, 3, 3, 2] times)—24 (35, 41, 50, 58, 62) sts.

SIZES S (M, L) ONLY

Row 11 (WS): Ch 1, hdc2tog, work in pattern st as established across, turn—23 (34, 40) sts.

SIZES M (L) ONLY

Row 12 (RS): Work in pattern st as established to last 2 sts, hdc2tog, turn—33 (39) sts.

Rows 13–18 (24): Maintaining color sequence as established, rep rows 1 and 2 (3 [6] times)—27 (27) sts.

Row 19 (25): Rep row 13—26 (26) sts.

SIZES XL (2X, 3X, 4X, 5X)

Row 9 (9, 7, 3, 1) (WS): Ch 1, hdc2tog, sk next st, work in pattern st as established across, turn—48 (56, 60, 68, 74) sts.

Row 10 (10, 8, 4, 2) (RS): Ch 1, work in pattern st as established to last 3 sts, sk next st, hdc2tog, turn—46 (54, 58, 66, 72) sts.

Rows 11 (11, 9, 5, 3)–20 (24, 24, 24, 24): Rep last 2 rows 5 (7, 8, 10, 11) times—26 (26, 26, 26, 28) sts at end of last row.

SIZE 5X ONLY

Row 25: Rep row 1—26 sts.

ALL SIZES

Rows 12 (20, 26, 21, 25, 25, 25, 26)–35 (38, 40, 41, 43, 44, 43, 43): Work even in pattern st as established.

RIGHT FRONT PANEL

Work same as Left Front to Begin Front Neckline Shaping.

Note: Maintain color changes as established; that is, continue to change colors every 2 rows while working remaining pattern rows.

BEGIN FRONT NECKLINE SHAPING

Row 1 (WS): Ch 1, work in pattern st as established to last 3 sts, sk next st, hdc2tog, turn—73 (85, 95, 107, 119, 129, 141, 153) sts.

Row 2 (RS): Work even in pattern st as established.

Rows 3–26: Maintaining color sequence as established, rep rows 1 and 2—49 (61, 71, 83, 95, 105, 117, 129) sts.

BEGIN ARMHOLE SHAPING AND CONTINUE FRONT NECKLINE SHAPING

Row 1 (WS): Ch 1, sl st in first 5 (6, 10, 10, 15, 18, 18, 23) sts, ch 1, work in pattern st as established to last 3 sts, sk next st, hdc2tog, turn—42 (53, 59, 71, 78, 85, 97, 104) sts.

Row 2 (RS): Ch 1, work in established pattern st to last 2 sts, hdc2tog, turn—41 (52, 58, 70, 77, 84, 96, 103) sts.

Row 3: Ch 1, hdc2tog, work in pattern st as established to last 3 sts, sk next st, hdc2tog, turn—38 (49, 55, 67, 74, 81, 93, 100) sts.

Rows 4–5 (5, 5, 7, 7, 9, 13, 15): Rep last 2 rows 1 (1, 1, 2, 2, 3, 5, 6) times—34 (45, 51, 59, 66, 69, 73, 76) sts at end of last row.

SIZES XL (3X, 4X) ONLY

Row 8 (10, 14): Rep row 2—58 (68, 72) sts.

SIZES S (M, L, 2X, 5X) ONLY

Row 6 (6, 6, 8, 16) (RS): Work even in pattern st as established.

CONTINUE FRONT NECKLINE SHAPING

SIZES S (M, L, XL, 2X, 3X, 4X) ONLY

Row 1 (WS): Ch 1, work in pattern st as established to last 3 sts, sk next st, hdc2tog, turn—32 (43, 49, 56, 64, 66, 70) sts.

Row 2 (RS): Work even in pattern st as established.

SIZES S (M, L, XL, 2X, 3X) ONLY

Rows 3–10 (10, 10, 8, 8, 6): Rep last 2 rows 4 (4, 4, 3, 3, 2) times—24 (35, 41, 50, 58, 62) sts at end of last row.

SIZES S (M, L) ONLY

Row 11 (WS): Ch 1, work in pattern st as established to last 2 sts, hdc2tog, turn—23 (34, 40) sts.

Row 12 (RS): Ch 1, hdc2tog, work in pattern st as established across, turn—33 (39) sts.

Rows 13–18 (24): Maintaining color sequence as established, rep last 2 rows 3 (6) times—27 (27) sts at end of last row.

Row 19 (25): Rep row 13—26 (26) sts.

SIZES XL (2X, 3X, 4X, 5X) ONLY

Row 9 (9, 7, 3, 1) (WS): Ch 1, work in pattern st as established to last 3 sts, sk next st, hdc2tog, turn—48 (56, 60, 68, 74) sts.

Row 10 (10, 8, 4, 2) (RS): Ch 1, hdc2tog, sk next st, work in pattern st as established across, turn—46 (54, 58, 66, 72) sts.

Rows 11 (11, 9, 5, 3)–20 (24, 24, 24, 24): Maintaining color sequence as established, rep last 2 rows 5 (7, 8, 10, 11) times—26 (26, 26, 26, 28) sts.

SIZE 5X ONLY

Row 25: Rep row 1—26 sts.

ALL SIZES

Row 12 (20, 26, 21, 25, 25, 25, 26)–35 (38, 40, 41, 43, 44, 43, 43): Work even in pattern st as established.

Fasten off.

FINISHING

Block pieces to finished measurements.

Using locking mattress stitch (see Special Technique section, page 200), sew side and shoulder seams.

BUTTON LOOP

Join yarn at bottom point of neckline shaping on one Front, ch 8, remove hook from ch st, insert hook from front to back into same st as joining, put ch st back on hook and draw through st, work 12 sc in ch-8 sp, sl st in same st as joining, cut yarn, pull cut end through loop, and weave in ends securely.

Rep Button Loop on other Front panel.

BUTTON PLACEMENT

Sew button to inside of Right Front at the point where Button Loop of Left Front meets. Sew button to outside of Left Front at the point where Button Loop of Right Front meets.

Weave in ends.

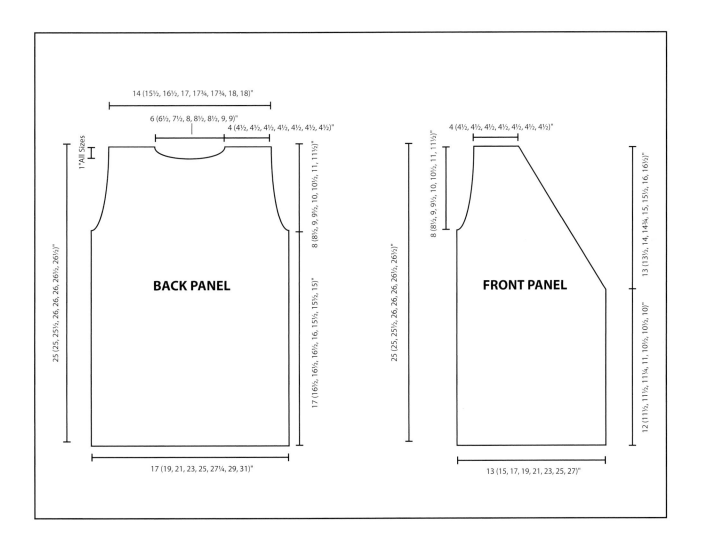

14 (15½, 16½, 17, 17¾, 17¾, 18, 18)"

6 (6½, 7½, 8, 8½, 8½, 9, 9)"

4 (4½, 4½, 4½, 4½, 4½, 4½, 4½)"

1" All Sizes

8 (8½, 9, 9½, 10, 10½, 11, 11½)"

BACK PANEL

25 (25, 25½, 26, 26, 26, 26½, 26½)"

17 (16½, 16½, 16, 15½, 15½, 15)"

17 (19, 21, 23, 25, 27¼, 29, 31)"

4 (4½, 4½, 4½, 4½, 4½, 4½, 4½)"

8 (8½, 9, 9½, 10, 10½, 11, 11½)"

13 (13½, 14, 14¾, 15, 15½, 16, 16½)"

FRONT PANEL

25 (25, 25½, 26, 26, 26, 26½, 26½)"

12 (11½, 11½, 11¼, 11, 10½, 10½, 10)"

13 (15, 17, 19, 21, 23, 25, 27)"

SOLID TANK

A good tank top is a must-have staple for your wardrobe and here we give you those classic tank lines with eye-catching detailing around the neckline, armholes, and hem for a clean, finished look. Layer it, dress it up ... however you wear it, make sure you make this one in a few different colors so you have one for every occasion from a day at the office to a weekend trip to a night out on the town.

SKILL LEVEL: Intermediate
SIZES: S (M, L, XL, 2X, 3X, 4X, 5X)
Sample shown in size small

FINISHED MEASUREMENTS

To Fit Bust: 32 (36, 40, 44, 48, 52, 56, 60) inches/81.5 (91.5, 101.5, 112, 122, 132, 142, 152.5) cm

Finished Bust: 34½ (38, 42, 46, 50, 54½, 58, 62) inches/87.5 (96.5, 106.5, 117, 127, 138.5, 147.5, 157.5) cm

Finished Length: 25¾ (25¾, 26¼, 26¾, 26¾, 27¼, 27¾, 27¾) inches/65.5 (65.5, 66.5, 68, 68, 69, 70.5, 70.5) cm

MATERIALS AND TOOLS

- Sample uses Crystal Palace, Panda Silk (52% Bamboo, 43% Superwash Merino Wool, 5% Combed Silk; 1.75 ounces/50 g = 204 yards/187m): 6 (7, 7, 8, 9, 9, 10, 10) skeins in color Mars Red #3033 or 1224 (1428, 1428, 1632, 1836, 1836, 2040, 2040) yards/1122 (1309, 1309, 1496, 1683, 1683, 1870, 1870) m of superfine weight yarn

- Crochet hooks: 2.75mm (size C-2) and 3.25mm (size D-3) or sizes to obtain gauge
- Yarn needle

BLOCKED GAUGES

Sc linen st var 1 with smaller hook: 41 sts = 5 inches/12.5 cm; 26 rows = 3¾ inches/9.5 cm

Bottom Border pattern with smaller hook: 31 sts = 5 inches/12.5cm

Always take time to check your gauge.

GAUGE SWATCHES

Bottom Border stitch swatch

Row 1: Work 31 Fsc, turn.

Row 2: Ch 1, sc in first st, *ch 1, sk next st, sc in next st; rep from * across, turn.

Row 3: Ch 1, hdc in first st, ch 1, yo, insert hook in next ch-1 sp, yo and draw up a loop even with loops on hook (3 loops on hook), yo, insert hook in Fsc one row below next sc, yo and draw up a loop even with loops on hook (5 loops on hook), yo, insert hook in next ch-1 sp, yo and draw up a loop even with loops on hook, yo and draw through all 7 loops on hook, ch 1, *yo, insert hook in same ch-1 sp as last st, yo and draw up a loop even with loops on hook (3 loops on hook), yo insert hook in Fsc one row below next sc, yo and draw up a loop even with loops on hook (5 loops on hook), yo, insert hook in next ch-1 sp, yo and draw up a loop even with loops on hook, yo and draw through al 7 loops on hook, ch 1; rep from * across to last sc, hdc in last sc, turn.

Row 4: Ch 1, hdc in first st, ch 1, work Beginning feather, ch 1, *feather, ch 1; rep from * across to last st, hdc in last st, turn.

Main Pattern stitch swatch

Transition row (RS): Ch 1, sc in each of first 2 sts, [2 sc in next st, sc in next 2 sts] 9 times, 2 sc in next st, sc 1.

Rows 1–26: Work in sc linen st var 1 pattern.

STITCH GUIDE

Foundation single crochet (Fsc): Ch 2, insert hook in 2nd ch from hook, yo and draw up a loop, yo and draw through 1 loop (first "chain" made), yo and draw through 2 loops on hook (first sc made), * insert hook under 2 loops of the "chain" just made, yo and draw up a loop, yo and draw through 1 loop ("chain" made), yo and draw through 2 loops on hook (sc made); rep from * for indicated number of foundation stitches.

Beginning feather: Yo, insert hook in last ch-1 space of previous rnd, yo and draw up a loop even with loops on hook (3 loops on hook), yo, insert hook in st or ch-1 sp one row below same sp, yo and draw up a loop even with loops on hook (5 loops on hook), yo, insert hook in next ch-1 sp, yo and draw up a loop even with loops on hook, yo and draw through all 7 loops on hook.

Feather: Yo, insert hook in same ch-1 sp as last feather, yo and draw up a loop even with loops on hook (3 loops on hook), yo, insert hook in skipped st or ch-1 sp one row below same sp, yo and draw up a loop even with loops on hook (5 loops on hook), yo, insert hook in next ch-1 sp, yo and draw up a loop even with loops on hook, yo and draw through all 7 loops on hook.

PATTERN STITCH

Bottom Border

For Master Chart Key, see page 206.

Feathered columns (any odd number of sts)

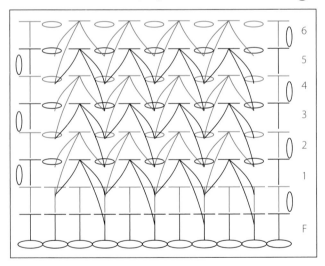

 Feathered columns stitch chart

Row 1: Work designated number of Fsc.

Row 2: Ch 1, sc in first st, *ch 1, sk next st, sc in next st; rep from * across, turn.

Row 3: Ch 1, hdc in first st, ch 1, yo, insert hook in next ch-1 sp, yo and draw up a loop even with loops on hook (3 loops on hook), yo, insert hook in Fsc one row below next sc, yo and draw up a loop even with loops on hook (5 loops on hook), yo, insert hook in next ch-1 sp, yo and draw up a loop even with loops on hook, yo and draw through all 7 loops on hook, ch 1, *yo, insert hook in same ch-1 sp as last st, yo and draw up a loop even with loops on hook (3 loops on hook), yo insert hook in Fsc one row below next sc, yo and draw up a loop even with loops on hook (5 loops on hook), yo, insert hook in next ch-1 sp, yo and draw up a loop even with loops on hook, yo and draw through al 7 loops on hook, ch 1; rep from * across to last Fsc, hdc in last Fsc, turn.

Row 4: Ch 1, hdc in first st, ch 1, work Beginning feather, ch 1, *feather, ch 1; rep from * across to last st, hdc in last st, turn.

Single crochet linen stitch variation 1 (sc linen st var 1) (worked on a multiple of 2 + 1 sts) **B**

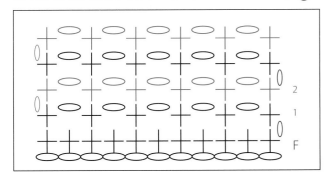

B Single crochet linen stitch variation 1 stitch chart

Row 1 (RS): Ch 1, sc in first st, *ch 1, sk next st, sc in next st; rep from * across, turn.

Row 2: Ch 1, sc in first st, *ch 1, sk next ch-1 sp, sc in next st; rep from * across, turn.

Rep row 2 for pattern.

SPECIAL TECHNIQUE

Locking mattress stitch (see Special Techniques, page 200)

INSTRUCTIONS

FRONT

BOTTOM BORDER

Row 1: With smaller hook, work 107 (119, 131, 143, 155, 169, 181, 193) Fsc, turn.

Row 2: Ch 1, sc in first st, *ch 1, sk next st, sc in next st; rep from * across, turn.

Row 3: Ch 1, hdc in first st, ch 1, yo, insert hook in next ch-1 sp, yo and draw up a loop even with loops on hook (3 loops on hook), yo, insert hook in Fsc one row below next sc, yo and draw up a loop even with loops on hook (5 loops on hook), yo, insert hook in next ch-1 sp, yo and draw up a loop even with loops on hook, yo and draw through all 7 loops on hook, ch 1, *yo, insert hook in same ch-1 sp as last st, yo and draw up a loop even with loops on hook (3 loops on hook), yo insert hook in Fsc one row below next sc, yo and draw up a loop even with loops on hook (5 loops on hook), yo, insert hook in next ch-1 sp, yo and draw up a loop even with loops on hook, yo and draw through all 7 loops on hook, ch 1; rep from * across to last Fsc, hdc in last Fsc, turn.

Row 4: Ch 1, hdc in first st, ch 1, work Beginning feather, ch 1, *feather, ch 1; rep from * across to last st, hdc in last st, turn.

MAIN BODY

Row 1 (RS): Ch 1, sc in each of first 4 (4, 4, 4, 4, 5, 5, 5) sts, [2 sc in next st, sc in each of next 2 sts] 33 (37, 41, 45, 49, 53, 57, 61) times, 2 sc in next st, sc in each of next 3 (3, 3, 3, 3, 4, 4, 4) sts, turn—141 (157, 173, 189, 205, 223, 239, 255) sts.

Row 2: Ch 1, sc in first st, *ch 1, sk next st, sc in next st; rep from * across, turn.

Row 3: Ch 1, sc in first st, *ch 1, sk next ch-1 sp, sc in next st; rep from * across, turn.

Rows 4–126 (122, 122, 122, 118, 118, 118, 114): Rep row 3.

BEGIN ARMHOLE AND NECKLINE SHAPING

FIRST SIDE

Row 1 (RS): Ch 1, sl st in first 9 (11, 12, 12, 15, 15, 15, 17) sts, ch 1, work in pattern st as established across next 55 (59, 66, 74, 77, 86, 94, 100) sts, turn, leaving 77 (87, 95, 103, 113, 112, 130, 138) sts unworked—55 (59, 66, 74, 77, 86, 94, 100) sts.

Row 2 (WS): Ch 1, sc2tog, work in pattern st as established to last 2 sts, sc2tog, turn—53 (57, 64, 72, 75, 84, 92, 98) sts.

Row 3 (RS): Ch 1, sk first st, sc2tog, work in pattern st as established to last 3 sts, sk next st, sc2tog, turn—49 (53, 60, 68, 71, 80 88, 94) sts.

Rows 4–9 (9, 11, 13, 13, 13, 13, 13): Rep last 2 rows 3 (3, 4, 5, 5, 5, 5, 5) more times—31 (35, 36, 38, 41, 50, 58, 64) sts at end of last row.

SIZES XL (2X, 3X, 4X, 5X) ONLY

CONTINUE ARMHOLE SHAPING

Row 14 (WS): Ch 1, work in pattern st as established to last 2 sts, sc2tog, turn—37 (40, 49, 57, 63) sts.

Row 15 (RS): Ch 1, sk first st, sc2tog, work in pattern st as established to end of row, turn—35 (38, 47, 55, 61) sts.

SIZES 2X (3X, 4X, 5X) ONLY

Rows 16–17 (23, 27, 31): Rep last 2 rows 1 (4, 6, 8) more times—35 (35, 37, 37) sts at end of last row.

SIZES S (M, L) ONLY

CONTINUE NECKLINE SHAPING

Row 10 (10, 12) (WS): Ch 1, sc2tog, work in pattern st as established to end of row, turn—30 (34, 35) sts.

Row 11 (11, 13) (RS): Ch 1, work in pattern st as established to last 3 sts, sk next st sc2tog, turn—28 (32, 33) sts.

SIZES S (M) ONLY

Rows 12 and 13: Rep last 2 rows (once)—25 (29) sts.

ALL SIZES

Rows 14 (14, 14, 16, 18, 24, 28, 32)–48 (52, 55, 58, 62, 66, 69, 73): Work even in pattern st as established. Fasten off.

SECOND SIDE

With RS facing, sk first 13 (17, 17, 17, 21, 21, 21, 21) unworked sts at center of neckline, join yarn in next st; first st of row 1 is worked in same st as joining.

Row 1 (RS): Ch 1, work in pattern st as established across next 55 (59, 66, 74, 77, 86, 94, 100) sts, turn, leaving last 9 (11, 12, 12, 15, 15, 15, 17) sts unworked—55 (59, 66, 74, 77, 86, 94, 100) sts.

Row 2 (WS): Ch 1, sc2tog, work in pattern st as established to last 2 sts, sc2tog, turn—53 (57, 64, 72, 75, 84, 92, 98) sts.

Row 3 (RS): Ch 1, sk first st, sc2tog, work in pattern st as established to last 3 sts, sk next st, sc2tog, turn—49 (53, 60, 68, 71, 80 88, 94) sts.

Rows 4–9 (9, 11, 13, 13, 13, 13, 13): Rep last 2 rows 3 (3, 4, 5, 5, 5, 5) times—31 (35, 36, 38, 41, 50, 58, 64) sts.

SIZES XL (2X, 3X, 4X, 5X) ONLY

CONTINUE ARMHOLE SHAPING

Row 14 (WS): Ch 1, sc2tog, work in pattern st as established to end of row, turn—37 (40, 49, 57, 63) sts.

Row 15 (RS): Ch 1, work in pattern st as established to last 3 sts, sk next st, sc2tog, turn—35 (38, 47, 55, 61) sts.

SIZES 2X (3X, 4X, 5X) ONLY

Rows 16–17 (23, 27, 31): Rep last 2 rows 1 (4, 6, 8) times—35 (35, 37, 37) sts

SIZES S (M, L) ONLY

CONTINUE NECKLINE SHAPING

Row 10 (10, 12) (WS): Ch 1, work in pattern st as established to last 2 sts, sc2tog, turn—30 (34, 35) sts.

Row 11 (11, 13) (RS): Ch 1, sc2tog, sk next st, work in pattern st as established to end of row, turn—28 (32, 33) sts.

SIZES S (M) ONLY

Rows 12 and 13: Rep last 2 rows (once)—25 (29) sts at end of last row.

ALL SIZES

Rows 14 (14, 14, 16, 18, 24, 28, 32)–48 (52, 55, 58, 62, 66, 69, 73): Work even in pattern st as established. Fasten off.

BACK

Work as for Front to Armhole Shaping.

BEGIN ARMHOLE SHAPING

Row 1 (RS): Ch 1, sl st in first 9 (11, 12, 12, 15, 15, 15, 17) sts, ch 1, work in pattern st as established across to last 9 (11, 12, 12, 15, 15, 15, 17) sts, turn, leaving last 9 (11, 12, 12, 15, 15, 15, 17) sts unworked—123 (135, 149, 165, 175, 193, 209, 221) sts.

Row 2 (WS): Ch 1, sc2tog, work in pattern st as established to last 2 sts, sc2tog, turn—121 (133, 147, 163, 173, 191, 207, 219) sts.

Row 3 (RS): Ch 1, sk first st, sc2tog, work in pattern st as established to last 3 sts, sk next st, sc2tog, turn—117 (129, 143, 159, 169, 187, 203, 215) sts.

Rows 4–9 (9, 11, 15, 17, 23, 27, 31): Rep last 2 rows 3 (3, 4, 6, 7, 10, 12, 14) times—99 (111, 119, 123, 127, 127, 131, 131) sts.

Rows 10 (10, 12, 16, 18, 24, 28, 32)–40 (44, 46, 50, 54, 58, 60, 64): Work even in pattern st as established.

BEGIN BACK NECKLINE SHAPING

FIRST SIDE

Row 1 (RS): Ch 1, work in pattern st as established across 37 (41, 45, 47, 47, 47, 49, 49) sts, turn, leaving 62 (70, 74, 76, 80, 80, 82, 82) sts unworked—37 (41, 45, 47, 47, 47, 49, 49) sts.

Row 2: Ch 1, sk first st, sc2tog, work in pattern st as established to end of row, turn—35 (39, 43, 45, 45, 45, 47, 47) sts.

Row 3: Ch 1, work in pattern st as established to last 3 sts, sk next st, sc2tog, turn—33 (37, 41, 43, 43, 43, 45, 45) sts.

Rows 4–7: Rep last 2 rows 2 more times—25 (29, 33, 35, 35, 35, 37, 37) sts at end of last row.

Row 8: Work even in pattern st as established.

SIZES S (M, XL, 2X, 3X) ONLY

Fasten off.

SIZES L (4X, 5X) ONLY

Row 9: Work even in pattern st as established.

Fasten off.

SECOND SIDE

With RS facing, sk first 25 (29, 29, 29, 33, 33, 33, 33) unworked sts at center of neckline, join yarn in next st; first st of row 1 is worked in same st as joining.

Row 1 (RS): Ch 1, work in pattern st as established to end of row, turn—37 (41, 45, 47, 47, 47, 49, 49) sts.

Row 2: Ch 1, work in pattern st as established to last 3 sts, sk next st, sc2tog, turn—35 (39, 43, 45, 45, 45, 47, 47) sts.

Row 3: Ch 1, sk first st, sc2tog, work in pattern st as established to end of row, turn—33 (37, 41, 43, 43, 43, 45, 45) sts.

Rows 4–7: Rep last 2 rows 2 more times—25 (29, 33, 35, 35, 35, 37, 37) sts at end of last row.

Row 8: Work even in pattern st as established.

SIZES S (M, XL, 2X, 3X) ONLY

Fasten off.

SIZES L (4X, 5X) ONLY

Row 9: Work even in pattern st as established.

Fasten off.

FINISHING

Block pieces to finished measurements.

Sew shoulder and side seams with locking mattress stitch (see Special Techniques section, page 200).

NECKLINE AND ARMHOLE BORDER

With larger hook, join yarn in side of first st after seam, insert hook in same st as joining, yo and draw up a loop (2 loops on hook), insert hook in side of third st in from end of next row, yo and draw up a loop to height of first loop on hook (3 loops on hook), insert hook in side of st of next row, yo and draw up a loop (4 loops on hook), yo and draw through all 4 loops on hook, ch 1, *insert hook in same st just worked, yo and draw up a loop (2 loops on hook), insert hook in side of third st in from end of row, yo and draw up a loop to height of first loop on hook (3 loops on hook), insert hook inside of st of next row, yo and draw up a loop (4 loops on hook), yo and draw through all 4 loops on hook, ch 1; rep from * evenly around neckline. Fasten off. Join with duplicate stitch.

Rep Border around each armhole.

Gently re-block neckline and armhole borders if needed.

Weave in ends.

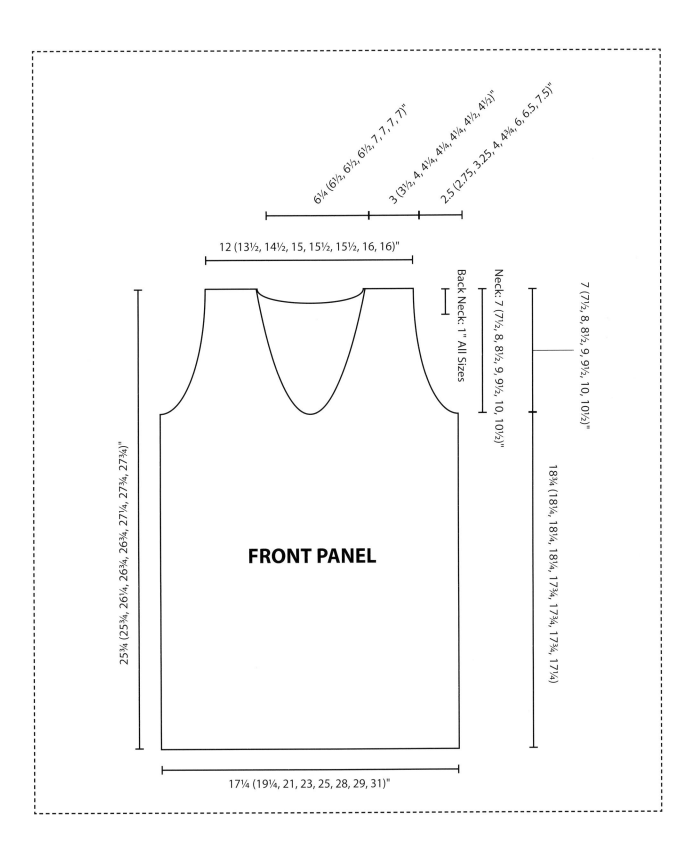

6¼ (6½, 6½, 6½, 7, 7, 7, 7)"

3 (3½, 4, 4¼, 4¼, 4¼, 4½, 4½)"

2.5 (2.75, 3.25, 4, 4¾, 6, 6.5, 7.5)"

12 (13½, 14½, 15, 15½, 15½, 16, 16)"

Back Neck: 1" All Sizes

Neck: 7 (7½, 8, 8½, 9, 9½, 10, 10½)"

7 (7½, 8, 8½, 9, 9½, 10, 10½)"

18¾ (18¼, 18¼, 18¼, 17¾, 17¾, 17¾, 17¼)

25¾ (25¾, 26¼, 26¾, 27¼, 27¾, 27¾)"

FRONT PANEL

17¼ (19¼, 21, 23, 25, 28, 29, 31)"

LACE TANK

This piece combines the classic tank top shape that is a staple for any wardrobe with our unique Non-stick lace pattern stitch. Wear your tank top layered with a contrasting color to show off your lace stitches, or wear it under a jacket to give just a hint of feminine lace for a great daytime or evening look.

SKILL LEVEL: Intermediate
SIZES: S (M, L, XL, 2X, 3X, 4X, 5X)
Sample shown in size small

FINISHED MEASUREMENTS

To Fit Bust: 32 (36, 40, 44, 48, 52, 56, 60) inches/81.5 (91.5, 101.5, 112, 122, 132, 142, 152.5) cm
Finished Bust: 35 (39, 43½, 47½, 52, 56, 60, 64) inches/89 (99, 110.5, 120.5, 132, 142, 152.5, 162.5) cm
Finished Length: 25 (25, 25½, 26, 26, 26½, 27, 27½) inches/63.5 (63.5, 65, 66, 66, 67.5, 68.5, 70) cm

MATERIALS AND TOOLS

- Sample uses Crystal Palace, Panda Silk (52% Bamboo, 43% Superwash Merino Wool, 5% Combed Silk; 1.75 ounces/50 g = 204 yards/187 m): 5 (6, 6, 7, 7, 8, 8, 9) skeins color Ocean #3036 or 1020 (1224, 1224, 1428, 1428, 1632, 1632, 1836) yards/935 (1122, 1122, 1309, 1309, 1496, 1496, 1683) m of superfine weight yarn

- Crochet hook: 3.25mm (size D-3) or size to obtain gauge
- Yarn needle

BLOCKED GAUGE

Non-stick lace pattern: 47 sts = 6½ inches/16.5 cm; 14 rows = 5¾ inches/14.5 cm

Always take time to check your gauge.

GAUGE SWATCH

Non-stick lace stitch swatch

Row 1: Work 47 Fsc, turn.

Row 2: First-tr in first st, *yo, [insert hook in next st, yo and pull up a loop to height of First-tr] 5 times (7 loops on hook), yo and draw through 6 loops on hook, yo and draw through rem 2 loops on hook, 4 sc in under top layer of last 6 loops of cluster; rep from * across to last st, tr in last st, turn.

Row 3: Ch 1, sc in each st across, turn.

Rows 4–15: Rep rows 2 and 3 (6 times).

Fasten off.

STITCH GUIDE

Foundation single crochet (Fsc): Ch 2, insert hook in 2nd ch from hook, yo and draw up a loop, yo and draw through 1 loop (first "chain" made), yo and draw through 2 loops on hook (first sc made), * insert hook under 2 loops of the "chain" just made, yo and draw up a loop, yo and draw through 1 loop ("chain" made), yo and draw through 2 loops on hook (sc made); rep from * for indicated number of foundation sts.

First treble crochet (First-tr): Sc in first st, ch 3. Note: Use this st whenever the first st of a row is a tr.

Treble crochet 2 together (tr2tog): Yo (twice), insert hook in next st, yo and draw up a loop, yo and draw through 2 loops on hook, yo, insert hook in next st, yo and draw up a loop, yo and draw through 4 loops on hook, yo and draw through 2 loops on hook.

PATTERN STITCH

For Master Chart Key, see page 206.

Non-stick lace variation 1 (worked on a multiple of 5 + 2 sts) Ⓐ

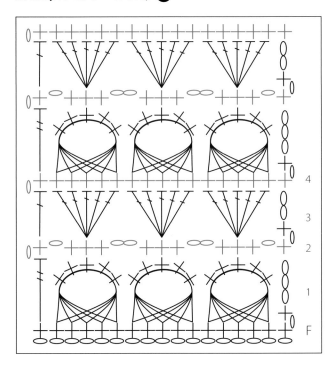

Ⓐ Non-stick lace variation 1 stitch chart

Row 1 (RS): First-tr in first st, *yo, [insert hook in next st, yo and pull up a loop to height of First-tr] 5 times (7 loops on hook), yo and draw through 6 loops on hook, yo and draw through rem 2 loops on hook, 4 sc in under top layer of last 6 loops of cluster; rep from * across to last st, tr in last st, turn.

Row 2: Ch 1, sc in each st across, turn.

Rep rows 1 and 2 for pattern.

SPECIAL TECHNIQUE

Locking mattress stitch (see Special Techniques, page 200)

NOTES

1. Left Side and Right Side refer to left and right side as worn.
2. When instructed to work in a pattern stitch "as established," work the next row of pattern stitch and ensure that the stitches line up as in previous rows.
3. When decreasing in broomstick lace pattern stitch, fill ends of row with tr before and after pattern sts.

INSTRUCTIONS

FRONT

Foundation Row: Work 127 (142, 157, 172, 187, 202, 217, 232) Fsc, turn.

Rows 1–48 (46, 46, 46, 44, 44, 44, 44): Work even in Non-stick lace pattern st.

BEGIN ARMHOLE AND NECKLINE SHAPING

FIRST SIDE

Row 1 (RS): Ch 1, sl st in first 8 (10, 11, 14, 14, 15, 21, 22) sts, First-tr, work in pattern st as established across next 47 (50, 57, 62, 67, 74, 75, 82) sts, tr in next st, turn, leaving last 70 (80, 87, 94, 104, 111, 119, 126) sts unworked—49 (52, 59, 64, 69, 76, 77, 84) sts.

Row 2 (WS): Ch 1, sc in first st, sc2tog, work in pattern st as established to last 3 sts, sc2tog, sc in last st, turn—47 (50, 57, 62, 67, 74, 75, 82) sts.

Row 3 (RS): First-tr in first st, sk next st, tr2tog, work in pattern st as established to last 4 sts, tr2tog, sk next st, tr in last st, turn—43 (46, 53, 58, 63, 70 71, 78) sts.

Rows 4–9 (9, 11, 11, 11, 11, 11, 11): Rep last 2 rows 3 (3, 4, 4, 4, 4, 4, 4) times—25 (28, 29, 34, 39, 46, 47, 54) sts at end of last row.

SIZES S (M) ONLY

CONTINUE NECKLINE DECREASES

Row 10 (WS): Ch 1, sc in first st, sc2tog, work in pattern st as established to end of row, turn—24 (27) sts.

Row 11 (RS): Ch 1, work in pattern st as established to last 4 sts, tr2tog, sk next st, tr in last st, turn—22 (25) sts.

SIZES XL (2X, 3X, 4X, 5X) ONLY

CONTINUE ARMHOLE SHAPING

Row 12 (WS): Ch 1, work in pattern st as established to last 3 sts, sc2tog, sc in last st, turn—33 (38, 45, 46, 53) sts.

Row 13 (RS): Ch 1, First-tr, sk next st, tr2tog, work in pattern st as established to end of row, turn—31 (36, 43, 44, 51) sts.

SIZES 2X (3X, 4X, 5X) ONLY

Rows 14–17 (21, 21, 25): Rep last 2 rows 2 (4, 4, 6) times—30 (31, 32, 33) sts at end of last row.

ALL SIZES

Rows 12 (12, 12, 14, 18, 22, 22, 26)–18 (20, 21, 22, 24, 25, 26, 27): Work even in pattern st as established. Fasten off.

SECOND SIDE

With RS facing, skip first 13 (18, 17, 16, 21, 20, 21, 20) unworked sts at center of neckline, join yarn in next st; first st of row 1 is worked in same st as joining.

Row 1 (RS): First-tr in first st, work in pattern st as established across next 47 (50, 57, 62, 67, 74, 75, 82) sts, tr in next st, turn, leaving rem 8 (10, 11, 14, 14, 15, 21, 22) sts unworked—49 (52, 59, 64, 69, 76, 77, 84) sts.

Row 2 (WS): Ch 1, sc in first st, sc2tog, work in pattern st as established to last 3 sts, sc2tog, sc in last st, turn—47 (50, 57, 62, 67, 74, 75, 82) sts.

Row 3: First-tr in first st, sk next st, tr2tog, work in pattern st as established to last 4 sts, tr2tog, sk next st, tr in last st, turn—43 (46, 53, 58, 63, 70 71, 78) sts.

Rows 4–9 (9, 11, 11, 11, 11, 11, 11): Rep last 2 rows 3 (3, 4, 4, 4, 4, 4, 4) times—25 (28, 29, 34, 39, 46, 47, 54) sts at end of last row.

SIZES S (M) ONLY

CONTINUE NECKLINE DECREASES

Row 10 (WS): Ch 1, work in pattern st as established to last 3 sts, sc2tog, sc in last st, turn—24 (27) sts.

Row 11 (RS): Ch 1, First-tr, sk next st, tr2tog, work in pattern st as established to end of row, turn—22 (25) sts.

SIZES XL (2X, 3X, 4X, 5X) ONLY

CONTINUE ARMHOLE SHAPING

Row 12 (WS): Ch 1, sc in first st, sc2tog, work in pattern st as established to end of row, turn—33 (38, 45, 46, 53) sts.

Row 13 (RS): Ch 1, work in pattern st as established to last 4 sts, tr2tog, sk next st, tr in last st, turn—31 (36, 43, 44, 51) sts.

SIZES 2X (3X, 4X, 5X) ONLY

Rows 14–17 (21, 21, 25): Rep last 2 rows 2 (4, 4, 6) times—30 (31, 32, 33) sts at end of last row.

ALL SIZES

Rows 12 (12, 12, 14, 18, 22, 22, 26)–18 (20, 21, 22, 24, 25, 26, 27): Work even in pattern st as established. Fasten off.

BACK

Work as for Front to Armhole Shaping

BEGIN ARMHOLE SHAPING

Row 1 (RS): Ch 1, sl st in first 8 (10, 11, 14, 14, 15, 21, 22) sts, First-tr in first st, work in pattern st as established to last 9 (11, 12, 15, 15, 16, 22, 23) sts, tr in next st, turn, leaving last 8 (10, 11, 14, 14, 15, 21, 22) sts unworked—111 (122, 135, 144, 159, 172, 175, 188) sts.

Row 2 (WS): Ch 1, sc in first st, sc2tog, work in pattern st as established to last 3 sts, sc2tog, sc in last st, turn—109 (120, 133, 142, 157, 170, 173, 186) sts.

Row 3 (RS): First-tr in first st, sk next st, tr2tog, work in pattern st as established to last 4 sts, tr2tog, sk next st, tr in last st, turn—105 (116, 129, 138, 153, 166, 169, 182) sts.

Rows 4–9 (9, 11, 13, 17, 21, 21, 25): Rep last 2 rows 3 (3, 4, 5, 7, 9, 9, 11) times—87 (98, 105, 108, 111, 112, 115, 116) sts at end of last row.

Rows 10 (10, 12, 14, 18, 22, 22, 26)–18 (20, 21, 22, 24, 25, 26, 27): Work even in pattern st as established.
Fasten off.

FINISHING

Block pieces to schematic measurements.
Using locking mattress stitch, sew shoulder and side seams.
Weave in ends.

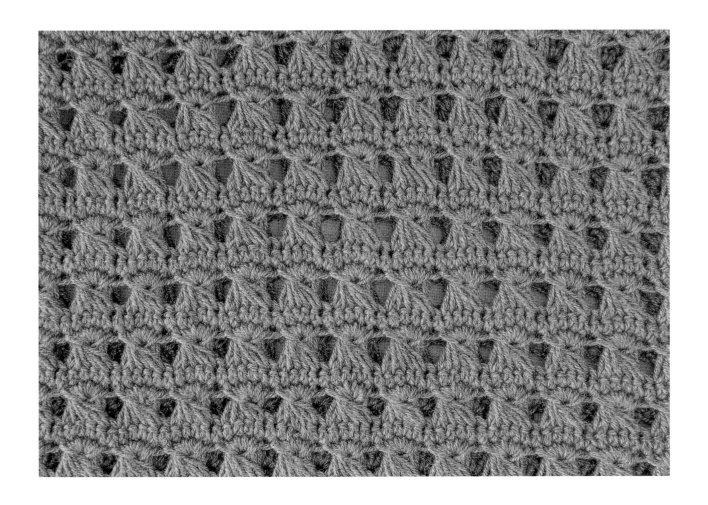

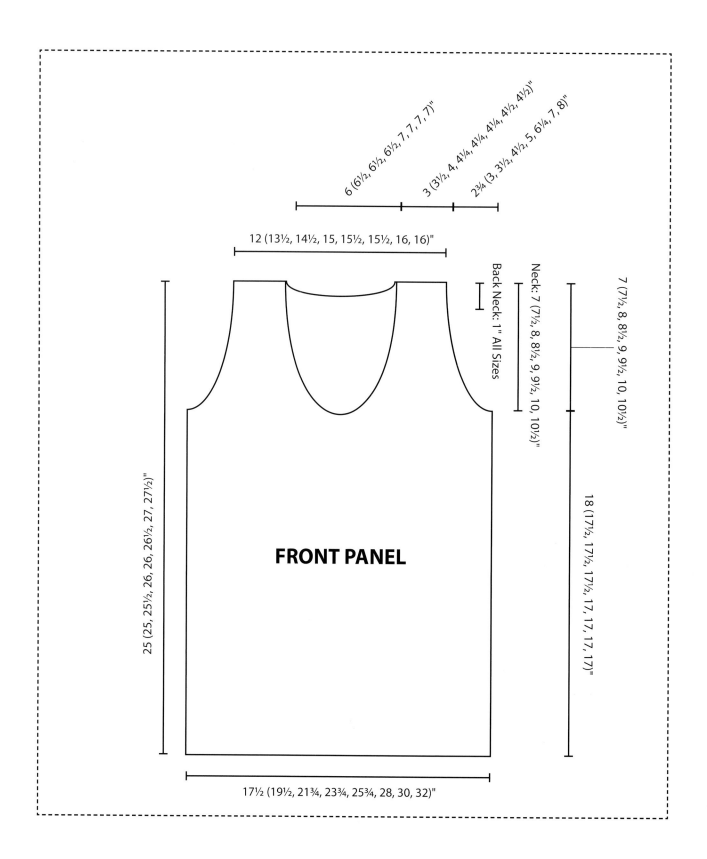

6 (6½, 6½, 7, 7, 7, 7)"

3 (3½, 4, 4¼, 4¼, 4¼, 4½)"

2¾ (3, 3½, 4½, 5, 6¼, 7, 8)"

12 (13½, 14½, 15, 15½, 15½, 16, 16)"

Back Neck: 1" All Sizes

Neck: 7 (7½, 8, 8½, 9, 9½, 10, 10½)"

7 (7½, 8, 8½, 9, 9½, 10, 10½)"

25 (25, 25½, 26, 26, 26½, 27, 27½)"

FRONT PANEL

18 (17½, 17½, 17½, 17, 17, 17, 17)"

17½ (19½, 21¾, 23¾, 25¾, 28, 30, 32)"

ACCESSORIES

CABLED TRIO:

SHORT SLEEVE CARDI
ARM WARMERS
BOOT TOPPERS

Stylish details like the graphic offset V-Cable stitches, tapered ribbed collar, elongated ribbed waist, and ribbed armhole borders give this sleeveless cardi a bit of an edge. While those same eye-catching details carry over to the coordinating arm warmers and boot toppers, creating an overall look that is classy and cohesive.

BLOCKED GAUGES

Herringbone hdc pattern st with larger hook: 30 sts = 6¼ inches/16 cm; 17 rows = 4¼ inches/11 cm

V-Cables Panel pattern st with larger hook: 18 sts = 3½ inches/9 cm; 18 rows = 4½ inches/11.5 cm

Sc ribbing pattern with smaller hook: 32 sts = 5 inches/12.5 cm; 29 rows = 4¼ inches/11 cm

Always take time to check your gauge.

GAUGE SWATCHES

Herringbone hdc stitch swatch

Row 1: With larger hook, work 30 Fhdc, turn.

Rows 2–17: Work in Herringbone hdc pattern st.

V-Cables stitch swatch

Row 1 (RS): With larger hook, work 18 Fhdc, turn.

Rows 2–17: Work rows 2–5 of V-Cables pattern st (4 times).

Row 18: Ch 1, hdc in each st across.

Sc ribbing stitch swatch

Row 1: With smaller hook, 32 Fsc, turn.

Rows 2–29: Work in sc ribbing pattern st.

STITCH GUIDE

Foundation single crochet (Fsc): Ch 2, insert hook in 2nd ch from hook, yo and draw up a loop, yo and draw through 1 loop (first "chain" made), yo and draw through 2 loops on hook (first sc made), *insert hook under 2 loops of the "chain" just made, yo and draw up a loop, yo and draw through 1 loop ("chain" made), yo and draw through 2 loops on hook (sc made); rep from * for indicated number of foundation sts.

Foundation half double crochet (Fhdc): Ch 3, yo, insert hook in 3rd ch from hook, yo and draw up a loop, yo and draw through 1 loop (first "chain" made), yo and draw through all 3 loops on hook (first hdc made), *yo, insert hook under 2 loops of the "chain" just made, yo and draw up a loop, yo and draw through 1 loop ("chain" made), yo and draw through all 3 loops on hook (hdc made); rep from * for indicated number of foundation sts.

Half double crochet 2 together (hdc2tog): Yo, insert hook in next st and pull up a loop, insert hook in next st and pull up a loop, yo and draw through all 4 loops on hook.

Single crochet 2 together (sc2tog): Insert hook in next st and pull up a loop, insert hook in next st and pull up a loop, yo and draw through all 3 loops on hook.

Front Post treble crochet (FPtr): Yo (twice), insert hook from front to back and then to front again around post of indicated stitch 2 rows below, yo and draw up a loop, [yo and draw through 2 loops on hook] 3 times.

2-over-2 FPtr left cross cable (worked over 4 sts): Sk next 2 sts, FPtr around the post of each of next 2 sts 2 rows below; working in front of FPtr just made, FPtr around the post of each of 2 skipped sts 2 rows below.

PATTERN STITCHES

For Master Chart Key, see page 206.

Herringbone half double crochet (Hhdc)

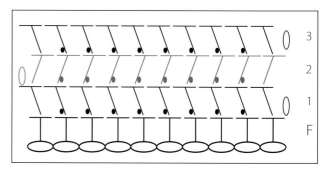

 Herringbone half double crochet stitch chart

Row 1: Ch 1, hdc in first st, *yo, insert hook in next st, yo and draw up a loop through st and first loop on hook, yo, draw up a loop through both loops on hook; rep from * across to last st, hdc in last st, turn.

Rep row 1 for pattern.

V-Cables Panel (worked over 18 sts) **B**

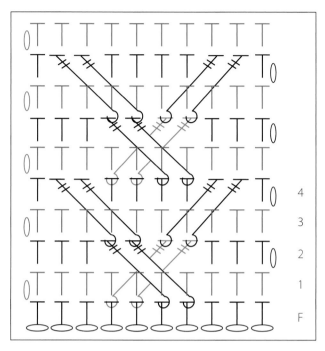

B V-Cables Panel stitch chart

Row 1 (RS): Hdc in each st across.

Row 2 (WS): Hdc in each st across.

Row 3 (RS): Hdc in next st, [hdc in each of next 2 sts, work 2-over-2 FPtr left cross cable, hdc in each of next 2 sts] twice, hdc in next st.

Row 4 (WS): Rep row 2.

Row 5 (RS): Hdc in next st, [sk next 2 sts, FPtr around the post of each of next 2 FPtr sts 2 rows below, hdc in each of next 4 sts, FPtr around the post of each of previous FPtr sts 2 rows below] twice, hdc in next st.

Rep rows 2–5 for pattern.

Single crochet ribbing (sc ribbing) **C**

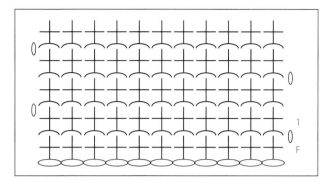

C Single crochet ribbing stitch chart

Row 1: Ch 1, sc in both loops of first st, sc-tbl in each st across to last st, sc in both loops of last st, turn.

Rep row 1 for pattern.

SPECIAL TECHNIQUE

Locking mattress stitch (see Special Techniques, page 200)

NOTES

Short Sleeve Cardi

1. When instructed to work in st 2 rows below, insert hook in or around indicated stitch in the row numbered 2 less than the row you are working. For example, if you are working row 5, a stitch "2 rows" below is in row 5 – 2 = row 3.

2. Left Side and Right Side refer to left and right side as worn.

3. On front panels, V-Cables Panel pattern stitch is worked on the 18 sts on the front border edge, and all other stitches are worked as Herringbone Hdc pattern stitch. When instructed to "work in pattern st as established," maintain the 18 stitch and 4-row pattern repeat for V-Cables Panel pattern stitch as well as the Herringbone Hdc pattern stitch.

4. Always skip stitch in current row behind each post stitch worked.

Arm Warmers

1. Ribbing section is made from side to side, then stitches are worked into the side of the end stitches of the ribbing rows for the forearm/wrist section.
2. Forearm/wrist section is worked in turned rounds. Turned rounds are worked back and forth like rows but joined with a slip stitch like rounds before turning.
3. When instructed to work in st 2 rows below, insert hook in or around indicated stitch in the row numbered 2 less than the row you are working. For example, if you are working row 5, a stitch "2 rows" below is in row 5 – 2 = row 3.
4. Always skip stitch in current row behind each post stitch worked.

Boot Toppers

1. When instructed to work in stitch 2 rows below, insert hook in or around indicated stitch in the row numbered 2 less than the row you are working. For example, if you are working row 5, a stitch "2 rows" below is in row 5 – 2 = row 3.
2. Always skip stitch in current row behind each post stitch worked.

CABLED TRIO SHORT SLEEVE CARDI

SKILL LEVEL: Intermediate
SIZES: S (M, L, XL, 2X, 3X, 4X, 5X)
Sample shown in size large

FINISHED MEASUREMENTS

To Fit Bust: 32 (36, 40, 44, 48, 52, 56, 60) inches/81.5 (91.5, 101.5, 112, 122, 132, 142, 152.5) cm
Finished Bust: 36 (40, 44, 48, 52, 56, 60, 64) inches/91.5 (101.5, 112, 122, 132, 142, 152.5, 162.5) cm
Finished Length: 30 (30, 30½, 31, 31, 31, 31½, 31½) inches/76 (76, 77.5, 79, 79, 79, 80, 80) cm

MATERIALS AND TOOLS

■ Sample shown in Knit Picks Stroll Fingering (75% Superwash Merino Wool, 25% Nylon; 3.5 ounces/100g = 231 yards/211 m): 7 (8, 9, 10, 10, 11, 12, 13) skeins in color Firecracker Heather #24587 or 1617 (1848, 2079, 2310, 2310, 2541, 2772, 3003) yards/1477 (1688, 1899, 2110, 2110, 2321, 2532, 2743) m of superfine weight yarn

■ Crochet hooks: 3.25mm (size D-3) and 3.5mm (size E-4) or sizes to obtain gauge
■ Yarn needle
■ Pins or locking stitch markers
■ Separating zipper: 23 (22½, 22½, 22½, 22, 21½, 21½, 21) inches/58.5 (57, 57, 57, 56, 54.5, 54.5, 53.5) cm long

INSTRUCTIONS

BACK PANEL

RIBBING

Row 1: With smaller hook, work 19 Fsc, turn.

Rows 2–124 (136, 151, 165, 178, 192, 205, 219): Work in sc ribbing pattern stitch. Do not fasten off. At end of last row, rotate work ¼ turn to the right for working in row-end sts of ribbing.

MAIN BODY

Row 1 (RS): With larger hook, ch 1, working in row-end sts of ribbing, hdc in each of first 7 (9, 9, 10, 10, 11, 12, 13) sts, [hdc2tog, hdc in next st] 36 (39, 44, 48, 52, 56, 60, 64) times, hdc2tog, hdc in each of next 7 (8, 8, 9, 10, 11, 11, 12) sts, turn—87 (96, 106, 116, 125, 135, 144, 154) sts.

Rows 2–80 (78, 78, 78, 76, 74, 74, 72): Work in Hhdc pattern st.

BEGIN BACK ARMHOLE SHAPING

Row 1 (RS): Ch 1, sl st in each of first 5 (6, 6, 6, 6, 5, 5, 7) sts, ch 1, hdc2tog, work in pattern st across to last 8 (9, 9, 9, 8, 8, 10) sts, hdc2tog, turn, leaving last 5 (6, 6, 6, 6, 5, 5, 7) sts unworked—75 (82, 92, 102, 111, 123, 132, 138) sts.

Row 2: Ch 1, hdc in first st, hdc2tog, work in pattern st across to last 3 sts, hdc2tog, hdc in last st, turn—73 (80, 90, 100, 109, 121, 130, 136) sts.

Row 3: Ch 1, hdc in first st, [hdc2tog in next 2 sts] twice, work in pattern st across to last 5 sts, [hdc2tog in next 2 sts] twice, hdc in last st, turn—69 (76, 86, 96, 105, 117, 126, 132) sts.

SIZES L (XL, 2X, 3X, 4X, 5X) ONLY

Rows 4–5 (7, 9, 13, 15, 17): Rep last 2 rows 1 (2, 3, 5, 6, 7) times—80 (84, 87, 87, 90, 90) sts.

ALL SIZES

Rows 4 (4, 6, 8, 10, 14, 16, 18)–28 (30, 32, 34, 36, 38, 40, 42): Work in pattern st.

Fasten off.

LEFT FRONT PANEL

RIBBING

Row 1: With smaller hook, work 19 Fsc, turn.

Rows 2–62 (69, 75, 82, 89, 96, 103, 109): Work in sc ribbing pattern st.

Do not fasten off. At end of last row, rotate work ¼ turn to the right for working in row-end sts of ribbing.

MAIN BODY

Row 1 (RS): With larger hook, ch 1, working in row-end sts of ribbing, hdc in each of first 6 (7, 7, 7, 8, 8, 9, 9) sts, [hdc2tog, hdc in next st] 16 (18, 20, 22, 24, 26, 28, 30) times, hdc2tog, hdc in each of next 6 (6, 6, 7, 7, 8, 8, 8) sts, turn—45 (50, 54, 59, 64, 69, 74, 78) sts.

Row 2 (WS): Ch 1, work row 2 of V-Cables Panel over first 18 sts, then continue in Hhdc pattern st across, turn.

Row 3: Ch 1, work in Hhdc pattern st across to last 18 sts, work row 3 of V-Cables Panel over last 18 sts, turn.

Rows 4–80 (78, 78, 78, 76, 74, 74, 72): Work in V-Cables pattern st and Hhdc pattern st as established.

BEGIN ARMHOLE AND FRONT NECKLINE SHAPING

Row 1 (RS): Ch 1, sl st in each of first 5 (6, 6, 6, 6, 5, 5, 7) sts, ch 1, hdc2tog, work in pattern st across to last 3 sts, hdc2tog, hdc in last st, turn—38 (42, 46, 51, 56, 62, 67, 69) sts.

Row 2 (WS): Ch 1, hdc in first st, hdc2tog, work in pattern st to last 3 sts, hdc2tog, hdc in last st, turn—36 (40, 44, 49, 54, 60, 65, 67) sts.

Row 3: Ch 1, hdc in first st, [hdc2tog in next 2 sts] twice, work in pattern st to last 3 sts, hdc2tog, hdc in last st, turn—33 (37, 41, 46, 51, 57, 62, 64) sts.

SIZES L (XL, 2X, 3X, 4X, 5X) ONLY

Rows 4–5 (7, 9, 13, 15, 17): Rep last 2 rows 1 (2, 3, 5, 6, 7) times—36 (36, 36, 32, 32, 29) sts.

Row 4 (4, 6, 8, 10, 14, 16, 18) (WS): Ch 1, hdc in first st, hdc2tog, work in pattern st across to end of row, turn—32 (36, 35, 35, 35, 31, 31, 28) sts.

Row 5 (5, 7, 9, 11, 15, 17, 19) (RS): Ch 1, work in pattern st across to last 3 sts, hdc2tog, hdc in last st, turn—31 (35, 34, 34, 34, 30, 30, 27) sts.

Rows 6 (6, 8, 10, 12, 16, 18, 20)–17 (19, 19, 19, 23, 25, 25, 25): Rep last 2 rows 6 (7, 6, 5, 6, 5, 4, 3) times—19 (21, 22, 24, 22, 20, 22, 21) sts.

SIZES XL (2X, 4X) ONLY

Row 20 (24, 26): Ch 1, hdc in first st, hdc2tog, work in pattern st across to end of row, turn—23 (21, 21) sts.

ALL SIZES

Rows 18 (20, 20, 21, 25, 26, 27, 26)–28 (30, 32, 34, 36, 38, 40, 42): Work even in pattern st.

Fasten off.

RIGHT FRONT PANEL

RIBBING

Row 1: With smaller hook, work 19 Fsc, turn.

Rows 2–62 (69, 75, 82, 89, 96, 103, 109): Work in sc ribbing pattern stitch.

Do not fasten off. At end of last row, rotate work ¼ turn to the right for working in row-end sts of ribbing.

MAIN BODY

Row 1 (RS): With larger hook, ch 1, working in row-end sts of ribbing, hdc in each of first 6 (7, 7, 7, 8, 8, 9, 9) sts, [hdc2tog, hdc in next st] 16 (18, 20, 22, 24, 26, 28, 30) times, hdc2tog, hdc in each of next 6 (6, 6, 7, 7, 8, 8, 8) sts turn—45 (50, 54, 59, 64, 69, 74, 78) sts.

Row 2 (WS): Ch 1, work in Hhdc pattern st across to last 18 sts, work row 2 of V-Cables Panel over last 18 sts, turn.

Row 3: Ch 1, work row 3 of V-Cables Panel over first 18 sts, work in Hhdc pattern st across, turn.

Rows 4–80 (78, 78, 78, 76, 74, 74, 72): Work in V-Cables pattern st and Hhdc pattern st as established.

BEGIN ARMHOLE AND FRONT NECKLINE SHAPING

Row 1 (RS): Ch 1, hdc in first st, hdc2tog, work in pattern st across to last 8 (9, 9, 9, 9, 8, 8, 10) sts, hdc2tog, turn, leaving last 6 (7, 7, 7, 7, 6, 6, 8) sts unworked—38 (42, 46, 51, 56, 62, 67, 69) sts.

Row 2 (WS): Ch 1, hdc in first st, hdc2tog, work in pattern st to last 3 sts, hdc2tog, hdc in last st, turn—36 (40, 44, 49, 54, 60, 65, 67) sts.

Row 3: Ch 1, hdc in first st, hdc2tog, work in pattern st across to last 5 sts, [hdc2tog over next 2 sts] twice, hdc in last st, turn—33 (37, 41, 46, 51, 57, 62, 64) sts.

SIZES L (XL, 2X, 3X, 4X, 5X) ONLY

Rows 4–5 (7, 9, 13, 15, 17): Rep last 2 rows 1 (2, 3, 5, 6, 7) times—36 (36, 36, 32, 32, 29) sts.

ALL SIZES

Row 4 (4, 6, 8, 10, 14, 16, 18) (WS): Ch 1, work in pattern st across to last 3 sts, hdc2tog, hdc in last st, turn—32 (36, 35, 35, 35, 31, 31, 28) sts.

Row 5 (5, 7, 9, 11, 15, 17, 19) (RS): Ch 1, hdc in first st, hdc2tog, work in pattern st to end of row, turn—31 (35, 34, 34, 34, 30, 30, 27) sts.

Rows 6 (6, 8, 10, 12, 16, 18, 20)–17 (19, 19, 19, 23, 25, 25, 25): Rep last 2 rows 6 (7, 6, 5, 6, 5, 4, 3) more times—19 (21, 22, 24, 23, 20, 22, 21) sts at end of last row.

SIZES XL (2X, 4X) ONLY

Row 20 (24, 26): Ch 1, work in pattern st across to last 3 sts, hdc2tog, hdc in last st, turn—23 (22, 21) sts.

ALL SIZES

Rows 18 (20, 20, 21, 25, 26, 27, 26)–28 (30, 32, 34, 36, 38, 40, 42): Work even in pattern st.

Fasten off.

SLEEVE CAP (MAKE 2)

Row 1: With smaller hook, work 19 (19, 19, 23, 26, 26, 26, 26) Fsc, turn.

Rows 2–77 (82, 87, 92, 97, 102, 107, 111): Work in sc ribbing pattern stitch.

Fasten off.

COLLAR

Row 1: With smaller hook, work 3 Fsc, turn.

BEGIN FIRST SIDE SHAPING

Row 2: Ch 1, 2 sc in both loops of first st, sc-tbl in next st, sc in both loops of last st, turn—4 sts.

Row 3: Work even in sc ribbing pattern st.

Row 4: Ch 1, 2 sc in both loops of first st, sc-tbl in each st across to last st, sc in both loops of last st, turn—5 sts.

Row 5: Rep row 3.

Rows 6–47: Rep last 2 rows (21 times)—26 sts.

Rows 48–108 (118, 132, 142, 160, 172, 182, 188): Work even in sc ribbing pattern st.

BEGIN SECOND SIDE SHAPING

Row 109 (119, 133, 143, 161, 173, 183, 189): Work in sc ribbing pattern st across to last 2 sts, sc2tog, turn—25 sts.

Row 110 (122, 136, 146, 164, 176, 186, 192): Work even in sc ribbing pattern st.

Rows 111 (123, 137, 147, 165, 177, 187, 193)–154 (164, 178, 188, 206, 218, 228, 234): Rep last 2 rows—4 sts at end of last row.

Row 155 (165, 179, 189, 207, 219, 229, 235): Work even in sc ribbing pattern st.

Fasten off.

FINISHING

Block all pieces to schematic measurements.

Using locking mattress stitch technique (see Special Technique section, page 200), sew shoulder and side seams.

Set Sleeve Cap into armholes, and sew in place.

Pin center point of straight edge of Collar to center of back neckline; pin corners of same edge of Collar to bottom front corners of garment; place pins to evenly distribute collar rows around front garment border; sew Collar in place. Sew zipper into front of garment.

Weave in ends.

CABLED TRIO
ARM WARMERS

SKILL LEVEL: Intermediate
SIZES: S (M, L, XL)
Sample shown in size medium

FINISHED MEASUREMENTS

Length: 13 inches/33cm
To Fit Forearm Circumference: 8 (11, 14, 17) inches/20.5 (28, 35.5, 43) cm

MATERIALS AND TOOLS

▪ Sample shown in Knit Picks Stroll Fingering (75% Superwash Merino Wool, 25% Nylon; 3.5 ounces/100g = 231 yards/211 m): 2 (3, 3, 4) skeins in color Firecracker Heather #24587 or 462 (693, 693, 924) yards/422 (633, 633, 844) m of superfine weight yarn

▪ Crochet hooks: 3.25mm (size D-3) and 3.5mm (size E-4) or sizes to obtain gauge
▪ Yarn needle

INSTRUCTIONS
RIGHT ARM

CUFF RIBBING

Row 1: With smaller hook, work 32 Fsc, turn.

Rows 2–47 (64, 93, 99): Work in sc ribbing pattern st. Do not fasten off. At end of last row, rotate work ¼ turn to the right for working in row-end sts of ribbing.

FOREARM

Rnd 1 (RS): With larger hook, ch 1, working in row-end sts on long edge of ribbing, hdc in each of first 5 (4, 1, 4) sts, [hdc2tog, hdc in each of next 5 (4, 4, 4) sts] 5 (9, 13, 15) times, hdc2tog, hdc in each of next 5 (4, 1, 3) sts, join with sl st in first hdc, turn—41 (54, 68, 83) sts.

Rnd 2 (WS): Ch 1, work in Hhdc pattern st in each of first 2 (5, 8, 12) sts, work row 2 of V-Cables Panel over next 18 sts, work in Hhdc pattern st in each of next 2 (5, 8, 12) sts (Top of Arm completed), work in Hhdc pattern st in each of next 19 (26, 34, 41) sts (Bottom of Arm completed), join with sl st in first st, turn.

Rnd 3: Ch 1, work in Hhdc pattern st in each of first 19 (26, 34, 41) Bottom of Arm sts, work in Hhdc pattern st in each of first 2 (5, 8, 12) Top of Arm sts, work row 3 of V-Cables Panel over next 18 sts, work in Hhdc pattern st in each of last 2 (5, 8, 12) sts, join with sl st in first st, turn.

Rnds 4–26: Work in Hhdc pattern st and V-Cables pattern st as established.

THUMB OPENING

Work now progresses in rows.

Rows 1–10: Work in Hhdc pattern st and V-Cables pattern st as established without joining.

HAND

Hand is worked in turned rnds.

Rnds 1–6: Work in Hhdc pattern st and V-Cables pattern st as established, joining and turning at the end of each rnd. Fasten off.

LEFT ARM

CUFF RIBBING

Row 1: With smaller hook, work 32 Fsc, turn.

Rows 2–47 (64, 82, 99): Work in sc ribbing pattern st.

Do not fasten off. At end of last row, rotate work ¼ turn to the right for working in row-end sts of ribbing.

FOREARM

Rnd 1 (RS): With larger hook, ch 1, hdc in each of first 5 (4, 1, 4) sts, [hdc2tog, hdc in each of next 5 (4, 4, 4) sts] 5 (9, 13, 15) times, hdc2tog, hdc in each of next 5 (4, 1, 3) sts, join with sl st in first hdc, turn—41 (54, 68, 83) sts.

Rnd 2 (WS): Ch 1, work in Hhdc pattern st in each of first 19 (26, 34, 41) sts (Bottom of Arm completed), work in Hhdc pattern st in first 2 (5, 8, 12) sts, work row 2 of V-Cables Panel over next 18 sts, work in Hhdc pattern st in each of next 2 (5, 8, 12) sts (Top of Arm completed), join with sl st in first st, turn.

Rnd 3: Ch 1, work in Hhdc pattern st in each of first 2 (5, 8, 12) sts, work row 3 of V-Cables Panel over next 18 sts, work in Hhdc pattern st in each of next 2 (5, 8, 12) sts (Top of Arm completed), work in Hhdc pattern st in each of next 19 (26, 34, 41) Bottom of Arm sts, join with sl st in first st, turn.

Rnds 4–26: Work even in Hhdc pattern st and V-Cables pattern st as established.

THUMB OPENING

Work now progresses in rows.

Rows 1–10: Work even in Hhdc pattern st and V-Cables pattern st as established without joining.

HAND

Hand is worked in turned rnds.

Rnds 1–6: Work even in Hhdc pattern st and V-Cables pattern st as established, joining at turning at the end of each rnd. Fasten off.

FINISHING

With WS facing, sew Cuff Ribbing seam; fold Cuff Ribbing in half lengthwise and sew to inside edge of ribbing.

Weave in ends.

CABLED TRIO BOOT TOPPERS

SKILL LEVEL: Intermediate
SIZES: S (M, L, XL)
Sample shown in size medium

FINISHED MEASUREMENTS

To Fit Calf Circumference: 13 (16, 18, 20) inches/33 (40.5, 45.5, 51) cm
Cuff Width: 5 inches/12.5 cm
Leg Length: 6 inches/15 cm.

MATERIALS AND TOOLS

- Sample uses Knit Picks Stroll Fingering (75% Superwash Merino Wool, 25% Nylon; 3.5 ounces/100 g = 231 yards/211 m): 2 (3, 3, 3) skeins in color Firecracker Heather #24587 or 462 (693, 693, 693) yards/422 (633, 633, 633) m of superfine weight yarn

- Crochet hooks: 3.25mm (size D-3) and 3.5mm (size E-4) or sizes to obtain gauge
- Yarn needle

INSTRUCTIONS

BOOT TOPPER (MAKE 2)

Row 1: With larger hook, work 55 Fhdc, turn.
Row 2 (WS): Ch 1, work row 2 of V-Cables Panel across first 26 sts, work Hhdc pattern st across rem 29 sts, turn.
Row 3: Ch 1, work Hhdc pattern st across first 29 sts, work row 3 of V-Cables Panel across last 26 sts, turn.
Rows 4–52 (64, 72, 80): Work in Hhdc pattern st and V-Cables pattern st as established.
Fasten off.

FINISHING

With RS of V-Cables pattern st facing, fold Boot Topper in half lengthwise and sew seam along Hhdc section; turn Boot Topper inside out with WS of V-Cables pattern stitch facing (seam just sewn will now be on inside of work). Sew seam along V-Cables pattern st section.
Weave in ends.

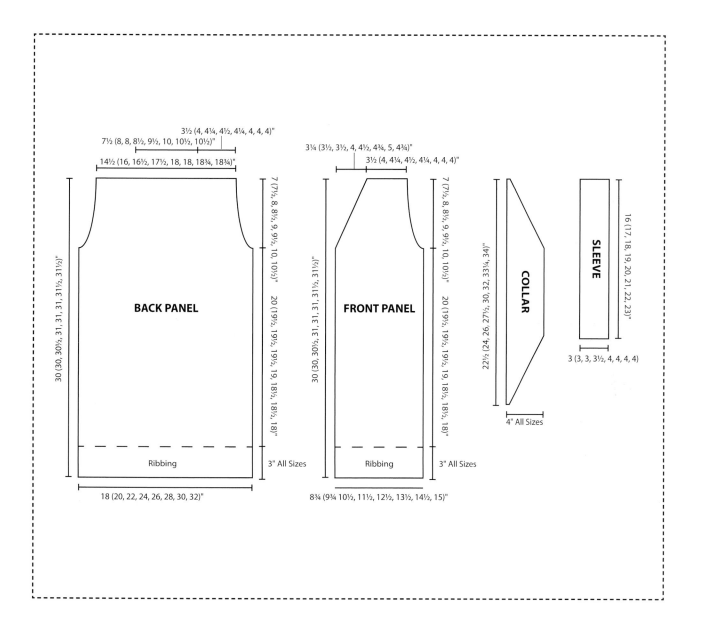

3½ (4, 4¼, 4½, 4¼, 4, 4, 4)"

7½ (8, 8, 8½, 9½, 10, 10½, 10½)"

14½ (16, 16½, 17½, 18, 18, 18¾, 18¾)"

BACK PANEL

7 (7½, 8, 8½, 9, 9½, 10, 10½)"

20 (19½, 19½, 19½, 19, 18½, 18½, 18)"

30 (30, 30½, 31, 31, 31, 31½, 31½)"

Ribbing

3" All Sizes

18 (20, 22, 24, 26, 28, 30, 32)"

3¼ (3½, 3½, 4, 4½, 4¾, 5, 4¾)"

3½ (4, 4¼, 4½, 4¼, 4, 4, 4)"

FRONT PANEL

7 (7½, 8, 8½, 9, 9½, 10, 10½)"

20 (19½, 19½, 19½, 19, 18½, 18½, 18)"

30 (30, 30½, 31, 31, 31, 31½, 31½)"

Ribbing

3" All Sizes

8¾ (9¾ 10½, 11½, 12½, 13½, 14½, 15)"

COLLAR

22½ (24, 26, 27½, 30, 32, 33¼, 34)"

4" All Sizes

SLEEVE

16 (17, 18, 19, 20, 21, 22, 23)"

3 (3, 3, 3½, 4, 4, 4, 4)

CAPELETTE

Sometimes elegance is best expressed in the simplest forms. Easy single crochet and half double crochet ribbing combine to create a highly graphic fabric that sculpts the classic silhouette of this capelette. Add a dash of your own style with a bold, beautiful button or a simple shawl pin.

SKILL LEVEL: Beginner

SIZES: S/M (L/XL, 2X/3X, 4X/5X)

Sample shown in size small/medium

FINISHED MEASUREMENTS

To Fit Bust: 32-36 (40-44, 48-52, 56-60) inches/81.5-91.5 (101.5-112, 122-132, 142-152.5) cm

Length across Bottom Edge: 48 (54, 64, 72) inches/122 (137, 162.5, 183) cm

Length across Top Edge: 36 (40½, 48, 54) inches/91.5 (103, 122, 137) cm

Width: 16 (16, 21¼, 21¼) inches/40.5 (40.5, 54, 54) cm

MATERIALS AND TOOLS

■ Sample shown in Malabrigo Arroyo (100% Superwash Merino; 3.53 ounces/100 g = 335 yards/306 m): 3 (4, 4, 5) skeins in color Borraja #58 or 1005 (1340, 1340, 1675) yards/918 (1224, 1224, 1530) m of lightweight yarn

■ Crochet hook: 3.5mm (size E-4) or size to obtain gauge

■ Yarn needle

■ One 3-inch/7.6 cm decorative button

■ One 5/8-inch/1.6 cm shirt button to be used as a post button

BLOCKED GAUGES

Sc ripple ribbing pattern: 30 sts = 5 inches/12.5 cm; 32 rows = 8 inches/20.5 cm

Hdc ripple ribbing pattern: 30 sts = 5½ inches/14 cm; 30 rows = 10 inches/25.5 cm

Always take time to check your gauge.

GAUGE SWATCH

Hdc/sc ripple ribbing stitch swatch

Foundation Row: Work 30 Fsc, work 30 Fhdc, turn.

Row 1: Ch 1, work 2 hdc in both loops of first st, work row 2 of hdc ripple ribbing across first 30 sts, work row 2 of sc ripple ribbing across next 30 sts, ending with 2 sc in both loops of last st, turn.

Row 2: Ch 1, 2 sc in both loops of first st, work row 1 of sc ripple ribbing across first 30 sts, work row 1 of hdc ripple ribbing across next 30 sts ending with 2 sc in both loops of last st, turn.

Rows 3–31: Rep last 2 rows.

STITCH GUIDE

Foundation single crochet (Fsc): Ch 2, insert hook in 2nd ch from hook, yo and draw up a loop, yo and draw through 1 loop (first "chain" made), yo and draw through 2 loops on hook (first sc made), *insert hook under 2 loops of the "chain" just made, yo and draw up a loop, yo and draw through 1 loop ("chain" made), yo and draw through 2 loops on hook (sc made); rep from * for indicated number of foundation sts.

Foundation half double crochet (Fhdc): Ch 3, yo, insert hook in 3rd ch from hook, yo and draw up a loop, yo and draw through 1 loop (first "chain" made), yo and draw through all 3 loops on hook (first hdc made), *yo, insert hook under 2 loops of the "chain" just made, yo and draw up a loop, yo and draw through 1 loop ("chain" made), yo and draw through all 3 loops on hook (hdc made); rep from * for indicated number of foundation sts.

Half double crochet through back loop only (hdc-tbl): Yo, insert hook in back loop of indicated st, yo and draw up a loop, yo and draw through 3 loops on hook.

Single crochet through back loop only (sc-tbl): Insert hook in back loop of indicated st, yo and draw up a loop, yo and draw through 2 loops on hook.

PATTERN STITCHES

For Master Chart Key, see page 206.

Hdc ripple ribbing (worked on a multiple of 15 sts) Ⓐ

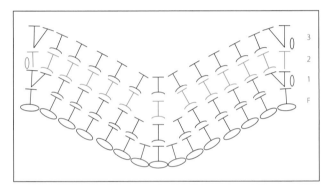

Ⓐ Hdc ripple ribbing stitch chart

Row 1: Hdc in both loops of first st, hdc-tbl in each st across to last st, hdc in both loops of last st, turn.

Row 2: Ch 1, 2 hdc in both loops of first st, hdc-tbl in each of next 5 sts, [sk next st, hdc-tbl in next st] twice, hdc-tbl in each of next 4 sts, 2 hdc-tbl in next st, *2 hdc-tbl in next st, hdc-tbl in each of next 5 sts, [sk next st, hdc-tbl in next st] twice, hdc-tbl in each of next 4 sts, 2 hdc-tbl in next st; rep from * across to last st, 2 hdc in both loops of last st, turn. Rep rows 1 and 2 for pattern.

Sc ripple ribbing (worked on a multiple of 15 sts) Ⓑ

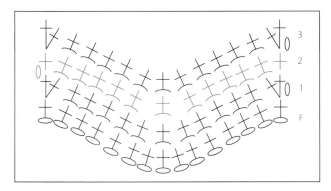

Ⓑ Sc ripple ribbing stitch chart

Row 1: Sc in both loops of first st, sc-tbl in each st across to last st, sc in both loops of last st, turn.
Row 2: Ch 1, 2 sc in both loops of first st, sc-tbl in each of next 5 sts, [sk next st, sc-tbl in next st] twice, sc-tbl in each of next 4 sts, 2 sc-tbl in next st, *2 sc-tbl in next st, sc-tbl in each of next 5 sts, [sk next st, sc-tbl in next st] twice, sc-tbl in each of next 4 sts, 2 sc-tbl in next st; rep from * across to last st, 2 sc in both loops of last st, turn.
Rep rows 1 and 2 for pattern.

NOTES

1. Capelette is made from side to side.
2. Finished piece is worn with sc sts at top edge.

INSTRUCTIONS

Foundation Row: Work 30 (30, 45, 45) Fsc, work 60 (60, 75, 75) Fhdc, turn—90 (90, 120, 120) sts.
Row 1: Ch 1, work 2 hdc in both loops of first st, work row 2 of hdc ripple ribbing across next 59 (59, 74, 74) sts, work row 2 of sc ripple ribbing across next 29 (29, 44, 44) sts, work 2 sc in both loops of last st, turn.

Row 2: Ch 1, work 2 sc in both loops of first st, work row 1 of sc ripple ribbing across next 29 (29, 44, 44) sts, work row 1 of hdc ripple ribbing across next 59 (59, 74, 74) sts, work 2 hdc in both loops of last st, turn.
Rows 3–143 (161, 191, 215): Rep last 2 rows.
Fasten off.

BUTTON LOOP

With WS facing, join yarn to underside of Capelette where hdc sts transition to sc sts on one front edge. Make a ch approx 1½–2 inches/3.8–5 cm long (depending on the size of your button). Join tinto a ring with sl st in original join, turn; sc evenly around ch loop; join last st with sl st in original join. Fasten off.

FINISHING

Block to finished width only—not length—allowing ribbing to stretch to fit wearer's shoulders.
Sew button to section where hdc transitions to sc sts opposite button loop.
Weave in ends.

HOODED WRAP VEST

We've elevated the hooded scarf to the next level. First, we widened the scarf section to cover your upper body like a stole. Next we added buttons to the front edge of the wrap section for the look of a vest when worn with a belt or layered under a coat. Finally, we created the fabric for this piece using a feather and fan version of our unique Non-stick lace pattern stitch. The result is a beautiful accessory piece you will wear for its clever functionality as well as its breathtaking good looks.

SKILL LEVEL: Intermediate
SIZES: One size

FINISHED MEASUREMENTS
Wrap Section: 16 inches/40.5 cm wide x 73 inches/185.5 cm long
Hood Section: 10 inches/25.5 cm x 23 inches/58.5 cm

MATERIALS AND TOOLS
- Sample uses Buffalo Wool Company, Sock yarn (90% Superwash Merino, 10% Bison Down; 400 yards/366 m = 3.5 ounces/100 g): 4 skeins in color Mykonos Blue or 1600 yards/1464 m of superfine weight yarn

- Crochet hook: 3.25mm (size D-3) or size to obtain gauge
- Yarn needle
- Six 1 ⅛-inch/2.9 cm decorative buttons

BLOCKED GAUGE

Non-stick lace feather and fan pattern: 48 sts = 8 inches/20.5 cm; 13 rows = 6 inches/15 cm
Always take time to check your gauge.

GAUGE SWATCH

Foundation Row: Work 48 Fsc, turn.

Row 1–14: Work even in Non-stick lace feather and fan pattern stitch.

STITCH GUIDE

Foundation single crochet (Fsc): Ch 2, insert hook in 2nd ch from hook, yo and draw up a loop, yo and draw through 1 loop (first "chain" made), yo and draw through 2 loops on hook (first sc made), *insert hook under 2 loops of the "chain" just made, yo and draw up a loop, yo and draw through 1 loop ("chain" made), yo and draw through 2 loops on hook (sc made); rep from * for indicated number of foundation sts.

First double treble crochet (First-dtr): Sc in first st, ch 4. Note: Use this stitch whenever the first stitch of a row is a dtr.

Double treble crochet (dtr): Yo (3 times), insert hook in indicated st, yo and draw up a loop, [yo and draw through 2 loops on hook] 4 times.

PATTERN STITCH

For Master Chart Key, see page 206.

Non-stick lace feather and fan (worked on a multiple of 15 + 3 sts) Ⓐ

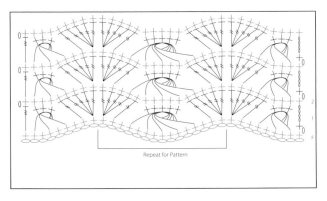

Ⓐ Non-stick lace feather and fan stitch chart

Row 1 (RS): First-dtr, yo, insert hook in next st, yo and pull up a loop to height of First-dtr, (sk next st, insert hook in next st, yo and pull up a loop to height of First-dtr) twice (5 loops on hook), yo and draw through 4 loops on hook, yo and draw through rem 2 loops on hook, 2 sc under last 4 loops ("eye" of loops), sk next st, dtr in next st, 4 dtr in next st, *4 dtr in next st, dtr in next st, yo, (sk next st, insert hook into next st, yo and pull up a loop to height of dtr) 5 times (7 loops on hook), yo and draw through 6 loops on hook, yo and draw through remaining 2 loops on hook, 4 sc under last 6 loops ("eye" of loops), sk next st, dtr in next st, 4 dtr in next st; rep from * to last 9 sts, 4 dtr in next st, dtr in next st, yo, (sk next st, insert hook in next st, yo and pull up a loop to height of dtr) 3 times (5 loops on hook), yo and draw through 4 loops on hook, yo and draw through rem 2 loops on hook, 2 sc under last 4 loops ("eye" of loops), sk next st, dtr in last st, turn.

Row 2: Ch 1, sc in each st across, turn.

Rep rows 1 and 2 for pattern.

Buttonhole: Hdc in each of next 6 sts, ch 5, drop loop on hook, insert hook in first of last 6 hdc, place working loop back on hook and draw through hdc, work 7 sc in ch-5 sp, sl st in same st as 6th hdc.

NOTE

Left Side and Right Side refer to left and right side as worn.

INSTRUCTIONS

BODY SECTION

Foundation Row: Work 438 Fsc, turn.

Rows 1–34: Work even in pattern st.

Fasten off.

HOOD

With RS facing, working across opposite side of Foundation Row, sk first 150 sts, join yarn with sl st in next st; first st of row 1 is worked in same st as joining.

Row 1: Work in pattern st across first 138 sts, turn, leaving rem sts unworked.

Rows 2–22: Work even in pattern st.

Fasten off.

FINISHING

Block to finished dimensions.

Fold hood in half widthwise, and sew top closed using locking mattress stitch.

BUTTON BAND

With RS facing, join yarn with sl st in bottom right-hand corner of Right Front; first st is made in same st as joining.

Right Side (Buttonholes): Ch 1, hdc in each of first 6 sts, make buttonhole, *hdc in each of next 9 sts, make buttonhole; rep from * across to last 6 sts, hdc in each of last 6 sts.

Hood (Border): Working across row-end sts of Hood, work 5 hdc in each row-end dtr, hdc in each row-end sc across hood.

Left Side (Button Band): Hdc in each st across to to bottom left-hand corner.

Fasten off.

FINISHING

Block Button Band and Border to finished dimensions.

Sew buttons in place along Left Side opposite buttonholes.

Weave in ends.

HOODED SCARF

Versatility is the name of the game when it comes to accessories, and this hooded scarf fits that bill perfectly. Hood up or down, this piece will keep you warm while looking stylish.

SKILL LEVEL: Intermediate

SIZES: One size

FINISHED MEASUREMENTS

Hood Section: 24 inches/61 cm x 12 inches/30.5 cm

Scarf Section: 72½ inches/184 cm x 5½ inches/14 cm

MATERIALS AND TOOLS

- Sample uses Malabrigo Silky Merino (50% Silk, 50% Baby Merino Wool; 1.75 ounces/50 g = 150 yards/137 m): 5 skeins in color Archangel #850 or approx 750 yards/685 m of lightweight yarn

- Crochet hook: 3.75mm (size F-5) or size to obtain gauge
- Yarn needle
- Stitch markers

BLOCKED GAUGE

Starburst pattern stitch: 30 sts = 5¾ inches/14.5 cm; 10 rows = 5 inches/12.5 cm

Always take time to check your gauge.

GAUGE SWATCH

Foundation Row: Work 30 Fsc, turn.

Rows 1–10: Work even in starburst pattern stitch. Fasten off.

STITCH GUIDE

Foundation single crochet (Fsc): Ch 2, insert hook in 2nd ch from hook, yo and draw up a loop, yo and draw through 1 loop (first "chain" made), yo and draw through 2 loops on hook (first sc made), *insert hook under 2 loops of the "chain" just made, yo and draw up a loop, yo and draw through 1 loop ("chain" made), yo and draw through 2 loops on hook (sc made); rep from * for indicated number of foundation sts.

First double crochet (First-dc): Sc in first st, ch 2. Note: Use this st whenever the first st of a row is a dc.

First star cluster: Yo, insert hook into next st, yo and draw up a loop, yo and draw through 2 loops on hook (2 loops on hook), yo, insert hook into same st, yo and draw up a loop, yo and draw through 2 loops on hook (3 loops on hook), skip next 2 sts, yo and insert hook in next st, yo and draw up a loop, yo and draw through 2 loops on hook (4 loops on hook), yo, insert hook into same st, yo and draw up a loop, yo and draw through 2 loops on hook (5 loops on hook), yo and draw through all 5 loops on hook.

Next star cluster: Ch 3, yo, insert hook in top of last star cluster made, yo and draw up a loop, yo and draw through 2 loops on hook (2 loops on hook), yo and insert hook in same st as second half of last star cluster worked, yo and draw up a loop, yo and draw through 2 loops on hook (3 loops on hook), yo, insert hook in same st and draw up a loop, yo and draw through 2 loops on hook (4 loops on hook), sk next 3 sts, yo, insert hook in next st, yo and draw

up a loop, yo and draw through 2 loops on hook (5 loops on hook), yo, insert hook in same st, yo and draw up a loop, yo and draw through 2 loops on hook (6 loops on hook), yo and draw through all 6 loops on hook.

Last star cluster: Ch 3, yo, insert hook in top of last star cluster made, yo and draw up a loop, yo and draw through 2 loops on hook (2 loops on hook), yo and insert hook in same st as second half of last star cluster worked, yo and draw up a loop, yo and draw through 2 loops on hook (3 loops on hook), yo, insert hook in same st and draw up a loop, yo and draw through 2 loops on hook (4 loops on hook), sk next st, yo, insert hook in last st, yo and draw up a loop, yo and draw through 2 loops on hook (5 loops on hook), yo, insert hook in last st again, yo and draw up a loop, yo and draw through 2 loops on hook (6 loops on hook), yo and draw through all 6 loops on hook.

2-double crochet cluster (2-dc cluster): Yo, insert hook in indicated stitch, yo and draw up a loop, yo and draw through 2 loops on hook, yo, insert hook in same st, yo and draw up a loop, yo and draw through 2 loops on hook, yo and draw through 3 loops on hook.

Double crochet split cluster (dc-split cluster): Yo, insert hook in last st worked, yo and draw up a loop, yo and draw through 2 loops on hook (2 loops on hook), yo, insert hook in same st, yo and draw up a loop, yo and draw through 2 loops on hook (3 loops on hook), sk next 3 sts, yo, insert hook in next st, yo and draw up a loop, yo and draw through 2 loops on hook (4 loops on hook), yo insert hook in same st, yo and draw up a loop, yo and draw through 2 loops on hook (5 loops on hook), yo and draw through all 5 loops on hook.

Last star-split cluster: Ch 3, yo, insert hook in top of last star cluster made, yo and draw up a loop, yo and draw through 2 loops on hook (2 loops on hook), yo and insert hook in same st as second half of last star cluster worked, yo and draw up a loop, yo and draw through 2 loops on hook (3 loops on hook), yo, insert hook in same st and draw up a loop, yo and draw through 2 loops on hook (4 loops on hook), sk next 3 sts, insert hook in last st, yo and draw up a loop, yo and draw through 2 loops on hook (5 loops on hook), yo, insert hook in last st again, yo and draw up a loop, yo and draw through 2 loops on hook (6 loops on hook), yo and draw through all 6 loops on hook.

PATTERN STITCH

For Master Chart Key, see page 206.

Starburst pattern stitch (multiple of 4 + 2 sts) Ⓐ

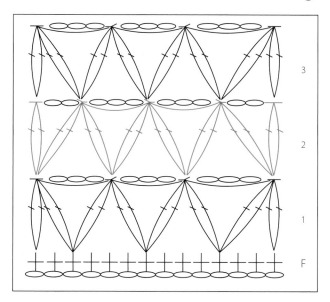

Ⓐ Starburst pattern stitch chart

Row 1: Work First star cluster, *work Next star cluster; rep from * across to last 2 sts, work Last star cluster, turn.

Row 2: Work First-2-dc cluster, ch 2, work dc-split cluster, *work Next star cluster, rep from * across to last 4 sts, work Last star-split cluster, ch 2, work 2-dc cluster in last st, turn. Rep rows 1 and 2 for pattern.

SPECIAL TECHNIQUES

Locking mattress stitch (see Special Techniques, page 200)

INSTRUCTIONS

SCARF

Foundation Row: Work 378 Fsc, turn.

Row 1 (RS): First-dc in first st, dc in next st, work First star cluster, *work Next star cluster, rep from * across to last 4 sts, work Last star cluster, dc in each of last 2 sts, turn.

Row 2: First-dc in first st, dc in next st, work 2-dc cluster, ch 2, work dc-split cluster, *work Next star cluster, rep from * across to last 6 sts, work Last star-split cluster, ch 2, work 2-dc cluster in next st, dc in each of last 2 sts, turn.

Rows 3–10: Rep rows 1 and 2 (4 times).

Row 11 (RS): Ch 1, work 378 sc evenly spaced across row to match Foundation Row.

Fasten off.

HOOD

With RS facing, skip first 126 sts, place marker in next st; skip next 124 sts, place marker in next st. Hood sts will be worked between these 2 markers.

With RS facing, join yarn in first marked st; first st of row 1 is worked in same st as joining.

Row 1: First-dc in first st, dc in next st, work First star cluster, *work Next star cluster; rep from * across to last 4 sts, work Last star cluster, dc in each of last 2 sts, turn.

Row 2: First-dc in first st, dc in next st, work 2-dc cluster, ch 2, work dc-split cluster, *work Next star cluster; rep from * across to last 6 sts, work Last star-split cluster, ch 2, work 2-dc cluster in next st, dc in each of last 2 sts, turn.

Rows 3–20: Rep rows 1 and 2 (9 times).

Row 21 (RS): Ch 1, work 126 sc evenly spaced across row to match last row of Scarf section. Fasten off.

FINISHING

Block to finished measurements.

Fold Hood in half widthwise, and sew top seam.

Weave in ends.

THREESOME SET #1:

CUFFED BEANIE HAT
COWL
WRIST WARMERS

We used twisted stitches and single crochet ribbing to give you a classic set you can count on to get you through cold temps while still looking stylish. We patterned the beanie in a wide range of sizes so you can keep all of your friends and family warm while looking good!

BLOCKED GAUGES

Diagonal post pattern: 18 sts = 3¼ inches/8.5 cm; 25 rows = 6 inches/15 cm

Sc ribbing pattern: 26 sts and 32 rows = 4 inches/10 cm
Always take time to check your gauge.

GAUGE SWATCH

Diagonal post stitch swatch

Foundation Row: Work 46 Fhdc, turn.

Rows 1–24: Work in diagonal post pattern stitch.

STITCH GUIDE

Foundation single crochet (Fsc): Ch 2, insert hook in 2nd ch from hook, yo and draw up a loop, yo and draw through 1 loop (first "chain" made), yo and draw through 2 loops on hook (first sc made), *insert hook under 2 loops of the "chain" just made, yo and draw up a loop, yo and draw through 1 loop ("chain" made), yo and draw through 2 loops on hook (sc made); rep from * for indicated number of foundation sts.

Foundation half double crochet (Fhdc): Ch 3, yo, insert hook in 3rd ch from hook, yo and draw up a loop, yo and draw through 1 loop (first "chain" made), yo and draw through all 3 loops on hook (first hdc made), *yo, insert hook under 2 loops of the "chain" just made, yo and draw up a loop, yo and draw through 1 loop ("chain" made), yo and draw through all 3 loops on hook (hdc made); rep from * for indicated number of foundation sts.

Front Post treble crochet (FPtr): Yo (twice), insert hook from front to back and to front again around the post of next st, yo and draw up loop, [yo and draw through 2 loops on hook] 3 times.

Half double/treble crochet left twist (Hdc/tr left twist): Skip next st, hdc in next st, working in front of hdc just made, FPtr around the post of last skipped st 2 rows below.

PATTERN STITCHES

For Master Chart Key, see page 206.

Diagonal post stitch worked in rows (worked on a multiple of 9 + 1 sts) Ⓐ

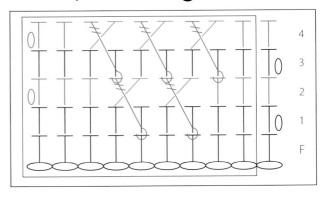

Ⓐ Diagonal post stitch chart worked in rows

Row 1 (WS): Ch 1, hdc in each st across, turn.

Row 2 (RS): Ch 1, hdc in first st, *hdc in each of next 2 sts, [work Hdc/tr left twist] 2 times, hdc in each of next 3 sts; rep from * across, turn.

Row 3: Rep row 1.

Row 4: Ch 1, hdc in first st, *hdc in next st, [work Hdc/tr left twist] 3 times, hdc in each of next 2 sts; rep from * across, turn.

Rep rows 1–4 for pattern.

Diagonal post stitch worked in turned rnds (worked on a multiple of 9 sts)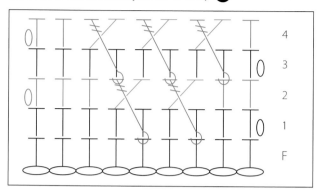

 Diagonal post stitch chart worked in turned rnds

Rnd 1 (RS): Ch 1, hdc in each st around, join with sl st in first hdc, turn.

Rnd 2 (WS): Ch 1, hdc in each st around, join with sl st in first hdc, turn.

Rnd 3: Ch 1, *hdc in each of next 2 sts, [work Hdc/tr left twist] 2 times, hdc in each of next 3 sts; rep from * around, join with sl st in first hdc, turn.

Rnd 4: Rep rnd 2.

Rnd 5: Ch 1, *hdc in next st, [work Hdc/tr left twist] 3 times, hdc in each of next 2 sts; rep from * across, turn.

Rep rows 2–5 for pattern.

Single crochet ribbing (sc ribbing)

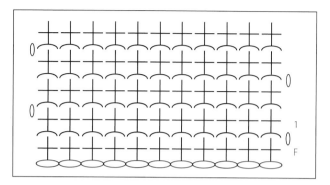

 Single crochet ribbing stitch chart

Row 1: Ch 1, sc in both loops of first st, sc-tbl in each st across to last st, sc in both loops of last st, turn.

Rep row 1 for pattern.

SPECIAL TECHNIQUE

Locking mattress stitch (see Special Techniques, page 200)
Join with duplicate stitch (see Special Techniques, page 199)

NOTES

Wrist Warmers

1. Forearm and Hand sections are worked in turned rnds. Turned rnds are worked back and forth like rows but joined with a sl st like rnds before turning.

2. Pattern can be made to a custom fit by adding or subtracting rows from any of the three sections in the written pattern.

Cuffed Beanie Hat

1. Band Ribbing section is made from side to side, then sts are worked into the side of the end sts of the ribbing rows for the Main Hat section.

THREESOME SET #1: CUFFED BEANIE HAT

SKILL LEVEL: Intermediate
SIZES: S (M, L, XL)
Sample shown in size medium

FINISHED MEASUREMENTS

To Fit Head Circumference: 20 (22, 24, 26) inches/51 (56, 61, 66) cm

Finished Hat Circumference: 19 (21, 23, 25) inches/48.5 (53.5, 58.5, 63.5) cm

Finished Hat Height: 9 (9, 10, 10) inches/23 (23, 25.5, 25.5) cm deep

MATERIALS AND TOOLS

▨ Sample uses Knit Picks Stroll Sock (75% Superwash Merino Wool, 25% Nylon; 1.75 ounces/50 g = 231 yards/211 m): 2 skeins in color Fedora #25030 or 462 yards/422 m superfine weight yarn

▨ Crochet hook: 3.25mm (size D-3) or size to obtain gauge
▨ Yarn needle

INSTRUCTIONS

BAND RIBBING

Row 1: Leaving a long sewing length, work 26 Fsc, turn.

Rows 2–133 (145, 154, 168): Work in sc ribbing pattern st. Do not fasten off. At end of last row, rotate work ¼ turn to the right for working in row-end sts of ribbing.

MAIN HAT

Work now progresses in rnds.

Rnd 1 (transition row): Ch 1, hdc in each of first 6 (4, 9, 3) sts, [hdc2tog, hdc in each of next 3 (3, 3, 5) sts] 24 (27, 27, 23) times, hdc2tog, hdc in each of next 5 (4, 8, 2) sts, join with sl st in first hdc, turn—108 (117, 126, 144) sts.

Rnds 2–17 (17, 21, 21): Work Diagonal post st pattern worked in turned rnds.

BEGIN TOP SHAPING

Rnd 1: Ch 1, starting in first st, *hdc2tog, hdc in each of next 7 sts; rep from * around, join with sl st in first hdc, turn—96 (104, 112, 128) sts.

Rnd 2: Ch 1, starting in first st, *hdc in each of next 2 sts, [work Hdc/tr left twist] 2 times, hdc in each of next 2 sts; rep from * around, join with sl st in first hdc, turn.

Rnd 3: Ch 1, starting in first st, *hdc2tog, 6 hdc; rep from * around, join with sl st in first hdc, turn—84 (91, 98, 112) sts.

Rnd 4: Ch 1, starting in first st, *hdc in next st, [work Hdc/tr left twist] 3 times; rep from * around, join with sl st in first hdc, turn .

Rnd 5: Ch 1, starting in first st, *hdc2tog, hdc in each of next 5 sts; rep from * around, join with sl st in first hdc, turn—72 (78, 84, 96) sts.

Rnd 6: Ch 1, starting in first st, *hdc in each of next 2 sts, [work Hdc/tr left twist] 2 times; rep from * around, join with sl st in first hdc, turn.

Rnd 7: Ch 1, starting in first st, *hdc2tog, hdc in each of next 4 sts; rep from * around, join with sl st in first hdc, turn—60 (65, 70, 80) sts.

Rnd 8: Ch 1, starting in first st, *hdc in next st, [work Hdc/tr left twist] 2 times; rep from * around, join with sl st in first hdc, turn.

Rnd 9: Ch 1, starting in first st, *hdc2tog, hdc in each of next 3 sts; rep from * around, join with sl st in first hdc, turn—48 (52, 56, 64) sts.

Rnd 10: Ch 1, starting in first st, *hdc in each of next 2 sts, work Hdc/tr left twist; rep from * around, join with sl st in first hdc, turn.

Rnd 11: Ch 1, starting in first st, *hdc2tog, hdc in each of next 2 sts; rep from * around, join with sl st in first hdc, turn—36 (39, 42, 48) sts.

Rnd 12: Ch 1, starting in first st, *hdc in next st, work Hdc/tr left twist; rep from * around, join with sl st in first hdc, turn.

Rnd 13: Ch 1, starting in first st, *hdc2tog, hdc in next st; rep from * around, join with sl st in first hdc, turn—24 (26, 28, 32) sts.

Rnd 14: Ch 1, starting in first st, *hdc2tog over next 2 sts; rep from * around, join with sl st in first hdc, turn—12 (13, 14, 16) sts. Break yarn leaving 6-inch/15 cm tail. Thread tail on yarn needle, draw tail through remaining stitches, and pull snug to close top of hat. Use yarn needle to pull tail through to inside of hat. Secure tail.

FINISHING

Using long sewing length, with WS of ribbing facing, sew Ribbing Seam. Block beanie. Weave in ends.

THREESOME SET #1: COWL

SKILL LEVEL: Intermediate
SIZES: Short (long)
Sample shown in size long

FINISHED MEASUREMENTS

One size: 8¼ inches/21 cm x 49 (65½) inches/124.5 (166.5) cm

MATERIALS AND TOOLS

■ Sample uses Knit Picks Stroll Sock (75% Superwash Merino Wool, 25% Nylon; 1.75 ounces/50 g = 231 yards/211 m): 3 (4) skeins in color Fedora #25030 or 693 (924) yards/633 (844) m superfine weight yarn

■ Crochet hook: 3.25mm (size D-3) or size to obtain gauge
■ Yarn needle

INSTRUCTIONS

Row 1: Work 46 Fhdc, turn.

Rows 2–205 (273): Work in Diagonal post pattern st.

FINISHING

Block to finished measurements.

Sew row 1 to row 205 (273).

Weave in ends.

THREESOME SET #1: WRIST WARMERS

SKILL LEVEL: Intermediate
SIZES: S (M, L, XL, 2X)
Sample shown in size medium

FINISHED MEASUREMENTS

Finished Forearm/Hand Circumference: 6¼ (7½, 8½, 9½, 10¾) inches/16 (19, 21.5, 24, 27.5) cm
Finished Length: 8½ inches/21.5 cm

MATERIALS AND TOOLS

- Sample uses Knit Picks Stroll Sock (75% Superwash Merino Wool, 25% Nylon; 1.75 ounces/50 g = 231 yards/211 m): 1 (1, 2, 2, 2) skeins in color Fedora #25030 or 231 (231, 462, 462, 462) yards/211 (211, 422, 422, 422) m of superfine weight yarn

- Crochet hook: 3.25mm (size D-3) or size to obtain gauge
- Yarn needle

INSTRUCTIONS

WRIST WARMER (MAKE 2)

FOREARM

Worked in turned rnds.

BORDER

Foundation rnd: Work 34 (41, 46, 52, 59) Fhdc, join with sl st in first Fhdc, turn.

Rnds 1–5: Ch 1, hdc in each st around, join with sl st in first hdc, turn.

Fold Border in half lengthwise and work next rnd through sts of Border rnd 5 and base of foundation rnd.

FOREARM

Rnd 1: Ch 1, hdc in each st around, join with sl st in first hdc, turn.

Rnd 2: Ch 1, hdc in each of first 4 (3, 1, 4, 3) sts, *hdc in each of next 2 sts, (work Hdc/tr left twist) 2 times, hdc in each of next 3 sts; rep from * around to last 4 (3, 1, 4, 3) sts, hdc in each of last 4 (3, 1, 4, 3) sts, join with sl st in first hdc, turn.

Rnd 3: Rep rnd 1.

Rnd 4: Ch 1, hdc in each of first 4 (3, 1, 4, 3) sts, *hdc in next st, (work Hdc/tr left twist) 3 times, hdc in each of next 2 sts; rep from * around to last 4 (3, 1, 4, 3) sts, hdc in each of last 4 (3, 1, 4, 3) sts, join with sl st in first hdc, turn.

Rnds 5–16: Rep last 4 rows.

Rnds 17 and 18: Rep rnds 1 and 2.

THUMB OPENING

Work now progresses in rows.

Rows 1–8: Maintaining pattern as established, work in Diagonal post pattern worked in rows. At end of last row, join with sl st in first hdc.

HAND

Work now progresses in rnds.

Rnds 1–7: Rep rnds 1–7 of Forearm.

Rnd 8: Ch 1, hdc in each st around, join with duplicate stitch.

FINISHING

Block to finished measurements.

Weave in ends.

THREESOME SET #2:

BRIMMED BEANIE HAT
SCARF
WRIST WARMERS

Lightweight yarn meets a luxuriously comfy stitch pattern to give this set a warm and cozy feel that also looks stylish and chic. We patterned this set in a wide range of sizes: the wrist warmers can be made longer or shorter by adjusting the pattern repeats between sections, and the brimmed beanie can be made into a cloche style hat by leaving off the brim. Whatever your style, you make it to fit you!

BLOCKED GAUGES

Feathered columns pattern: 41 sts = 8¼ inches/21 cm; 21 rows = 5½ inches/14 cm

Feathers and chains pattern: 36 sts = 6 inches/15 cm; 25 rows = 6½ inches/16.5 cm

Sc ribbing pattern with smaller hook: 26 sts = 3¾ inches/9.5 cm; 27 rows = 3½ inches/9 cm

Always take time to check your gauge.

STITCH GUIDE

Foundation single crochet (Fsc): Ch 2, insert hook in 2nd ch from hook, yo and draw up a loop, yo and draw through 1 loop (first "chain" made), yo and draw through 2 loops on hook (first sc made), *insert hook under 2 loops of the "chain" just made, yo and draw up a loop, yo and draw through 1 loop ("chain" made), yo and draw through 2 loops on hook (sc made); rep from * for indicated number of foundation sts.

Foundation half double crochet (Fhdc): Ch 3, yo, insert hook in 3rd ch from hook, yo and draw up a loop, yo and draw through 1 loop (first "chain" made), yo and draw through all 3 loops on hook (first hdc made), *yo, insert hook under 2 loops of the "chain" just made, yo and draw up a loop, yo and draw through 1 loop ("chain" made), yo and draw through all 3 loops on hook (hdc made); rep from * for indicated number of foundation sts.

Beginning feather: Yo, insert hook in last ch-1 space of previous rnd, yo and draw up a loop even with loops on hook (3 loops on hook), yo, insert hook in st or ch-1 sp one row below same sp, yo and draw up a loop even with loops on hook (5 loops on hook), yo, insert hook in next ch-1 sp, yo and draw up a loop even with loops on hook, yo and draw through all 7 loops on hook.

Feather: Yo, insert hook in same ch-1 sp as last feather, yo and draw up a loop even with loops on hook (3 loops on hook), yo, insert hook in skipped st or ch-1 sp one row below same sp, yo and draw up a loop even with loops on hook (5 loops on hook), yo, insert hook in next ch-1 sp, yo and draw up a loop even with loops on hook, yo and draw through all 7 loops on hook.

Last feather: Yo, insert hook in same ch-1 sp as last feather, yo and draw up a loop even with loops on hook (3 loops on hook), yo, insert hook in skipped st or ch-1 sp one row below same sp, yo and draw up a loop even with loops on hook (5 loops on hook), yo, insert hook in same ch-1 sp as first loop of Beginning feather and draw up a loop even with loops on hook, yo and draw through all 7 loops on hook.

Decrease feather (Dec feather): Yo, insert hook in same ch-1 sp as last feather, yo and draw up a loop even with loops on hook (3 loops on hook), yo, insert hook in skipped st or ch-1 sp one row below same sp, yo and draw up a loop even with loops on hook (5 loops on hook), [yo, insert hook in next ch-1 sp, yo and draw up a loop even with loops on hook] twice (9 loops on hook), yo and draw through all 9 loops on hook.

Front Post half double crochet (FPhdc): Yo, insert hook from front to back and to front again around the post of the indicated st, yo and draw up a loop, yo and draw through all 3 loops on hook.

Back Post half double crochet (BPhdc): Yo, insert hook from back to front and to back again around the post of the indicated st, yo and draw up a loop, yo and draw through all 3 loops on hook.

Joining Front Post half double crochet: Yo, insert hook in side of next st one row below, yo, insert hook from front to back and to front again around the post of the indicated st, yo and draw up a loop, yo and draw through all 5 loops on hook.

Joining Back Post half double crochet: Yo, insert hook in side of next st one row below, yo, insert hook from back to front and to back again around the post of the indicated st, yo and draw up a loop, yo and draw through all 5 loops on hook.

Joining Hdc: Yo, insert hook in side of next st one row below, yo, insert hook in next available stitch, yo and draw up a loop, yo and draw through all 5 loops on hook.

PATTERN STITCHES

For Master Chart Key, see page 206.

Feathered columns worked flat (worked on a multiple of 2 + 1 sts)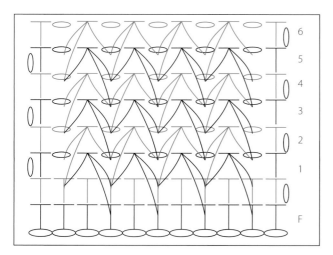

Ⓐ Feathered columns worked flat stitch chart

Feathered columns worked in turned rounds (worked on an even number of sts)

Rnd 1: Ch 1, yo, insert hook in last ch-1 sp of last rnd, yo and draw up a loop even with loops on hook (3 loops on hook), yo, insert hook in Fsc one row below same sp, yo and draw up a loop even with loops on hook (5 loops on hook), yo, insert hook in next ch-1 sp, yo and draw up a loop even with loops on hook, yo and draw through all 7 loops on hook (first feather made), ch 1, * yo, insert hook in same ch-1 sp as last st, yo and pull up a loop even with loops on hook (3 loops on hook), yo, working over next sc, insert hook in Fsc one row below, yo and draw up a loop even with loops on hook (5 loops on hook), yo, insert hook in next ch-1 sp, yo and draw up a loop even with loops on hook, yo and draw through all 7 loops on hook, ch 1; repeat from * around, join with sl st in first feather made, turn.

Rnd 2: Ch 1, work Beginning feather, ch 1, *feather, ch 1; rep from * around to last ch-1 sp, work Last feather, join with sl st in Beginning feather, turn.

Rep rnd 2 for pattern.

Feathers and chains worked in rows (worked on a multiple of 14 + 9 sts)

Row 1: Ch 1, sc in first st, *ch 1, sk next st, sc in next st; repeat from * across, turn.

Row 2: Ch 1, hdc in first st, [ch 1, yo, insert hook in next ch-1 sp, yo and draw up a loop even with loops on hook (3 loops on hook), yo, insert hook in Fhdc one row below next sc, yo and draw up a loop even with loops on hook (5 loops on hook), yo, insert hook in next ch-1 sp, yo and draw up a loop even with loops on hook, yo and draw through all 7 loops on hook] 3 times, ch 1, hdc in next sc, *ch 5, sk next 5 sts, hdc in next st, [ch 1, yo, insert hook in next ch-1 sp, yo and draw up a loop even with loops on hook (3 loops on hook), yo, insert hook in Fhdc one row below next sc, yo and draw up a loop even with loops on hook (5 loops on hook), yo, insert hook in next ch-1 sp, yo and draw up a loop even with loops on hook, yo and draw through all 7 loops on hook] 3 times, ch 1, hdc in next sc; rep from * across, turn.

Row 3: Ch 1, hdc in first st, ch 1, work Beg feather, ch 1, [feather, ch 1] twice, hdc in next st, *ch 5, sk next ch-5 sp, hdc in next st, work Beg feather, ch 1, [feather, ch 1] twice, hdc in next st; rep from * across, turn.

Rep row 3 for pattern.

Single crochet ribbing (sc ribbing) (any number of sts)

Row 1: Ch 1, sc in both loops of first st, sc-tbl of each st across to last st, sc in both loops of last st, turn.

SPECIAL TECHNIQUE

Duplicate stitch (see Special Techniques, page 199)

NOTES

Brimmed Beanie Hat

1. Hat is worked in turned rounds. Turned rounds are worked back and forth like rows but joined with a sl st like rounds before turning.

Wrist Warmers

1. Ribbing section is worked first from side to side, then stitches for Main Body are worked in side of ribbing rows.

2. Forearm to Thumb Opening worked in turning rounds; Thumb Opening worked in rows; then Hand worked in turning rounds. Turning rounds are worked back and forth like rows but joined with a sl st like rounds before turning.

3. Cuff Ribbing section is worked with smaller hook, remaining pattern worked with larger hook.

THREESOME SET #2: BRIMMED BEANIE HAT

SKILL LEVEL: Intermediate
SIZES: S (M, L, XL)
Sample shown in size medium

FINISHED MEASUREMENTS

To Fit Head Circumference: 20 (22, 24, 26) inches/51 (56, 61, 66) cm
Finished Head Circumference: 19½ (21½, 23½, 25½) inches/49.5 (54.5, 59.5, 65) cm
Finished Hat Depth: 8½ (9, 9½, 9½) inches/21.5 (23, 24, 24) cm

MATERIALS AND TOOLS

- Sample uses Cascade Heritage Sock (75% Superwash Merino Wool, 25% Nylon; 3.5 ounces/100 g = 437 yards/400 m): 1 skein in color Sapphire #5636 or 437 yards/400 m of superfine weight yarn

- Crochet hook: 3.25mm (size D-3) or size to obtain gauge
- Yarn needle
- Stitch markers

INSTRUCTIONS

Foundation rnd: Work 96 (106, 116, 126) Fhdc, join with sl st to first Fhdc, turn.

Set-up rnd: Ch 1, hdc in each st around, join with sl st to first hdc, turn.

Rnd 1: Ch 1, yo, insert hook in first st, yo and draw up a loop (3 loops on hook), yo, insert hook in st one row below st just worked, yo and draw up a loop even with loops on hook (5 loops on hook), sk next st, yo, insert hook in next st, yo and draw up a loop even with loops on hook (7 loops on hook), yo and draw through all 7 loops on hook, ch 1, *yo, insert hook in same st as last st, yo and pull up a loop even with loops on hook (3 loops on hook), yo, insert hook in st one row below st just worked, yo and draw up a loop even with loops on hook (5 loops on hook), sk next st, yo, insert hook in next st, yo and draw up a loop even with loops on hook (7 loops on hook), yo and draw through all 7 loops on hook; rep from * around to last st, yo, insert hook in same st as last st, yo and pull up a loop even with loops on hook, yo, insert hook in st one row below st just worked, yo and draw up a loop even with loops on hook, sk next st, yo, insert hook in first st worked of rnd, yo and draw up a loop even with loops on hook, yo and draw through all 7 loops on hook, ch 1, join with sl st in first st, turn.

Rnds 2–23 (25, 27, 27): Work rnd 2 of feathered columns worked in turned rounds pattern st.

BEGIN TOP OF HAT SHAPING

Rnd 1: Ch 1, [4 feather, Dec feather] 3 times, [3 feather, Dec feather] 7 times, join with sl st in first feather, turn—76 (86, 96, 106) sts.

Rnd 2: Ch 1, [3 feather, Dec feather] 3 times, [2 feather, Dec feather] 7 times, join with sl st in first feather, turn—56 (66, 76, 86) sts.

Rnd 3: Ch 1, [2 feather, Dec feather] 3 times, [1 feather, Dec feather] 7 times, join with sl st in first feather, turn—36 (46, 56, 66) sts.

Rnd 4: Ch 1, [1 feather, Dec feather] 3 times, [Dec feather] 7 times, join with sl st in first feather, turn—16 (26, 36, 46) sts.

SIZE MEDIUM ONLY

Rnd 5: Ch 1, [Dec feather] 6 times, feather, join with sl st in first feather, turn—14 sts.

SIZE XL ONLY

Rnd 5: Ch 1, [Dec feather] 10 times, join with sl st in first feather, turn—26 sts.

Rnd 6: Ch 1, [Dec feather] 6 times, feather, join with sl st in first feather, turn—14 sts.

Fasten off, leaving a 10-inch/25.5 cm tail for finishing top of hat. Thread yarn needle with yarn tail, and weave through remaining sts. Draw top of hat closed. Secure end by running through drawn sts.

BRIM

TOP LAYER

Worked around posts of Fhdc sts at bottom of hat.

With RS facing, join yarn with sl st around the post of any Fhdc st in foundation rnd at bottom of Hat; first st is made around same post as joining.

Row 1: Ch 1, FPhdc in each of first 32 (35, 38, 42) sts, turn.

Row 2: Ch 1, sc in each of first 32 (35, 38, 42) sts, BPhdc in each of next 4 sts in foundation rnd, turn.

Row 3: Ch 1, sc in each of first 36 (39, 42, 46) sts, FPhdc in each of next 4 sts in foundation rnd, turn.

Row 4: Ch 1, sc in each of first 40 (43, 46, 50) sts, work 1 Joining BPhdc, BPhdc in next st in foundation rnd, turn.

Row 5: Ch 1, sc in each of first 42 (45, 48, 52) sts, work 1 Joining FPhdc, FPhdc in next st in foundation rnd, turn.

Row 6: Ch 1, sc in each of first 44 (47, 50, 54) sts, work 1 Joining BPhdc, turn.

Row 7: Ch 1, sc in each of first 45 (48, 51, 55) sts, work 1 Joining FPhdc, turn.

Row 8: Ch 1, sc in each of first 46 (49, 52, 56) sts, turn.

Row 9: Ch 1, sk first st, sc in next st, sc2tog, sc in each st across to last 3 sts, sc2tog, sc in last st, turn—43 (46, 49, 53) sts.

Rows 10–12: Rep last row—34 (37, 40, 44) sts at end of last row. Fasten off.

BOTTOM LAYER

Worked in bottom of Fhdc sts at bottom of hat.

With RS facing, join yarn with sl st in bottom of Fhdc st in foundation rnd at bottom of hat directly below first st of Top Layer; first st made in same st as joining.

Row 1: Ch 1, sc in each of first 32 (35, 38, 42) sts, turn.

Row 2: Ch 1, sc in each of first 32 (35, 38, 42) sts, sc in each of next 4 sts in foundation rnd, turn.

Row 3: Ch 1, sc in each of first 36 (39, 42, 46) sts, work 1 Joining Hdc, sc in each of next 3 sts in foundation rnd, turn.

Row 4: Ch 1, sc in each of first 40 (43, 46, 50) sts, work 1 Joining Hdc, sc in next st in foundation rnd, turn.

Row 5: Ch 1, sc in each of first 42 (45, 48, 52) sts, work 1 Joining Hdc, sc in next st in foundation rnd, turn.

Row 6: Ch 1, sc in each of first 44 (47, 50, 54) sts, work 1 Joining Hdc, turn.

Row 7: Ch 1, sc in each of first 45 (48, 51, 55) sts, work 1 Joining Hdc, turn.

Row 8: Ch 1, sc in each of first 46 (49, 52, 56) sts, turn.

Row 9: Ch 1, sk first st, sc in next st, sc2tog, sc in each st across to last 3 sts, sc2tog, sc in last st, turn—43 (46, 49, 53) sts.

Rows 10–12: Rep row 9—34 (37, 40, 44) sts. Do not fasten off.

BEGIN JOINING TOP AND BOTTOM HALF

Rnd 1: With RS of Top Layer facing, ch 1, working through double thickness of Top Layer and Bottom Layer of Brim, sc in each st across Brim, hdc in bottom of each Fhdc around bottom of hat to opposite side of Brim, sc evenly along side of Brim, join with duplicate stitch in first sc.

FINISHING

Block beanie to shape if needed. Weave in ends.

THREESOME SET #2: SCARF

SKILL LEVEL: Intermediate
SIZES: One size

FINISHED MEASUREMENTS

One size: 6 inches/15 cm wide x 60 inches/152.5 cm long

MATERIALS AND TOOLS

- Sample uses Cascade Heritage Sock (75% Superwash Merino Wool, 25% Nylon; 3.5 ounces/100 g = 437 yards/400 m): 2 skeins in color Sapphire #5636 or 874 yards/800 m superfine weight yarn

- Crochet hook: 3.25mm (size D-3) or size to obtain gauge
- Yarn needle

INSTRUCTIONS

Foundation Row: Work 37 Fhdc, turn.

Rows 1–231: Work in feathers and chains pattern st.

Row 232: Ch 1, hdc in each st and each ch st across, turn.

Row 233: Ch 1, sc in each st across.

Fasten off.

FINISHING

Block to finished measurements.

Weave in ends.

THREESOME SET #2: WRIST WARMERS

SKILL LEVEL: Intermediate
SIZES: S (M, L, XL)
Sample shown in size small

FINISHED MEASUREMENTS

Finished Arm/Wrist Circumference: 8 (11, 14, 17) inches/20.5 (28, 35.5, 43) cm

Finished Length: 10 inches/25.5 cm in all sizes

MATERIALS AND TOOLS

▨ Sample uses Cascade Heritage Sock (75% Superwash Merino Wool, 25% Nylon; 3.5 ounces/100 g = 437 yards/400 m): 1 skein in color Sapphire #5636 or 437 yards/400 m of superfine weight yarn

▨ Crochet hooks: 2.75mm (size C-2) and 3.25mm (size D-3) or sizes to obtain gauge

▨ Yarn needle

INSTRUCTIONS

CUFF RIBBING

Row 1: With smaller hook, work 35 Fsc, turn.

Rows 2–66 (89, 118, 135): Work in sc ribbing pattern st. Do not fasten off. At end of last row, rotate work ¼ turn to the right for working in row-end sts of ribbing.

FOREARM

Forearm is worked in turned rnds.

Set-up rnd 1: With larger hook, ch 1, hdc in each row-end st across long edge of ribbing, join with sl st in first hdc, turn—66 (89, 118, 135) hdc.

Set-up rnd 2: Ch 1, hdc in each of first 7 (12, 11, 19) sts, [hdc2tog over next 2 sts] 26 (33, 48, 49) times, hdc in each of next 7 (11, 11, 18) sts, join with sl st in first hdc, turn—40 (56, 70, 86) sts.

Rnd 1: Ch 1, yo, insert hook in first st, yo and draw up a loop (3 loops on hook), yo, insert hook in st one row below st just worked, yo and draw up a loop even with loops on hook (5 loops on hook), sk next st, yo, insert hook in next st, yo and draw up a loop even with loops on hook (7 loops on hook), yo and draw through all 7 loops on hook, ch 1, *yo, insert hook in same st as last st, yo and pull up a loop even with loops on hook (3 loops on hook), yo, insert hook in st one row below st just worked, yo and draw up a loop even with loops on hook (5 loops on hook), sk next st, yo, insert hook in next st, yo and draw up a loop even with loops on hook (7 loops on hook), yo and draw through all 7 loops on hook; rep from * around to last st, yo, insert hook in same st as last st, yo and pull up a loop even with loops on hook, yo, insert hook in st one row below st just worked, yo and draw up a loop even with loops on hook, sk next st, yo, insert hook in first st worked of rnd, yo and draw up a loop even with loops on hook, yo and draw through all 7 loops on hook, ch 1, join with sl st in first st, turn.

Rnds 2–15: Work rnd 2 of feathered columns pattern st worked in turned rounds.

THUMB OPENING

Worked in rows.

Rows 1–8: Work in feathered columns pattern st worked in rows without joining.

HAND

Hand is worked in turned rnds.

Rnds 1–6: Work in feathered columns pattern st worked in turned rows.

FINISHING

With WS facing, sew Cuff Ribbing seam; fold Cuff Ribbing in half lengthwise and sew to inside edge of ribbing. Weave in ends.

SPECIAL
TECHNIQUES

*I*n this section, you will find written instructions and photo tutorials for stitches and techniques used most commonly throughout this book.

CARRY YARN UP SIDE OF WORK

Work to last stitch of row, work last stitch of row up to last "yo and draw through," pass carried yarn from front to back over working yarn and hold to back of work, yo and draw through remaining loops as usual; turn, pass carried yarn from front to back over working yarn, ch 1, continue with row. Repeat for each row, being careful of tension in carried yarn. If this yarn is pulled too snug, your fabric will not block properly. Similarly, if tension in carried yarn is too loose, your fabric may have holes along the side or loose strands of yarn.

COLOR CHANGE AT END OF ROW

Work to last stitch of row, work last stitch of row up to last "yo and draw through," yo with new yarn and draw through remaining loops. Hold both previous and new yarn tails snug to adjust tension of last stitch of previous color and first stitch of new color. Continue with next row in new color.

CUSTOM ZIPPER CREATION

If you cannot find a zipper that is the exact length you need for your garment, shortening a zipper is your next best option and is really a breeze. First, purchase a zipper that is as close to your required length as possible. Make sure your zipper is open and the separating mechanism is at the bottom. Next, measure your zipper from the base up and mark the length you want it to be. Add 1 inch (2.5 cm) to that measurement for a second mark. Cut the zipper at the second mark. Using pliers or kitchen shears, remove the teeth from each side of the zipper tape down to your first mark. This gives you 1 inch (2.5 cm) of fabric at the top of your zipper to fold over for a clean edge.

Once you have cut your zipper to size, a new zipper stop needs to be installed on both sides of the zipper tape. The stop is the metal or plastic tab at the top of the zipper that keeps the separating mechanism from coming off the top. The simplest way to do this is to whipstitch a stop between two of the top teeth on each side of the zipper tape. Using a sewing needle and thread similarly colored to your zipper, insert your needle from the back of the tape through the middle of the zipper tape between one of the last two teeth. Sew around the edge of the tape to back side and insert your needle again through the same hole. Continue to sew through this same hole 10–20 times until a thick ridge fully fills the space between the two zipper teeth. Secure your stitching and cut. Your newly stitched stop should be thick enough to keep the separating mechanism from sliding off the top of your cut zipper. Remember to do this to each side of the zipper tape.

Another option is to purchase a new stop. Zipper repair kits that include new stops are available at most sewing centers. Simply crimp the metal stop between the top two zipper teeth of each side of the zipper tape.

Now just sew in your zipper by hand or by machine as if it were always that length. You can now make zippers of any length! Nifty, eh?

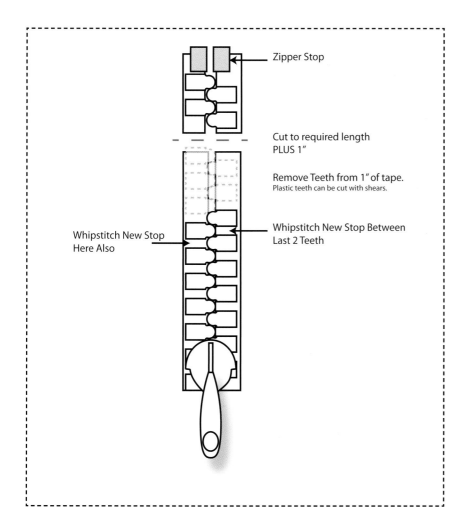

Zipper Stop

Cut to required length
PLUS 1"

Remove Teeth from 1" of tape.
Plastic teeth can be cut with shears.

Whipstitch New Stop Between
Last 2 Teeth

Whipstitch New Stop
Here Also

DUPLICATE STITCH

Work last stitch of row or round, and cut yarn, leaving about a 6-inch (15 cm) tail. Draw last loop of stitch still on the hook all the way through until tail passes through stitch. Skip next stitch (first stitch made in the round). With yarn needle, run end of tail under both loops of next stitch and pull yarn through. Insert needle back through where tail originally came from (last stitch made) and behind work. Snug yarn to cover skipped stitch with duplicate stitch just made. Weave in tail.

JOIN WITH DUPLICATE STITCH

Work to within one chain stitch of end of round, cut yarn leaving about a 6-inch (15 cm) tail. Draw last loop on hook all the way through last stitch made until tail passes through stitch. With yarn needle, run end of tail under both loops of first stitch of round and pull yarn through. Insert needle back through where tail originally came from (last chain stitch made) and behind work. Pull yarn gently to ensure chain stitch just made is same tension as other chain stitches. Weave in tail by first bringing yarn under first sc of round, then weaving in as usual.

LOCKING MATTRESS STITCH

❶ Lay work with RS down and edges to be sewn side by side. Stitches will be worked through the top loop only of both sides.

❷ First, insert needle from left to right through the first stitches of both panels at the bottom of your work to begin joining the two panels.

❸ Next, insert needle from right to left into the next stitch of the right panel and continue through the last stitch worked on the left panel.

❹ Next, insert needle from left to right into the next stitch of the left panel and continue through the last stitch worked of the right panel.

❺ Continue in this manner, gently pulling the yarn snug as you go to close the seam.

❻ Every few stitches, pull the yarn snug to secure and even out the seam.

Finish up by weaving in ends.

❶

❷

❸

❹

❺

❻

SETTING IN SLEEVES

With WS facing

1 Fold sleeve in half.

2 Pin center of sleeve at fold to shoulder seam. Pin bottom corner of sleeve to underarm seam.

3 Pin sleeve to armhole at points halfway between first three pins.

4 Continue pinning at points halfway between pins until sleeves are pinned securely in place around armhole. After all pins are secured, use locking mattress stitch technique to sew sleeves in place.

1

2

3

4

SEWING IN A ZIPPER

This technique works best if you place a small rotary mat or thin piece of acrylic glass or cardboard inside the garment to protect from pinning and sewing through the back of the garment. I used a quilting ruler.

1 First, with RS of garment facing, weave in two blocking wires on each side of the garment front—one wire woven along the first set of stitches closest to the edge, the other wire woven about 1 inch (2.5 cm) away.

2 Next, position the zipper under the opening in the front of the garment. Take care to center the zipper in the opening.

3 Pin first side of the zipper tape in place by pinning between the blocking wires. Your acrylic glass or rotary mat will really help here to prevent accidentally pinning and sewing through to the back of the garment. Note: Check that the zipper will move up and down without catching the edges of your garment.

4 Backstitch or whipstitch the zipper from the bottom edge to the top of the zipper, catching one or two stitches in each pass. Follow the stitch pattern closely to make your sewing as invisible as possible.

5 Leave the first side blocking wires in, and pin the second side of the zipper tape in place, again pinning between the blocking wires. Be sure to use your acrylic glass or rotary mat as a guide. Note: Stop and check occasionally that your pinning creates a straight zipper.

6 Unzip the zipper and sew the second side as you did the first side. Again, check here to ensure you can open and close the zipper with ease.

7 Remove guide wires, and your garment is ready to wear!

1

2

3

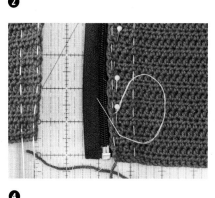

4

5

6

7

A SPECIAL NOTE ON INCREASING AND DECREASING

When instructed to "inc X number of sts," work 2 tr, 2 dc, or 2 sc in the first stitch according to the pattern row you are working on. For example: if you are about to work a row of Dc-V stitches, you would work 2 dc in the first st where the pattern reads "increase 1 st." If you are about to work a row that begins with a sc, you would work 2 sc in the first st where the pattern reads "increase 1 st."

When instructed to "dec X number of sts," use tr2tog, dc2tog, or sc2tog according to the pattern row you are working on. For example: if you are about to work a row that begins with a dc, you would dc2tog where the pattern reads "decrease 1 st." If you are about to work a row that begins with a sc, you would sc2tog where the pattern reads "dec 1 st."

If after a decrease the next stitch is a chain space, work one stitch in pattern stitch in the place of that chain space, then continue as instructed.

When a pattern instruction indicates to increase or decrease, then reads to continue working "in pattern st as established," this means you should maintain the pattern stitch as it has been worked up to this point in the pattern between your increases or decreases. When working in this manner, there are two important factors of the pattern stitch that you need to maintain:

1. Number of Rows to Repeat for Pattern Stitch
Most patterns are worked in a pattern stitch that has a certain number of rows that will be repeated to create the pattern stitch. This will be indicated in the Pattern Stitch section as "Repeat rows X–X for pattern stitch." When working in pattern stitch as established, you must ensure that this row repeat continues.

For example: If the instructions for a pattern stitch indicate to "Rep rows 1–4 for pattern st," you would maintain that 4-row repeat as you worked "in pattern stitch as established."

If the instructions for a pattern stitch end with "Rep rows 2–4 for pattern stitch," you would maintain that 3-row repeat as you worked "in pattern stitch as established."

2. Multiple of Stitches for Pattern Stitch
Most patterns are worked in a pattern stitch that has a pattern repeat in multiples of a certain number of stitches. This will be indicated in the Pattern Stitch section as "(worked on a multiple of X sts)" or "(worked on a multiple of X + X sts)." When working in pattern stitch as established, you must ensure that this stitch multiple continues.

For example: If the instructions for a pattern stitch indicates a stitch repeat as a "(multiple of 5 + 2 sts)," once you have increased a total of 5 stitches on each side of your established pattern, you will have enough increase stitches to begin working additional pattern repeats of the pattern stitch on the next row.

If the instructions for a pattern stitch indicates a stitch repeat as a "(multiple of 3 sts)," once you have increased a total of 3 sts on each side of your established pattern, you will have enough increase stitches to begin working additional pattern repeats of the pattern stitch on the next row.

In both examples, until another repeat of the pattern stitch can be established, you would work the same type of stitch (sc, dc, tr, etc.) in the increased stitches.

Similarly, if you are decreasing, to ensure you maintain the stitch multiple, you would work your decreases then work the same type of stitch (sc, dc, tr, etc.) until another repeat of the pattern stitch can be established.

For example: If you are decreasing in a pattern stitch with a stitch repeat of a "(multiple of 5 + 2 sts)" and that stitch pattern is mainly double crochet stitches, you would work your decreases as indicated in the pattern, then work double crochets until another repeat of the 5-stitch pattern repeat of the pattern stitch can be worked. Likewise, at the end of a row, you would work in pattern stitch as established, then work double crochets over any partial sections of the 5-stitch pattern repeat before you work your decreases.

FOUNDATION SINGLE CROCHET (FSC)

1 Chain 2.

2 Insert hook in 2nd chain from hook.

3 Yarn over and draw up a loop.

4 Yarn over and draw through 1 loop on hook (first "chain" made).

5 Yarn over and draw through 2 loops on hook (first single crochet made).

6 Insert hook under 2 loops of the "chain" just made.

7 Yarn over and draw up a loop.

8 Yarn over and draw through 1 loop ("chain" made).

9 Yarn over and draw through 2 loops on hook (single crochet made).

10 Repeat steps 6–9 for indicated number of foundation stitches.

1

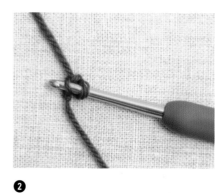

2

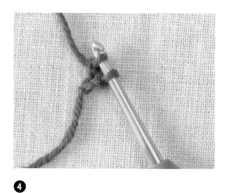

3

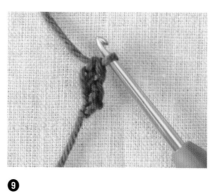

5

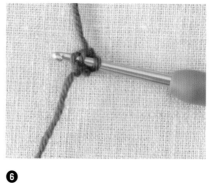

6

7

8

9

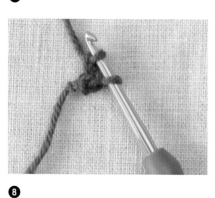

10

FOUNDATION HALF DOUBLE CROCHET (FHDC)

❶ Chain 3.

❷ Insert hook in 3rd chain from hook.

❸ Yarn over and draw up a loop.

❹ Yarn over and draw through 1 loop on hook (first "chain" made).

❺ Yarn over and draw through all 3 loops on hook (first hdc made).

❻ Yarn over, insert hook under 2 loops of the "chain" just made.

❼ Yarn over and draw up a loop.

❽ Yarn over and draw through 1 loop on hook ("chain" made).

❾ Yarn over and draw through all 3 loops on hook (hdc made).

❿ Repeat steps 6–9 for indicated number of foundation stitches.

❶

❷

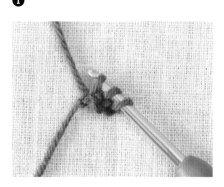

❸

❹

❺

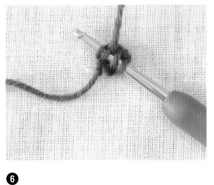

❻

❼

❽

❾

❿

MASTER CHART KEY

○ Chain (ch)

● Slip stitch (sl st)

+ Single crochet (sc)

Half double crochet (Hdc)

Double crochet (Hdc)

Treble crochet (tr)

Double treble crochet (Dtr)

Foundation single crochet (Fsc)

Foundation Half double (FHdc)

F Foundation Row

First double crochet (First-dc)

First treble crochet (First-tr)

Single crochet through
back loop only (Sc tbl)

Half double crochet through
back loop only (Hdc tbl)

3-double crochet Cluster (3-dc Cl)

5-double crochet Cluster (5-dc Cl)

Front Post double crochet (FPdc)

Back Post
double crochet (BPdc)

Front Post
treble crochet (FPtr)

Left leaning spike

Right leaning spike

Left Dc-cross
(worked over 3 sts)

Picot

Herringbone half
double crochet (Hhdc)

Spike stitch

Single crochet
V-St (Sc V-St)

Half double
crochet V-st (hdc-v)

Double
crochet V-st (dc-v)

6-over-6 FpQtr
Left cross cable
(worked over 13 sts)

MATERIALS LIST

Beginner Cardi
Cascade 220 Superwash Sport
http://www.cascadeyarns.com

Belted Ruana
Cascade 220 Superwash Sport
http://www.cascadeyarns.com

Cabled Trio
Knit Picks Stroll Sock
http://www.knitpicks.com

Cables and Lace Tunic
Knit Picks Stroll Sock
http://www.knitpicks.com

Capelette
Malabrigo Arroyo
http://malabrigoyarn.com

Cardi with Attached Scarf
Mirasol Nuna
http://knittingfever.com

Cloaked Hood Hoodie
Knit Picks Capretta
http://www.knitpicks.com

Cowl Neck Sweater Dress
Lion Brand Collection Superwash Merino
http://www.lionbrand.com

Cross Front Vest
Cascade 220 Superwash Sport
http://www.cascadeyarns.com

Drape Front Cardi
Knit Picks Capretta
http://www.knitpicks.com

Duster
Berroco Ultra Alpaca Fine
http://www.berroco.com

Hiking Vest
Mango Moon Bulu
http://www.mangomoonyarns.com

Hooded Scarf
Malabrigo Silky Merino
http://malabrigoyarn.com

Hooded Wrap Vest
Buffalo Wool Sock
http://thebuffalowoolco.com

Lace Tank
Crystal Palace Panda Silk
http://www.straw.com

Motif Maxi Skirt
Knit Picks Curio Crochet Thread
http://www.knitpicks.com

Off-the-Shoulder Dress
Malabrigo Sock
http://malabrigoyarn.com

Poncho Top
Mirasol Nuna
http://knittingfever.com

Sleeveless Hoodie
Cascade Heritage Silk
http://www.cascadeyarns.com

Solid Tank
Crystal Palace Panda Silk
http://www.straw.com

Three-Quarter Sleeve Cardi
Knit Picks Gloss Fingering
http://www.knitpicks.com

Three-Quarter Sleeve Pullover
Crystal Palace Mini Mochi Solid
http://www.straw.com

Threesome Set #1
Cascade Heritage Sock
http://www.cascadeyarns.com

Threesome Set #2
Knit Picks Stroll Fingering
http://www.knitpicks.com

Turtleneck Poncho
Cascade 220 Superwash Sport
http://www.cascadeyarns.com

Two-Way Top
Knit Picks Gloss Fingering
http://www.knitpicks.com

ACKNOWLEDGMENTS

It truly takes a team to bring a project like this across the finish line successfully. For all of their help, we would like to express our most sincere gratitude to the following people:

Linda Roghaar, Linda Roghaar Literary Agency—Thank you for being such a great supporter of our work and for being a true cheerleader when we needed it and a guide when we were feeling a bit adrift.

Karen Manthey, Tech Editor—Thank you for agreeing to work with us on this epic project. Your skill with crafting our patterns into their most elegant and precise forms has taught us so much, and we know our readers will reap the benefits with the best possible patterns.

The team at Lark and Sterling Publishing—Thank you for seeing a concept and a LOT of sketches and jumping in with both feet. This has been a dream come true for us, and your confidence in this book has made it possible.

Finally, to our FAB team of talented and driven contract crocheters: Your talented hands guided hooks and yarn to make our dreams come to life. Without your joy and passion for what you do, we never could have made this happen; and we are forever grateful that each and every one of you has come into our lives.

Amy C
Catherine R
Cookie G
Debbie M
Janelle P
Juanita Q
Kathy F
Lara O
Leandra L
LeeAnn W
Michelle M
Patrick L
Stephanie B

We are also very grateful for the generous support from these yarn companies for donating yarn for the samples in *Designer Crochet*:

Berroco
Buffalo Wool Company
Cascade Yarns
Crystal Palace Yarns
Knit Picks
Lion Brand
Malabrigo
Mango Moon
Knitting Fever (Mirasol)

Finally, and most importantly, I want to personally thank the man behind the designer (for over 20 years!), Jason Mullett-Bowlsby. Without your help, understanding, encouragement, infinite patience, love, and support, I absolutely would not have been able to make this epic project happen. Your skills as a photographer and graphic designer are evident throughout this book, but it is, perhaps, your innate ability to know just when I need more chocolate or when it is "time to leave the studio" that kept this project afloat. Thank you. I love you. Now can we go for a long hike?

ABOUT THE AUTHOR AND PHOTOGRAPHER

Shannon & Jason Mullett-Bowlsby are the DIY duo known as the Shibaguyz.

Shannon makes up half of the DIY duo known as the Shibaguyz behind the design studio of Shibaguyz Designz.

Shannon's award winning crochet & hand knitwear designs have been featured in and on the covers of both US and international publications. He currently has over 200 published patterns credited to his name since his first design was featured on the cover of a magazine in 2010. Shannon is also a veteran teacher and has been teaching adults for over 20 years. He is a Craft Yarn Council certified instructor and his quirky sense of humor and relatable teaching style have made him a sought after teacher in both local and national venues.

Jason, the other half of the Shibaguyz, is a professional fashion, commercial, and portrait photographer whose photos can be seen in many of the Shibaguyz' patterns and books as well as those of a number of other indie crochet and knit designers. Jason shares the teaching stage with Shannon for a number of their classes and is passionate about teaching designers and makers how to get the most out of their fiber photography.

One of Jason's favorite gigs is as a photographer at both local and national dog shows and has photographed such prestigious organizations as the Seattle Kennel Club and the Westminster Kennel Club dog shows. Even though Jason loves his work in fashion and portrait photography, his work with four-legged models is some of his most "ooooh" and "ahhhh" inducing work.

Shannon and Jason live in Seattle, Washington with their three Shiba Inu who, more or less, support their ventures as long as enough time is taken for walks and treats.

To see more of their work and to follow along on their adventures in fiber, photography, and Shibas, catch up with Shannon and Jason at Shibaguyz.com and ShibaguyzDesignz.com.

INDEX

Note: Page numbers in *italics* indicate projects.